THE COMPLETE
ENCYCLOPEDIA OF
FLIGHT

1848-1939

THE COMPLETE
ENCYCLOPEDIA OF
FLIGHT

1848-1939

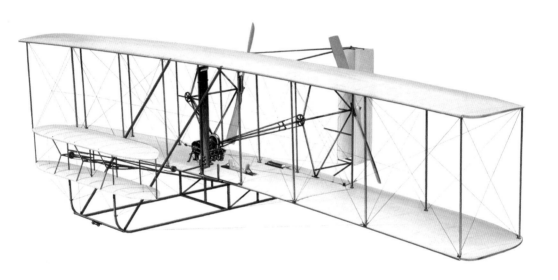

JOHN BATCHELOR & MALCOLM V. LOWE

REBO
PUBLISHERS

Published by Rebo International b.v., Lisse, The Netherlands
in association with Publishing Solutions (www) Ltd., Great Britain

© 2004 Rebo International b.v., Lisse, The Netherlands and Publishing Solutions (www) Ltd., Great Britain

Text: Malcolm V. Lowe
Illustrations: John Batchelor
M PRESS   Production, layout and typesetting: The Minster Press, Dorset, Great Britain
Cover design: The Minster Press, Dorset, Great Britain
Proofreading: Jeffrey Rubinoff

ISBN 90 366 1600 X

Contents

Introduction

The story of aviation since the first ground-breaking flight of the Wright brothers in December 1903 has been a tale of rapid technological advance and the blossoming of the new science of aeronautics into many areas of human activity. From small beginnings, aviation grew rapidly into the vitally important technology that it is opment of aeronautics, both before the great watershed of the Wright brothers' first flights, and after that time as aviation gained a foothold and eventually grew into the huge business that it is today. Aviation revolutionised warfare, made possible transportation to the farthest reaches of the earth, and grew into a vast number of

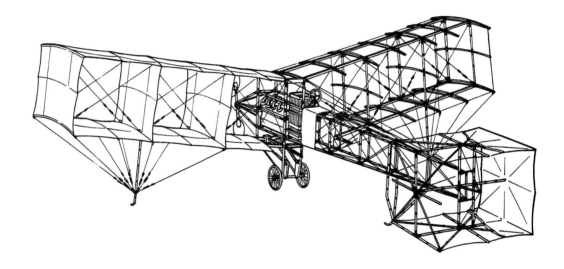

today. Aircraft revolutionised transportation and warfare in ways that few other single inventions or fields of human activity have been able to do. In concert with the development of the automobile, aviation came along in leaps and bounds virtually straight from its successful first application, helped along all the way with the invention of the internal combustion engine and its excellent power-to-weight ratio. The story of aviation in effect became a significant part of the story of the twentieth century. Many pioneers were involved in the devel- other tasks, some utilitarian, and some much less peaceful.

This book deals with the formative period of aviation involving the early pioneers and takes the fascinating story of aeronautical progress up to the start of World War Two. Many important aspects are covered or touched upon, illustrated all the way by the world-famous artwork of John Batchelor. It has been possible to include many significant aircraft and personalities within the general period referred to by this book, but any work of this size that covers such a wide area necessarily pays more attention to some and less to others, no doubt to the exclusion of some people's favorites. There have been so many different types of aircraft, from a myriad of manufacturers, that to include every one would be impossible without resorting to an almost infinite amount of writing, and so we have concentrated on an excellently representative selection of the great and the small. Further Volumes of this Encyclopaedia will cover World War Two and then bring the story of aviation up to the present.

Early Days

Mankind had dreamed of taking to the skies for centuries, long before genuine sustained manned flight ever became a reality. For many early dreamers and schemers, the way for Man to achieve flight was assumed to be by emulating the birds. Birds, after all, flew with ease. Why not therefore mimic the flight of birds in order to get a man off the ground? Although this thinking might have seemed sound, and it persisted for centuries, in reality little could have been further from the truth, and the idea of following the example of birds remained an enduring red herring in the quest for manned flight. Right up to the time of the Wright brothers, there remained some who were convinced that men flapping their arms, or a man sitting in a machine that flapped its wings, could lead to sustained flight. Fortunately there were also those who realised that there are significant differences between birds and human beings, not just in the obvious matter of appearance but also in what lies underneath the surface. Even the mechanics of how birds actually fly

remained a subject that was misunderstood for a long time. The great early artist and inventor, Leonardo da Vinci, studied birds a great deal. He did not, however, completely understand the complexities of the wing beats of birds. da Vinci came up with numerous aeronautical ideas, many of which seemed far-sighted in his day, but which must nowadays be viewed with some scepticism. That is not to underestimate da Vinci's importance, however. He, and the diversity of often religious men and theorists who went before and after him, all had an important influence in their aeronautical thinking to one extent or another on those who came along in more recent times. The science of aeronautics took a very long time to develop, and to uncover the ingredients needed for success. It was only thanks to the work of much more contemporary thinking men such as Sir George Cayley that the veil started to lift on what really was needed to get mankind into the air. Although birds did eventually contribute some important features to the conglomeration of ideas that finally led to manned flight, including wing cross-section and general configuration, Man eventually got into the skies by being taken aloft inside a mechanical invention called an aircraft that provided all the necessary power and lift, with the human beings inside it providing not the power, but the control and directional inputs.

To get that far needed what turned out to be a lot of experimentation, many dead ends, and the tenacity of individuals who were sometimes completely shunned (or even persecuted) in their own days. Some of these true pioneers, especially those in the nineteenth century, experimented on a shoestring budget, as a side-line to their normal day job. Early pioneers such as John Stringfellow in Somerset in the southwest of England, tried long and hard to find solutions. Stringfellow, Cayley and a number of other inventors are a part of our story in the forthcoming pages. Their contributions to the development of manned flight are all too often overlooked by historians who do not look back beyond the Wright brothers for the origins of sustained and powered manned flight. Nevertheless, some of the achievements of the early pioneers are still subject to debate. Stringfellow's flying machines of 1848 and 1868 are still argued over as to how successful they really were, and how they actually flew if indeed they successfully did at all. Such flying machines are best looked on from our viewpoint as flying MODELS rather than full-size aircraft. Sir George Cayley, however, has the accolade of actually getting a man into the air for the first time in an aircraft-like contraption. This was in 1853, within what was effectively a glider although it is sometimes regarded as the first heavier-than-air flying machine for its man-carrying capability. The 'pilot' for this endeavour was actually Cayley's coachman, and although he was the first adult human being to fly in this way, he was totally unimpressed and is said to have resigned his employment immediately.

What effectively stopped these early pioneers dead in their tracks was the lack of a viable form of propulsion for their creations. The nineteenth century, that great era of invention, was the age of steam power. Steam was fine for many applications, but all of them were very much ground-based or water-based. Steam was, in a nutshell, not suitable for powering aircraft. Most steam engines were large, unwieldy creations with a poor power-to-weight ratio that needed to be warmed up sometimes for a considerable time before they could do anything (where the term getting a 'full head of steam' comes from). To fuel them, wood or coal was needed, in large quantities. The thought of an aircraft powered by this type of propulsion might now seem absurd (particularly the idea of a pilot having to shovel coal or wood into a raging fire in mid-flight), but at the time steam was the only real possibility for the Victorian-era inventors. True, some steam engine manufacturers had managed to create small but nevertheless comparatively powerful steam engines, and in a limited number of cases steam ALMOST powered a number of potential man-carrying flying machines. Some inventors tried their hand with other types of power, such as gunpowder or gas, but with similarly generally disappointing (and occasionally explosive) results.

One form of aerial activity that was by then already established and successful was the science of ballooning. Starting in the 1780's with the pioneering work of the Montgolfier brothers in France, 'lighter-than-air' craft were developed over the next century or so and proved successful for getting human beings into the air with relative ease. During the American Civil War in the 1860's, American Thaddeus Lowe had become well-known for his use of balloons for observation, and balloons had been employed in several other conflicts as well. Further development along related lines saw the rise of the airship as another form of flying that was successful and comparatively safe. Both of these forms of flight are still with us today, although airships have had a bumpy ride and are not now the important form of transportation that they had become by the 1930's. The destruction of the German airship 'Hindenburg' at Lakehurst in the United States in 1937, when its flammable hydrogen gas-filled interior ignited, was one of several spectacular and devastating airship losses that have compromised this form of transport for more recent times. However, Mankind had also discovered another way of taking to the air, in the form of the unpowered glider. Gliding was well established by the start of the twentieth century. Indeed, the Wright brothers themselves had successfully experimented with gliders as an important part of the development work that led to their powered aircraft. Pioneers such as Otto Lilienthal, Percy Pilcher and a number of others were developing the art of gliding, often with contraptions that to our modern eyes look more akin to hang-gliders than the graceful long wing-span sailplanes that today grace the skies on still summer afternoons.

The invention that revolutionised the possibility of powered manned flight was the creation in the 1860's and patenting in the 1880's of the internal combustion engine. Several inventors can lay claim to this most remarkable and earth-shattering invention, but the German inventor Nikolaus A. Otto is certainly the man who must take most of the credit. The internal combustion engine was just what the pioneering aircraft designers needed, although it was at least two decades before the petrol engine could be per-fected sufficiently to give a viable power-to-weight ratio to allow for aerial activities. After that, the possibility of manned powered flight started to become a reality. In 1901 the American Samuel P. Langley flew a petrol engine-powered model aircraft, which was probably the most successful powered flying machine up to that time - although even this was not particularly successful on its initial flights, and needed further refinement. Nevertheless, the petrol internal combustion engine had entered the field of aeronautics for good, and the stage was set for the Wright brothers to leave their indelible mark on history.

The epic first genuine powered, sustained, controlled and manned flight in history by an aircraft took place on 17 December 1903. On that day Orville Wright successfully flew the Wright Flyer that he and his brother Wilbur had designed and built themselves – and which was powered by an internal combustion engine that was similarly of their own design and manufacture. The achievement of the Wright brothers in being the first to fly in this way has become legendary. They were well aware of all the experimentation that had gone on before them, and had studied much of what had been learned up to that time by the pioneers of their own time and of previous times. Interestingly, they subsequently attempted – following their successful first powered flights - to keep the mechanics of manned flight as much to themselves as possible, some would say for their own advantage. They became embroiled in some lengthy litigation over patents, especially but not exclusively with another great American aviation pioneer, Glenn Curtiss. Indeed, so secretive were the Wrights that some especially in Europe doubted their claims to success. It was not until Wilbur Wright made a series of demonstration flights in Europe during 1908 that it became obvious how far advanced aviation in the United States was, and how it was ahead in several respects from developments in Europe. This might have come as something of a shock to some of the American aviators; it certainly came as a big surprise to many in Europe.

Nevertheless, developments continued on both sides of the Atlantic Ocean, and one of the great pioneer aviators in Europe was the dashing Brazilian Alberto Santos-Dumont. His Hargrave box-kite inspired Santos-Dumont No.14-bis took the first internationally-ratified official world distance record for aircraft in November 1906 - although the distances that he was managing actually fell far short of what the Wright brothers were achieving in the United States by that time. In those early days of manned powered flight, mass production on the scale that eventually took place during, say, the Second World War was unthinkable. Nevertheless the very first aircraft-producing companies were founded during that era in France. Indeed, in the days prior to the First World War, the United States and France led the way in many areas of aeronautical development.

Although the Wright brothers had created the first successful aircraft design, their Wright Flyer was only the beginning of the development of viable and successful heavier-than-air craft. During the following years, various improvements were made to aircraft

design as greater knowledge of aerodynamics (and, simply, what it took to get an aircraft successfully into the air) became obvious to those in the growing field of aviation. The technology of flight moved forwards, sometimes less than smoothly, and sometimes into dead ends. However, many improvements were made, with more and more aircraft types being produced that offered improving levels of performance and reliability. One of the companies that helped to profoundly alter aircraft design and manufacture prior to World War One was the short-lived Deperdussin aircraft company of

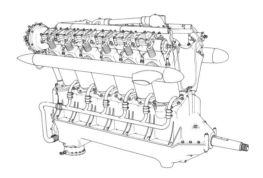

The Liberty engine

Armand Deperdussin. This French-based company produced a number of increasingly innovative aircraft, created by its talented and forward-looking designers. Particular requirements were streamlined design and high speed. The best representation of these ideas was the Deperdussin Monocoque of 1912/1913, which introduced a whole new appearance to aircraft design, with a beautifully-streamlined fuselage and undercarriage arrangement, coupled with a powerful rotary engine. The Monocoque's fuselage was just that, a revolutionary monocoque structure made from tulip-wood strips glued over a removable jig to make a strong shell-like structure that pre-dates the way many later aircraft were built. The heavy framework of longerons and cross-pieces over which fabric was fixed on many contemporary aircraft was not needed by the Monocoque. Lateral control, however, was still by warping of the aircraft's monoplane wing. Eventually, what we know today as ailerons for lateral control, and such fundamentals as a control column for the pilot, were developed and used ever more widely in aircraft design. Engine development too continued to move forward. One of the important pioneers of aircraft engines was the Frenchman Léon Levavasseur, whose Antoinette engines were significant sources of power for many early European aviators. In the United States, Glenn Curtiss made important advances with engine technology. Eventually the types of engine that created such an impact during the First World War started to come to the fore, including notably the rotary piston engine.

One of the great gifts of the famous aviator Alberto Santos-Dumont was his desire to make aviation available to ordinary people. His Demoiselle light aircraft was the first popular light plane, and he waived any rights to its plans in order to encourage amateur builders the world over. In later years a number of individuals and aircraft companies, notably Henri Mignet in France and the de Havilland company in Britain, also attempted to make aviation more generally available by producing aircraft or (in Mignet's case) plans of aircraft that were accessible to the mass market. Sadly such noble intentions did not always achieve their desired effects,

and for most people in the pre-Second World War era aviation was out of reach, and the preserve of those with the money or time (or, indeed, both) to indulge in aviation. Nevertheless aviation did find its way to a more general if ground-based audience through the exploits of the early aviators, who often became household names and generated great publicity through their varied exploits. One manifestation of this was the growth of air shows. Early aviation meetings attracted thousands of visitors who had the chance to see pioneer aviators in action. The first international aviation meeting was held in France at Reims during August 1909. Events such as the large spectacle at Los Angeles in January 1910, and air shows at Doncaster and Blackpool in northern England during 1909 were important early examples of their type. The ground-breaking aeronautical exhibitions in Paris from 1909 onwards set the bench-mark for expositions that showcased aviation and its continuing development. In parallel with this were developments in ground-based facilities for aircraft. The world's first recognised flying field had been, naturally enough, in France at the Port-Aviation in the vacinity of Paris, which opened during 1909. In the following years, landing grounds for aircraft started to become available in many locations, sometimes using existing facilities such as racecourses.

The First World War
When the world went to war in August 1914, successful manned powered aviation was only just over ten years old, and in many ways it was still in its infancy. In the four years of the First World War, aviation grew up in a

rapid and very brutal fashion. By the end of the war, aviation was well and truly established as a viable form of transport and, significantly, as a major tool of war. Although aircraft had been use in small conflicts and skirmishes prior to World War One, it was the global conflict that commenced during that distant summer of 1914 that effectively put military aviation 'on the map'. It has been there ever since.

At the start of World War One, military aviation was still in its formative years. By the end of the war all the major countries of the world recognised how important it was to have a military aviation element in their armed forces. Although the end of the war saw the scaling-down of these forces almost everywhere, aircraft had proven themselves as effective and indispensable tools of war, and in just about every way this importance has grown ever since.

Those countries that possessed military aviation elements at the start of World War One – and all the main protagonists had some kind of military aircraft – almost all possessed a mixture of frail but attractive biplanes, balloons and the odd airship. In more recent years it has become fashionable to refer to these early aircraft as being made from 'sticks and string', but little could be further from the case. Although their construction might seem antiquated by modern standards, these early aircraft were strong and were made from the best materials available at the time. A variety of woods were available for use in primary structural elements, with the completed aircraft usually being fabric-covered. This fabric was doped and finished to a high standard for maximum durability and strength.

SE5A. – 56 SQDN MARKINGS

The so-called 'string' was actually the highest grade wire available for rigging, the finished aircraft being rigged by fitters to the highest standards again for maximum strength.

At the start of the war some military establishments were larger than others, with those in Germany, France and Britain in the forefront. The Germans in particular had seen the potential of airships in warfare, and employed them to sometimes deadly effect during the conflict. In the initial stages aircraft were used mainly for reconnaissance and a variety of second-line duties such as liaison. Although these roles persisted throughout the war, there were forward-looking military men in most countries who recognised that aircraft could be employed for much more warlike tasks. Indeed, those at the sharp end who were daily flying these early aircraft over the battlefield soon began to ensure that they were armed. It was not long before aircraft started to take on far more warlike roles, and even before the end of 1914 aircraft were being used to drop bombs even some distances behind the enemy lines.

In the four years of the First World War these initial steps towards the large-scale usage of aircraft in warfare had developed into the situation that existed at the Armistice in November 1918, where aircraft were an established tool of war in all the various ways that combat aircraft had evolved during the conflict. This included bombing, both tactical above or just behind the battlefield, and strategic, many miles behind the front lines in which industrial centres and even civilian targets were attacked. Aircraft had been used for ground attack, fighting above the trenches, and scouting for ground forces and artillery spotting. Most notably, they had also evolved as true fighter aircraft, and the dogfight between opposing fighters in order to win air supremacy over the battlefield and beyond, had grown into a significant and very high-profile part of modern warfare. It had become acknowledged that whoever ruled the skies possessed a major advantage over the opposition. Fighters had been used to intercept bombers and airships both by day and night. Night fighting had developed its own sets of tactics, which were only markedly changed with the development of radar in the late 1930's and early 1940's.

In concert with the growing role of aircraft during the First World War came the development of the aircraft industry on a grand scale. Aircraft were suddenly required – and built – on a scale that would have been completely unthinkable only a handful of years before. Such aircraft as the Breguet 14, Sopwith Camel and SPAD S.XIII were built in large numbers. This type of production was enabled by the rapid growth of the aircraft industry and infrastructure in many countries. A rich diversity of aircraft design and manufacturing companies evolved. Many of these did not last very long, and the majority of those that persisted eventually amalgamated into larger entities or finally went out of business decades later. A small number persist to this day. With so many men away fighting the war, production of aircraft – like so many other war munitions – eventually encompassed many women workers. This was another important step towards the emancipation of women in a number of countries.

Mass production brought a host of equipment suppliers into the world of aviation, and an industry in its own right was created to supply everything from wheels to ordnance. A large variety of weapons were developed for aircraft to carry in anger once the war-like potential of aircraft had been recognised. From having no bombers of any recognised type at the start of the war, at the end of the war British aircraft were capable of dropping large quantities of bombs, and the first four-engined bomber for the Royal Air Force, the Handley Page V/1500, was just starting to appear. The development of aircraft as true warriors came with the creation of equipment suited to the increasing needs of military aviation. Such innovations as the Scarff ring mounting for machine guns, used in the observer/gunner position in many two-seat aircraft, exemplified the development of allied equipment to allow aircraft to fulfil the more demanding combat roles being asked of them. The most obvious example of this was the evolution of a viable interrupter mechanism, which allowed forward-firing machine guns in fighter aircraft to fire through the spinning disc of a propeller without shooting off the blades. This gave fighters the ability to have forward-firing machine guns concentrated more closely together in the forward fuselage, thus considerably increasing their effectiveness.

Mass production did not suit all manufacturers, and the means to achieving it were sometimes archaic. In a world where photocopiers and computers did not exist, plans had to be copied meticulously by hand, many components had to be created often by the most labour-intensive means, and in some cases a pattern aircraft was supplied to a subcontractor to copy rather than a set of plans being

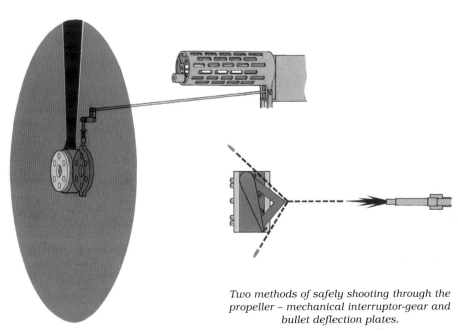

Two methods of safely shooting through the propeller – mechanical interruptor-gear and bullet deflection plates.

15

made available. In this type of environment the actual specifications of components and indeed complete aircraft were not subject to the type of rigorous tolerances that exist today. In this sense, our ancestors made it difficult for succeeding generations of historians to pin down the exact specifications of more than just a small number of aircraft types, and debate still exists over the true dimensions or operating capabilities of these aircraft. This book has therefore set out to give the most accurate figures available based where possible on manufacturer's or service specifications, but there remain aircraft types where more information is needed or might eventually be unearthed. The same is true where metric dimensions have been translated over the years into Imperial specifications, and vice versa, with the attendant loss of specificity that such calculations often create.

Aircraft fought over all the battlefronts in World War One. This involved service in northern Europe and in many other places. Wherever there was fighting to be done, aircraft were soon involved. In this way aircraft came to be operated under wartime conditions in the most rigorous of climates, those in the Middle East in particular playing havoc with sometimes already temperamental or unreliable equipment. In this way it became important for aircraft and their related equipment to be built to the highest specifications possible, another lesson that came home as a result of the war.

As mentioned earlier, the First World War had not only shown how important aircraft could be in warfare, the conflict also saw the establishment of military organisations to properly manage and operate military aircraft. The process had commenced prior to the war, with most of the major countries attaching their fledgling air elements to newly-formed branches of their often long-established army organisations. In some cases naval aviation grew as an off-shoot of established naval structures. The enormous growth of military aviation led to the need to formalise these structures, and in some cases an independent air force was the result. In Britain, a separate naval air arm, the Royal Naval Air Service, was created in July 1914. The Royal Flying Corps, an offshoot of the army, had existed since May 1912. On 1 April 1918 these came together to form the Royal Air Force, an early example of the

importance of military aviation elements being given their own autonomy within a leading country's military structures. In France, the Aéronautique Militaire (sometimes abbreviated to Aviation Militaire) was founded in 1910, with the Armée de l'Air being created in 1933/1934. In the United States, an aviation element of the Signal Corps was founded as early as 1907. This gave way to the U.S. Army Air Service in May 1918, and the U.S. Army Air Corps in July 1926. This service became the U.S. Army Air Force (technically called the U.S. Army Air Forces) just prior to the American entry into World War Two in 1941, while an independent air force did not arise in the United States until 1947.

Civil Aviation Developments after World War One

The foundations of air transport as we know it today were established in the years following World War One. The war had seen the aeroplane come of age in terms of technology and construction, and huge advances had been made during the war years in the design and manufacture of flying machines. Aircraft manufacturers and designers had learned much during the war, and the subsequent years of peace were to truly reap the harvest of this new-found knowledge. The years after the war witnessed the true birth of civil aviation, both in terms of the development of aircraft specifically designed for commercial operation, and in the creation of commercial companies to operate them. Initially, former military aircraft that had been 'civilianised' were used on the fledgling air routes that started to be established following the war. But increasingly aircraft companies across the world began to develop the new types of passenger-carrying aircraft that were the ancestors of today's airliners. These were aircraft that were designed specifically for carrying passengers or cargo, and as such they presented very particular challenges to their designers and manufacturers. They required good performance in terms of speed, range and load-carrying capacity, they had to fly in varying climates, and they had to do this efficiently and safely. Pioneers in a number of countries, such as Douglas in the USA and Fokker in the Netherlands, successfully developed families of airliners that were instrumental in the rapid growth of commercial aviation, and in helping to establish passenger-carrying air routes across the globe. Increasing development in the power output and efficiency of aero engines considerably aided these developments.

A plethora of airline companies, some large, some small, grew up as the fledgling civil commercial aircraft industry started to emerge in the 1920's. Many of these airlines eventually disappeared through failure or merger, but some of the bigger names are still with us today. The establishment of these companies was very much a leap in the dark in the early days of civil aviation, and many unsung pioneers behind the scenes were prepared to put up significant sums of money to establish these companies in what was at the time very much a completely new industry. Many of the air routes that were used by these airlines had been opened up and explored by intrepid individuals, some of whose names have become legends. Starting with the non-stop crossing of the Atlantic Ocean in 1919 by Alcock and Brown in a specially-prepared Vickers Vimy bomber, and continuing through the achievement of Charles Lindbergh on his solo crossing of the Atlantic in 1927, many pioneers risked their lives to trailblaze long-range flight and to prove new air routes, sometimes in the most inhospitable areas of the world. Today we take air travel to distant parts of the globe for granted, but in the 1920's this type of travel was only just being established for the very first time. It was thanks to the intrepid pioneers like Lindbergh, Alan Cobham, von Gronau and a number of others that the commercial air routes that we know so well today were established.

Much of this route-proving and exploration was intended for or indirectly helped along the establishment of commercial routes for passenger and freight-carrying airlines, but some of it was for the creation of mail routes for the transportation of mail speedily by air to distant destinations. In this sense the pioneering mail-carrying routes that were tentatively tried out before the First World War were properly established during the 1920's. This again was a pioneer of something that we take for granted today, the carriage of international mail and packages by air. Aviation effectively resulted in fast mail carriage across the vast distances of the United States, something that had not before been possible. Similarly, mail routes were pioneered in other parts of the world that were truly international in their nature. Some of this pioneering was carried out by countries such as Britain and France that were anxious to extend and speed up mail to distant parts of their far-flung empires. Some of it was just good old-fashioned exploration that nevertheless had big commercial spin-offs.

The inter-war period saw aviation become popularised through the exploits of many of the pioneers. Headline-making flights were accomplished in the name not just of commercial route-proving, exploration or other necessary goals, but also simply for the publicity value or to achieve some personal ambition or other. In this way some of the famous flights of the 1920's and 1930's were rather more valuable than others. One fact that was indisputable in the inter-war period was the increasing regulation of civil aviation. At the end of World War One there existed few hard and fast rules to govern civil aviation, and indeed comparatively few official regulatory bodies existed to achieve this. As the inter-war period developed, so the regulation of aviation in all its spheres gradually developed. Most countries adopted standards and rules to govern civil aviation and those who participated in it. Rudimentary forms of pilot's licences had been adopted in a number of countries before World War One for private flyers, but in the post-war world increasing regulation became necessary. Most countries eventually evolved official government regulatory bodies in the modern form. In the United States this became particularly necessary in order to keep tabs on the 'barnstorming' pilots (many of them ex-military World War One flyers) who were perhaps the most extreme examples of the unregulated world of post-First World War aviation.

In the sphere of civil commercial aviation, ever more high performance aircraft began to be introduced. By the early 1930's, the era of converting ex-military aircraft into ad-hoc airliners as in the post-First World War days was long gone. Some of the finest aircraft of their day, either military or civil, were the beautiful all-metal airliners that entered service during the 1930's. The needs of commercial airlines for higher performance airliners were a constant spur to aircraft manufacturers and engine designers, even in the darkest days of economic depression. In a number of celebrated cases, the new generation of civil transports exemplified by the Boeing Model 247 and the ubiquitous Douglas DC-3 enjoyed a performance that put some military aircraft to shame. Aircraft such as these were in the vanguard of the huge advances that were made in aircraft design and construction during the 1930's. Interestingly, some pre-World War Two airliners were of such good all-round performance that they had considerable potential as bombers as well. In several cases, aircraft such as the Junkers Ju 86 had military as well as civil commercial application. Even the renowned DC-3 had a direct military spin-off, the B-18 Bolo medium bomber.

The Road to War

The growing employment of aircraft in warfare without doubt changed the face of war forever. From the small beginnings of military aviation prior to World War One, and thence through the huge build-up of military air arms in World War One, aircraft developed into fighter, bomber, reconnaissance, transport, training and a host of other military tasks that would have surprised (and probably shocked) the early aviation pioneers. Continuing

JU 52/3M₁

development in the inter-war years witnessed ever-growing performance capabilities. These came about partly due to refinements in aircraft design and materials, and in the growing performance capabilities of aero engines. These developments, however, came about against the backdrop of seriously low defence budgets that were indulged in by many countries in the 1920's and early 1930's. Mass production on the scale that had arisen in World War One was quickly forgotten, resulting in manufacturers struggling to gain meaningful military orders. The situation was exacerbated by the economic climate in the inter-war period, the Wall Street Crash and Depression causing markets to shrink even more. It was not until the deteriorating political situation following the rise to power of Hitler's National Socialists in Germany during 1933, that a growing realization amongst military men and some politicians in a number of countries helped lead to rearmament. Unfortunately this rearmament took place too slowly in some countries to save them from disaster early in World War Two.

Great advances during the inter-war period took place in aeronautical design and construction, although some of the foundations for this had actually been put in place considerably earlier. One of the most important was in the large-scale adoption of metal in aircraft construction, for the structure of the aircraft and in notable cases for the aircraft's skin as well. There were several pioneers in this sphere, including Junkers and Dornier in Germany. It has sometimes been true that some of aviation's significant inventions and advances have received great fanfare at their birth, while others have met with much less

Hawker Hind

publicity. One of the latter, and it nevertheless transformed aviation, was the birth of the all-metal aeroplane. Virtually every type of aircraft up to the middle of World War One was made of wood (of various types), with fabric covering – metal was primarily used for rigging wires, and in some cases as a part of the structure. Thanks to pioneering work by Junkers, Dornier and others, the all-metal aircraft started to become reality long before the beautifully-streamlined all-metal stressed skin fighters of the Second World War. It eventually was enthusiastically taken up by many of the great designers and manufacturers, although some embraced it more rapidly than others.

Advances in materials alone could not guarantee success, however, and the development of stressed skin all-metal fighters in the run-up to World War Two came hand-in-hand with advances in aircraft design, streamlining, and the birth of more and more powerful engines. Continuing developments in related fields were also a big help, such as the creation of variable-pitch propellers and of course the key to many designers' dreams, the retractable undercarriage. The power available from engines also led to the huge increases in performance capability of civil and military aircraft as the 1930's wore on. The 1,030 hp Rolls-Royce Merlin inline piston engines that powered initial models of the superlative Supermarine Spitfire and Hawker Hurricane fighters of World War Two makes an interesting comparison to the power available to the Sopwith Camel, one of the greatest fighters of World War One. A number of engine types were used in the production run of the Camel, but fairly typical were the Clerget rotary engines of 130 hp.

In fact, the adoption of the monoplane layout for front-line military aircraft (and indeed for civil commercial aircraft as well) was not as straightforward as it might have seemed. The

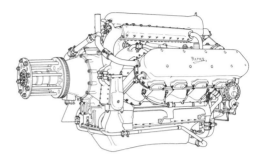

The Napier engine.

biplane fighter in particular evolved into an efficient and powerful military aircraft that continued to have its adherents well into the 1930's. Fortunately there were those rather more far-sighted designers such as the legendary R.J. Mitchell who was responsible with his Supermarine design team for the Spitfire. Mitchell saw the potential of the low-wing retractable undercarriage monoplane layout for future fighter design, and developed it into the superlative Spitfire. The biplane adherents nevertheless tried to wring the remaining capability from their chosen layout by fitting retractable undercarriages themselves, and continuing to point to the capabilities of the biplane layout including exceptional manoeuvrability. The monoplane camp eventually won the day, but in some countries the adoption of the retractable undercarriage monoplane fighter and bomber came too late and they were overwhelmed by better-equipped forces when World War Two commenced.

The inter-war period (and of course it was not known by that name at the time) was in fact an era of several significant wars in which aircraft played an important part. In the Far East, Japanese expansion resulted in brutal conflict with the Chinese. In Spain, the legitimately-elected government was challenged in 1936 by rebels whose cause was enthusiastically taken up by the Fascist powers of Germany and Italy. In both these conflicts and in a number of colonial skirmishes and other wars, aircraft came to play an important part. In the Spanish Civil War and in the fighting in the Far East in particular, aircraft were used on a number of significant occasions by the Axis powers (Japan, Italy and Germany) without remorse against civilian targets. This was a disturbing precursor of what was to come when World War Two broke out.

The fascinating aeronautical story of the greatest conflict in which aviation played a pivotal role, the Second World War, is the subject of the second Volume of this Encyclopaedia. In the telling of any historical narrative, authors and artists are indebted to many historians and colleagues for their assistance and practical help. As ever, it is a pleasant exercise to acknowledge friends and experts whose assistance and advice have been such an invaluable contribution towards the piecing together of much of the information and photographic content of this initial Volume of The Complete Encyclopaedia of Flight.

Particular recognition must go to Ed Banham, Derek Foley, Martin Hale, Jack Harris, Victor Lowe, Bob Richards, Jim Smith and Gordon Stevens for their assistance with information and illustrations, together with many overseas colleagues including Philippe Jalabert, Miroslav Khol, Hans Meier and Peter Walter. Special thanks also to Chris Slocock of Publishing

Avro Tutor. 1938

Solutions (www) Ltd. They have all been an important help in the telling of the story in this book. Aviation has been one of modern Man's greatest adventures, and fortunately it continues to be alive and well to this day.

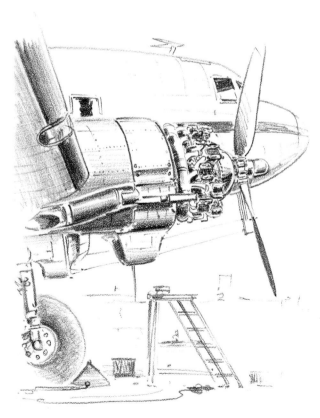

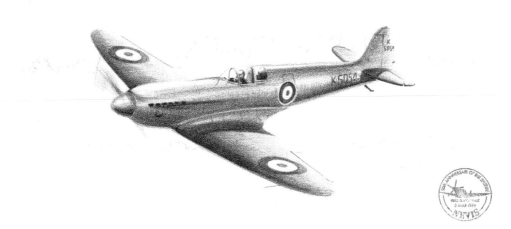

Spitfire Prototype Study for Nevis stamp   John Batchelor

Leonardo da Vinci

Mankind's desire to take to the skies is not a recent innovation. One of the earliest (but certainly not the first) of the many genuine proponents of manned flight was Leonardo da Vinci (1452-1519). da Vinci was the world-famous Florentine artist, who has been immortalised due to his famous painting the Mona Lisa. Yet da Vinci was busy in many other fields, and his interests in science and numerous related subjects brought him to study the mechanics of flight and the theoretical possibilities of manned flight. It is claimed that he made some 500 aeronautically-related drawings and sketches, and various writings on aeronautical subjects. This included such wide-ranging and far-reaching observations as the mechanics of the flight characteristics of birds (although he was not successful in identifying all of the complicated aspects of bird flight) and the way that these could be converted into structures to carry men aloft. Unfortunately for da Vinci the technology simply did not exist during his lifetime to transform his ideas and sketches into practical reality, and some of his proposals were too far-fetched to be realistic. His ideas for an early type of helicopter, for example, did not appreciate the basic dynamics of flight needed to make a helicopter work properly. Recent attempts to turn some of his other aeronautical ideas into reality have tended to meet limited success and illustrated the need for some re-design and reappraisal of his ideas. In reality, this would have been well beyond the capabilities of his own time, and he lived long before the appearance of viable sources of power (engines) and some suitable materials. Nevertheless, da Vinci left a legacy of ideas and observations, which provided an inspiration to subsequent thinkers and proved that a brilliant mind could grasp even in his era some of the basic principles needed for manned flight.

da Vinci's design for a corkscrew-type 'heilcopter'. if it had been built to carry people, might well have dwarfed its crew.

John Stringfellow

The Englishman John Stringfellow (1799-1883) was one of the most important of the aeronautical pioneers in the years leading up to the successful first controlled powered man-carrying flight by the Wright brothers in 1903. Based in Chard in the County of Somerset in southern England, Stringfellow was a practical pioneer who built a number of airworthy flying machines. In particular he worked tirelessly to find a suitable source of power for his aircraft designs. During the early Victorian era steam power was being successfully developed as a means of power for many ground-based applications, and so at the time steam propulsion was seen by many as a good potential source of power for flying machines. From the 1840's Stringfellow worked with another driving force for the creation of small, powerful steam engines, William Henson, on perfecting a suitable means of power for these craft. In the early 1840's Henson patented the design for a planned 'Aerial Steam Carriage'. This important development work culminated in 1848 when Stringfellow successfully flew a large powered aircraft model which made what is probably the first-ever sustained powered flight by a practical aircraft design – although it did not have a man aboard. This nonetheless represented a big breakthrough. Stringfellow's 1848 machine was later followed by a steam-powered triplane design that is claimed to have successfully flown at an exhibition in the Crystal Palace in London in 1868.

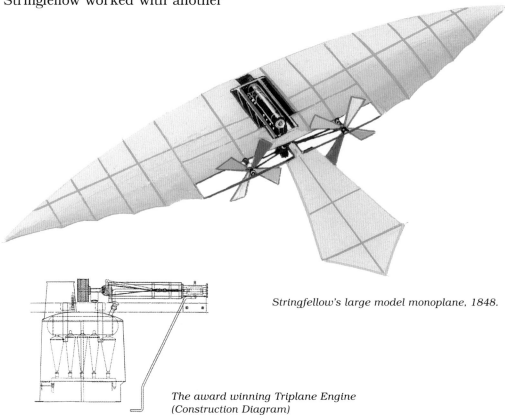

Stringfellow's large model monoplane, 1848.

The award winning Triplane Engine (Construction Diagram)

This was arguably the most successful powered flying up to that time anywhere in the world. It included the use of a 1 hp steam engine of exceptional design, and this power plant won a special award at the Crystal Palace event. Nevertheless, as before, no man was carried aloft by Stringfellow's machine. Although his work moved forward the potential of creating a viable, man-carrying flying machine, he did not achieve this feat himself. Indeed he did not live to see the ultimate fruits of his pioneering work, because he died 20 years before the famous flight of the Wright brothers in 1903.

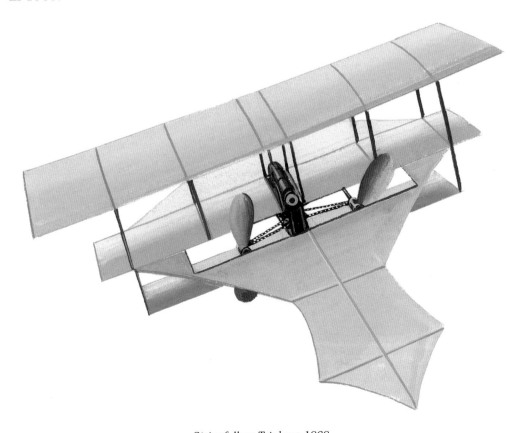

Stringfellow Triplane 1868.

Sir George Cayley

Regarded by many as the 'Father of Aviation', Sir George Cayley (1773-1857) achieved what was in its time the most thorough understanding yet of aerodynamics, but he also put his ideas into practice and gained several notable firsts. He was an aristocrat from the north of England, and he devoted much time to the theories and realities of the then emerging discipline of aerodynamics. In 1799 he engraved a silver disk with the design for an aircraft which was the earliest practical design for a heavier-than-air machine. He appreciated the problems with da Vinci's observations of the flight of birds, and instead came to understand the true mechanics of bird flight. He decided that successful flight for man could not be based exactly on the flight characteristics of birds. Indeed, Cayley was the first in history to realise that a successful aircraft would need rigid wings (rather than the flapping wings of birds, and the curious flapping ornithopters put forward by some eccentric early designers), allied to a separate source of power (e.g., an engine). However, he became sceptical of the use of steam power (as employed by pioneers such as Stringfellow) due to the comparatively poor power-to-weight ratio of steam engines and their general impracticality for use in flying machines. Sadly for Cayley no other viable source of power existed during his lifetime to power the aircraft that he designed. Nevertheless Cayley achieved many practical firsts. He built and flew in 1804, for the first time in the world, a successful model glider with full directional stability that had many modern features such as a fixed wing, and moveable direction-controlling tail surfaces. In 1849 he flew a triplane machine that carried a boy aloft, and in 1853 a full-size glider of monoplane design carried into the air his terrified coachman – now regarded as the first-ever flight of a human in a real aircraft-like contraption. However, the machine was not powered and it was not under the

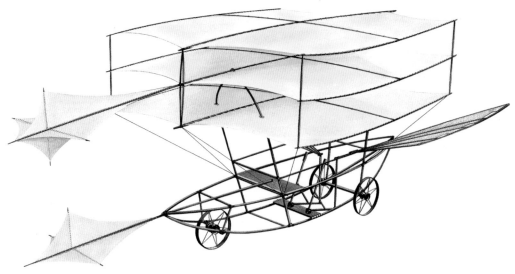

1849 boy-carrier.

full control of its occupant, who was largely along for the ride. Other achievements by Cayley were the first real understanding of airfoil sections and their vital role in wing design, the need for wing dihedral angle, and the requirement for an undercarriage to allow an aircraft to gain speed during a level take-off run.

Sir George Cayley, Bart. (1773-1857). This portrait is by Henry Perronet Briggs and is now in the National Portrait Gallery

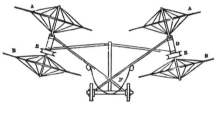

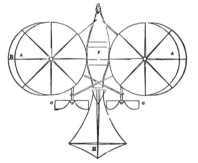

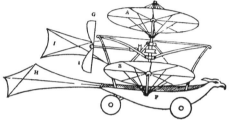

1843 Design for a Convertiplane.
Above left: front elevation (without airscrews).
Left: Plan, showing twin pusher airscrews.
Above: Side-elevation .
Rotor with blades open for helicoptering.

In praise of Sir George Cayley –

"About 100 years ago an Englishman, Sir George Cayley, carried the science of flying to a point which it had never reached before and which it scarcely reached again during the last century" – said Wilbur Wright (of Wright Flyer fame) in 1909.

"The aeroplane is a British invention: it was conceived in all essentials by George Cayley . . . the greatest genius of aviation" – said Charles Dollfus in France in 1923.

"The incontestable forerunner of aviation was an Englishman. Thus it is necessary to inscribe the name of Sir George Cayley in letters of gold on the first page of the aeroplane's history" – said Alphonse Berget in France in 1909.

"The principle of the airplane as we know it now, that of the rigid airplane, was first announced by Cayley" – said Theodore von Kármán in the USA in 1954.

Félix du Temple

Félix du Temple de la Croix was a French naval officer who broke new aeronautical ground when he became the first to create a man-carrying powered aircraft to actually leave the ground. He had already patented an aircraft design in 1857, and had achieved the 'first' of making the first-ever powered model aircraft to fly having actually taken-off under its own power. He experimented for some time with model aircraft layouts powered by clockwork and steam. In 1874 he successfully produced a full-size aircraft of some 56 feet wingspan (but some sources claim this to have been larger), which was powered by a hot-air piston engine. It made a short hop after running down a steep launching ramp, with a young sailor as its occupant. Whilst being powered, this man-carrying flight was not under any form of real control (although some rudimentary control to the aircraft's tail was included), and the occupant was present mainly for the ride. Nevertheless it was a major achievement to get a powered flying machine airborne with a human aboard, and in this sense du Temple succeeded where Stringfellow several years previously had been unable to achieve. In addition, du Temple pre-dated by several decades the achievements of other Frenchmen such as Louis Blériot and Léon Levavasseur in employing a tractor engine layout. This was eventually to become the conventional arrangement for most successful aircraft designs. Du Temple's flying machine was also a monoplane, again the type of layout that was (eventually) to find lasting favour amongst aircraft designers in the decades following the Wright brothers' first successful flights in 1903. It has also sometimes been claimed that du Temple's aircraft featured an undercarriage that was intended to be retractable – an amazingly far-sighted concept at that time.

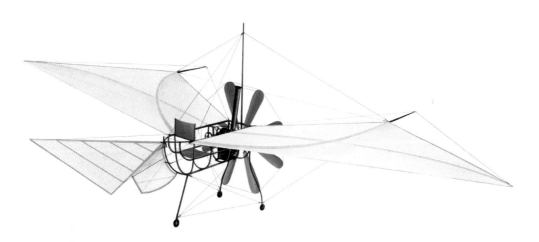

A more conventional layout for an aircraft than even the Wright Flyer of 1903,
the du Temple lacked only real controls, including lateral control (ailerons or wing-warping),
that would otherwise have made the French – and not the Americans - the first to genuinely fly.

Otto Lilienthal

German aviation pioneer Otto Lilienthal was the world's first true pilot of man-carrying heavier-than-air machines, and the most successful designer and exponent up to his era of manned glider designs. Nevertheless he also advocated powered flight using the flight of birds as the model, a concept that Sir George Cayley had thrown doubt upon decades before. Lilienthal's work with gliders was however ground-breaking. He not only designed and built practical gliders, he also realised that it was necessary to learn properly how to fly and control them. He therefore made the first practical man-carrying gliders in history. He built a number of different types of glider, and successfully made many hundreds of safe flights. In Lilienthal's designs, the pilot hung rather precariously from the glider's structure somewhat like a modern hang-glider design, and used movements of his body to control the glider in flight and allow it to change direction. Take-off was achieved by the pilot running forward until the glider became airborne. Lilienthal died in 1896 when he crashed after being caught by a sudden gust of wind.

Above:
Stamp issued by Romania in 1978. Drawn by John Batchelor.
This was also produced for the History of Transportation book.

Right:
Otto Lilienthal taking off from the Gollenburg in the Stöllner Hills in his monoplane hang-glider.

Samuel Langley

A significant aeronautical pioneer in the United States was Samuel P. Langley. Secretary of the Smithsonian Institution, Langley performed many years of research into aeronautics, and successfully flew in 1896 an important steam-powered model aircraft. The US government later commissioned Langley to create a full-size man-carrying machine. This was the second such official sponsorship of aeronautics (the first was made by the French, to French designer Clément Ader in 1892). Langley subsequently worked tirelessly to create a viable man-carrying aeroplane, and greatly inspired others including Orville and Wilbur Wright. Langley's various flying machines were called 'Aerodrome', a name now associated with an airfield rather than a flying machine. Although at first using steam-powered models, Langley importantly bridged the development gap between the redundant use of steam for flying machines, and the new, breath-taking technology of the petrol internal combustion engine. Langley worked with a number of pioneers who were developing the petrol engine for aeronautical applications, including Charles Manly and Stephen Balzer, and his later flying machines were petrol engine-powered. Langley's designs came to employ a tandem wing monoplane layout, and flight testing took place – somewhat bizarrely – from the top of

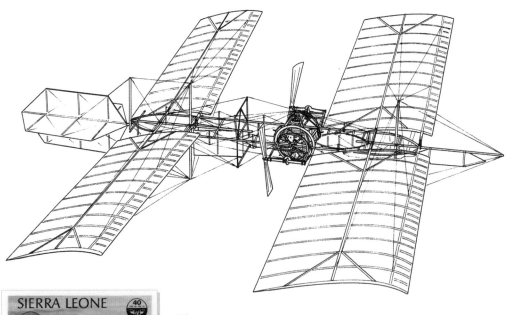

Above:
Showing the Langley Aerodrome, construction was of wood and fabric.

Left:
Stamp issued by Sierra Leone, 1985. Drawn by John Batchelor.

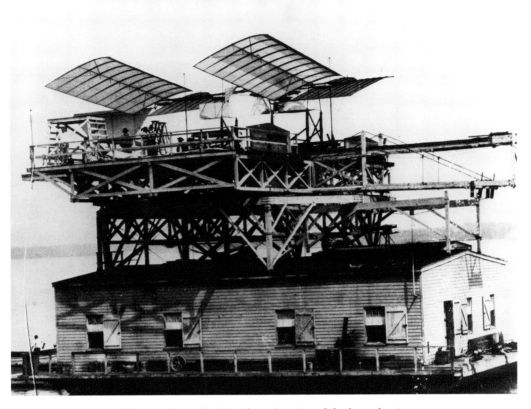

Picture shows the 'Aerodrome' on top of the houseboat.

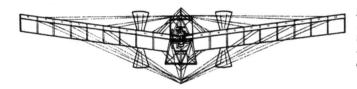

Front view of the Aerodrome. The 1914 Curtiss reconstruction of this aircraft had a wingspan of 48 ft 5 in (14.76 m), and a length of 52 ft 5 in (15.98 m).

a houseboat in the Potomac River. He successfully flew a petrol-engined model in 1901 which was quite possibly the first successful petrol-engined flying machine. However, it needed much re-design to give it true flying qualities, and a refined model flew successfully in August 1903. Langley's experiments with a full-size Aerodrome, however, met with disaster. Powered by a 52 hp Manly-Balzer engine, the Aerodrome A crashed into the Potomac River in October 1903. A further attempt in early December 1903, with Manly as pilot, saw the Aerodrome crash once more. The Aerodrome design did not incorporate correct flight controls, and Langley abandoned his promising experiments. The way was set for the Wright brothers to make the first controlled powered flight. Interestingly, Glenn Curtiss restored and improved the Langley Aerodrome in 1914. In its new, revised form, the Aerodrome successfully flew from off the surface of Lake Keuka, New York, without serious incident.

Wright Flyer

At 10.35 a.m. on Thursday, 17 December 1903, the history of the world was changed forever. At that time Orville Wright performed the first-ever manned, powered and controlled flight in a heavier-than-air craft. The Wright Flyer No.1 that he piloted successfully took off from a level launch rail, flew under control, and landed at approximately the same height that it had started from. This marked the event out from all other attempts that had taken place in the past. Although the flight lasted only 12 seconds and covered some 120 feet, it had world-wide significance. Later that day both Orville and his brother

Wilbur continued with three further successful flights. The place of these pioneering achievements was near to Kitty Hawk in North Carolina. In the coming months and years the Wright brothers continued to refine their designs – substituting, for example, the prone position of the pilot for a normal seat, and eventually introducing a conventional wheeled undercarriage. They became embroiled, however, in legal patent battles with some of their contemporaries. The Wright Flyer of the historic first flight in December 1903 was in effect the culmination of all the pioneering work that had taken place by many men in

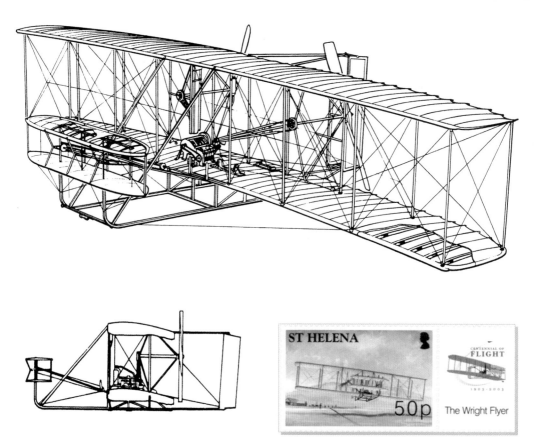

ST HELENA

CENTENNIAL OF FLIGHT

1903-2003

50p

The Wright Flyer

the past century or so into aerodynamics, aircraft design, and the components needed for successful powered flight. The Wright brothers were already successfully established in the bicycle trade in Dayton, Ohio, and they had spent several years studying the pioneering work in aeronautics that had taken place before them. The development of the internal combustion engine was a vital component to the success of the Wrights – at last the steam engine with its comparatively poor power-to-weight ratio was no longer needed for aircraft design. They had the talent and capabilities (and the necessary workshop) to make their own power plant (of some 12 hp) to power the Flyer. The success of the Wright Flyer opened the floodgates, and soon controlled powered manned flight was to become as commonplace as all of the other established means of transport.

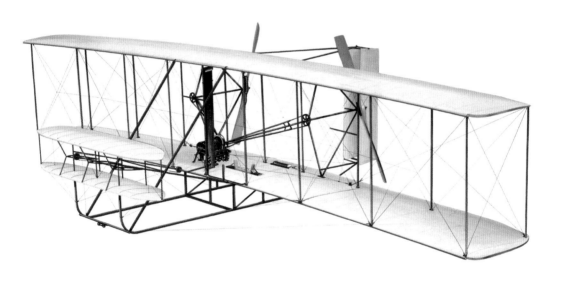

The Wright Flyer - note that the engine is off centre on the airframe so that the pilot lies next to it, thus equalising the weight distribution.

Specifications – Wright Flyer No.1

Wingspan	40 ft 4 in
Length	21 ft 1 in
Maximum flight distance	852 ft (on first flight day)
Maximum achieved flight	59 seconds (on first flight day)
Engine	One Wright-designed and built inline piston engine, of 12 hp
Crew	One

Levavasseur Antoinette VII

One of the great early pioneers of aviation in Europe was Frenchman Léon Levavasseur. Levavasseur was a pioneer of the internal combustion engine for aviation applications, having already achieved success with this type of engine for racing motorboats. His two basic engines, of 24 hp and 50 hp, powered many of the important European aircraft in the period up to around 1910, until the Gnome rotary piston engine and other descendants became pre-eminent sources of power for many European aircraft. Levavasseur was also an early, successful aircraft designer, and his most important contribution was the Antoinette series of elegant monoplanes with a tractor (rather than a pusher) engine/propeller layout. With Louis Blériot, Levavasseur was a true pioneer of this design arrangement, which in later years was to prove the classic evolved layout for many piston-engine aircraft designs. The Antoinette IV, which first appeared in October 1908, used somewhat primitive ailerons for lateral control, and is generally seen as the world's first truly successful monoplane. Nevertheless, wing-warping continued to be the means of ensuring lateral control in later Antoinette types. The most elegant Antoinette was the Antoinette VII, powered by one of Levavasseur's classic early V-8 piston engines. The fuselage of the Antoinette VII featured a long inverted triangular section, the large V-8 Antoinette engine being mounted prominently at the front. One of the famous pilots who flew the Antoinette was Frenchman Hubert Latham. He attempted (unsuccessfully) to make a first crossing of the English Channel in an Antoinette IV in July 1909, just days before Louis Blériot's successful attempt – but he did make several

Hubert Latham in his Antoinette leads Ralph Johnstone in his Wright Model B. Belmont Park, New York, October 1910.

Souvenir Postcard of Robert Thomas's flight in his Antoinette 1910.

other, far more successful flights and demonstrations in the Antoinette type. The Antoinette aircraft were named for Antoinette Gastambide, the daughter of a supporter and colleague of Levavasseur.

Specifications - Levavasseur Antoinette VII

Wingspan	42 ft
Length	37 ft 8.75 in
Maximum speed	43.5 mph at approximately 328 ft
Important flight time	included a flight of 1 hr 7 min
Engine	One Levavasseur Antoinette V-8 inline piston engine, of 50 hp or (possibly) 60 hp
Crew	One

Santos-Dumont No. 14-bis

Proving that aviation from the start was an international fraternity, one of Europe's first genuinely successful aeronautical pioneers was a Brazilian. Alberto Santos-Dumont was also one of early aviation's first truly popular characters, in comparison to the rather guarded and reserved Wright brothers. From a wealthy family in Brazil, Santos-Dumont took up an interest in aviation during the 1890's while in Europe. At first he was involved in ballooning. He later achieved great fame by building a successful, petrol-engined airship (his Airship No.6) that was one of the first actually successful manned powered flying machines. In 1901 it won for him a substantial prize of some 100,000 francs for a controlled flight around the Eiffel Tower in Paris. Turning to heavier-than-air flight, Santos-Dumont achieved great fame by being the first to make an officially-recognised powered controlled manned flight in Europe in an aircraft.

This was achieved in his No.14-bis biplane, which was a tail-first canard-configuration contraption using boxkite-type wings and a boxkite-like combined rudder-elevator at the front. The No.14-bis was thus a gloriously unconventional-looking machine, and it had only primitive controls, but it successfully made a short hop on 13 September 1906 as Europe's first powered manned heavier-than-air flight. Santos-Dumont subsequently flew the No.14-bis at the Bagatelle on the then-outskirts of Paris on 23 October 1906 for 197 feet to win a prize for the first flight in Europe of over 82 feet. Following this up on 12 November of that year in the same but slightly modified machine, Santos-Dumont achieved lasting fame. With the most auspicious of his several flights on that day, he succeeded in making the first officially-recognised powered manned controlled flight in Europe, when he flew 722 feet in just over 21 seconds of flight. With this

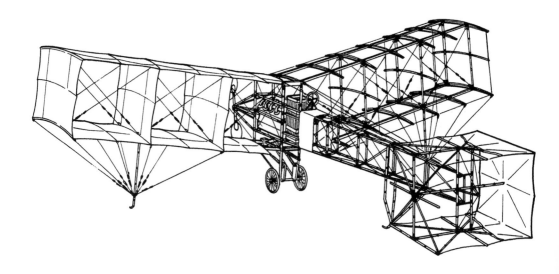

flight he won a prize offered by the Aéro-Club de France for the first flight of over 328 feet by a heavier-than-air machine. Santos-Dumont was a very popular figure in France, and he did much to bring an interest and belief in aviation to even some of those who were sceptical of this new form of transport.

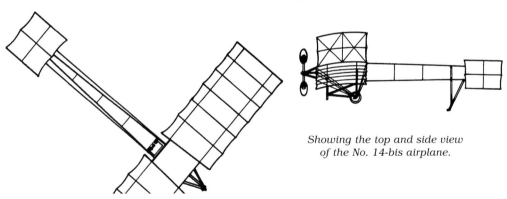

Showing the top and side view of the No. 14-bis airplane.

Specifications – Santos-Dumont No.14-bis

Wingspan	36 ft 9 in
Length	31 ft 10 in
Record-breaking distance	722 feet
Record-breaking flight time	just over 21 seconds
Engine	One Antoinette inline piston engine, of 50 hp
Crew	One

AEA Aerodrome No.3 'June Bug'

It was not long after the initial success of the Wright brothers before many would-be aviators and designers started to get themselves successfully into the air. In the United States, a number of patent battles soon erupted as the Wright brothers attempted to safeguard their designs, whilst others tried to construct viable flying machines of their own creation. An important if short-lived organisation in the USA that furthered aeronautical thought was the Aerial Experiment Association (AEA). This group contained such august members as Dr. Alexander Graham Bell (of telephone development fame), and Glenn Curtiss (who can claim the distinction of forming America's first viable aviation manufacturing company, the Curtiss Aeroplane Company). The AEA designed, built and flew several promising aircraft during 1908. One of these, the Aerodrome No.2 'White Wing', included moveable control surfaces on its outer wings, a great leap forward from the archaic wing-warping used by the Wright brothers. It was followed by Aerodrome No.3 named 'June Bug', which first flew in June 1908. This successful early flying machine was developed by Glenn Curtiss. On 4 July 1908, Curtiss won the Scientific American Trophy in the 'June Bug' for the first flight to exceed one kilometre (3,281 feet) in a straight line in the USA. This achievement put the United States at once back on a level with the achievements of early French aviators, who were themselves already pushing forward the boundaries of manned, powered and controlled aircraft.

Specifications – Aerodrome No.3 'June Bug'

Wingspan	42 ft 6 in
Length	27 ft 6 in
Maximum flight distance	2,000 yards
Maximum achieved flight	102.5 seconds
Engine	One Curtiss-origin 8-cylinder 'V' inline piston engine, of 40 hp
Crew	One

Avro Type F

In the formative years following the first successful manned, controlled and powered flights by the Wright brothers, most significant aeronautical developments took place in two countries – France and the United States. In other countries that eventually built up their own fine aviation traditions, such as Great Britain, progress was initially comparatively slow. One of several intrepid home-grown pioneers in Britain was A.V. Roe, and his company Avro was eventually to become one of the greatest aviation companies that the world has seen. From 1906 onwards the British newspaper the 'Daily Mail' began to sponsor aviation-related activities and awarded specific prizes for particular competitions. The first of these, held in London for model aeroplanes, was won by Roe with a rubber-band-powered biplane model. Suitably encouraged, Roe embarked on the development and construction of man-carrying aircraft. He progressed through various biplane and triplane projects, which proceeded with varying degrees of success. He was - arguably - the first Briton to fly successfully an aircraft of British invention and construction, with his triplane design in July 1909. By 1912 the Avro (A.V. Roe and Co.) company was well established, and it achieved a significant 'first' by creating the first aircraft in the world with a fully enclosed fuselage and enclosed accommodation for its pilot. Hitherto, all airworthy aircraft had left their occupant or occupants out in the open. The Avro Type F featured a properly enclosed fuselage of wood construction with fabric covering and celluloid windows, with a metal trapdoor in the roof. It first flew on 1 May 1912, but only one example was built. Rightly seen as the world's first cabin monoplane, the Type F was followed during 1912 by the Avro Type G biplane two-seater, which was the world's first cabin biplane. Overall, however, this very advanced fuselage design layout took a long time to be adopted on a wide scale.

Specifications – Avro Type F

Wingspan	28 ft
Length	23 ft
Maximum speed	65 mph at sea level
Maximum take-off weight	800 lb
Engine	One Viale radial piston engine, of 35 hp
Crew	One

Blériot XI

Perhaps the greatest name in early aviation in Europe is that of Louis Blériot. This celebrated Frenchman made a profound impact on the development of aviation, as a designer, pioneer pilot and constructor. With other pioneers such as Léon Levavasseur he was responsible for the eventual widespread adoption of the tractor monoplane layout of aircraft design (which puts the engine and propeller at the front) as opposed to the practice of many early aviators – including the Wright brothers – of having a pusher layout with the engine at the back. In this sense Blériot was far-sighted, and he worked for several years on perfecting the tractor monoplane layout. After brief collaboration with the Voisin brothers, he set out rather more successfully to build his own aircraft. His development work eventually culminated in the world-famous Blériot XI, which was initially exhibited in 1908 and first flew in early 1909. At a time when European aviation was starting to catch up with the many achievements gained by pioneers in the United States, the increasingly successful Blériot XI began to secure genuine European

accomplishments. On 25 July 1909, Blériot achieved aviation immortality by becoming the first to fly in a heavier-than-air machine across the English Channel. His flight from a field near Calais in France to Dover was barely achieved, and ended in a crash landing, but it gained international headlines. It also won for Blériot a £1,000 prize from the British 'Daily Mail' newspaper. The massive publicity and acclaim that attended Blériot's achievement guaranteed his success as an aviation entrepreneur. Large numbers of Blériot XI aircraft were ordered, and the type in several distinct versions gained widespread acceptance in both civilian and military service. Several European countries bought the Blériot XI for their fledgling military air arms. The type served in front-line observation roles (and sometimes carried improvised weapons), and it quite possibly saw very early military combat duties with Italian forces in 1911 (see Page 54). Blériot XI machines were also used for pilot training. Significant military air arms such as those of France and Britain were operating the type when

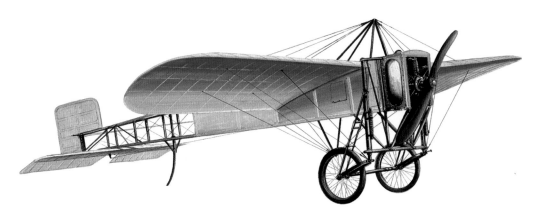

World War One commenced
in August 1914.

*One of the most celebrated early
flights was Louis Blériot's famous
crossing of the English Channel
in July 1909, an event that caught
the popular imagination and
did much to further the cause
of aviation.*

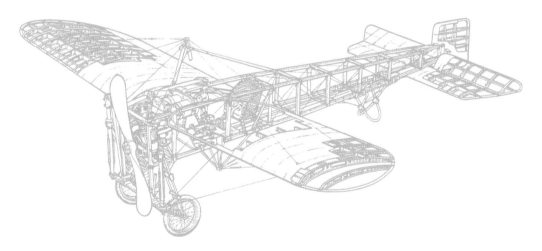

Specifications – Blériot XI (Cross-Channel type)

Wingspan	25 ft 7 in
Length	26 ft 3 in
Maximum speed	approximately 46 mph
Important flight distance	approximately 23.5 miles Calais-Dover
Engine	One Anzani semi-radial 'fan type' piston engine, of some 25 hp
Crew	One

Santos-Dumont Demoiselle

The notable and well-liked Brazilian aviation pioneer Alberto Santos-Dumont achieved lasting fame with his No.14-bis boxkite-like canard-configuration biplane (see Pages 38-39). However, successful though the No.14-bis was in achieving several 'firsts' and record flights, it was nonetheless something of a dead-end as far as long-term aerodynamic development was concerned. Santos-Dumont nevertheless had additional aviation concepts up his sleeve, and in 1907 he turned his attention to an aircraft that went on to achieve great and widespread acclaim. This was the Demoiselle (Dragonfly), which is often regarded by historians as the world's first light aircraft or even as the forerunner of the 'homebuilt' sector of aviation that exists to this day. The direct precursor of the Demoiselle line was the Santos-Dumont No.19, which first appeared in 1907 and was fine-tuned into a viable light plane design. This machine led onto the Santos-Dumont

No.20, which basically represented what became the best-known Demoiselle layout. The No.20 is believed to have first flown in March 1909, and it caused great excitement at the Paris aviation exhibition in the Grand Palais in September/October 1909. Santos-Dumont had a vision of making the ability to fly accessible to everyone who wished to take to the air, and to make the Demoiselle available to all – and so he waived any rights to the plans of the aircraft. This allowed amateur builders world-wide to have a go at building their own Demoiselle, sometimes with local modifications or improvements included. Limited factory production was carried out in Paris by the Clément-Bayard airship company at Issy-les-Moulineaux. With all the individual manufacturing that additionally took place world-wide, it is impossible to put an exact figure on the number of Demoiselle that were completed, but it is certainly true that the Demoiselle was one of the more wide-

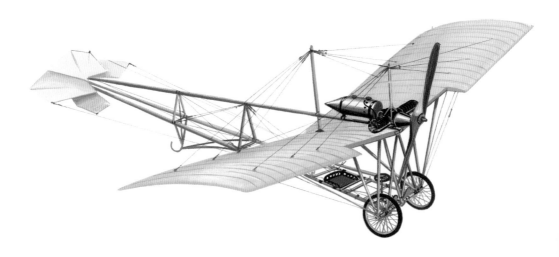

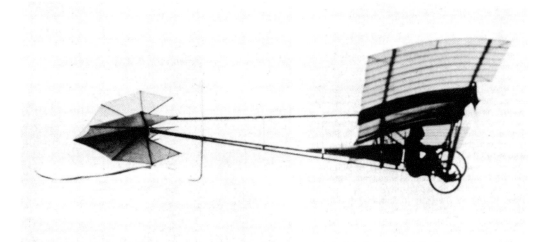

Santo-Dumont saling over St. Cyr near Versailles.
Conical fairing was probably an attempt to reduce pilot induced turbulence.

spread aircraft around the world in the period up to the outbreak of World War One. However, although advanced in its concept, the Demoiselle was still in important ways an aircraft of its time, with eventually-abandoned features such as wing-warping for lateral control. Some examples were employed by early flying schools, but there were nevertheless few serious accidents with the Demoiselle – a very handsome record. The specifications given here are typical for the 'homebuilt' Demoiselle.

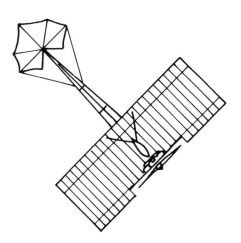

Plan view drawing of the Demoiselle, showing the simple but effective lines of this pioneering light aircraft.

Specifications – Santos-Dumont Demoiselle

Wingspan	18 ft
Length	20 ft
Maximum take-off weight	approximately 242 lb
Engine	One Darracq two-cylinder piston engine, of some 25 or 30 hp (other options available)
Crew	One

Farman Biplanes

By far the most active European country in the field of aeronautical development in the years after 1903 was France. The first-ever recognised commercial aircraft manufacturing company was formed by the Voisin brothers Gabriel and Charles in France in 1906, following an earlier liaison with Louis Blériot. An early associate was Englishman Henry Farman (who much later became a French citizen, and whose Christian name is often spelt Henri). Farman ordered a Voisin biplane (sometimes called the Voisin-Farman No.1) in 1907, and later made significant improvements to it. He also used it to achieve some ground-breaking long distance and 'endurance' flights. In subsequent years the talents of Henry and his brother Maurice Farman led to the creation of the Farman company of 1912, and a long series of successful production aircraft for military use ensued. Both brothers retained a certain autonomy within the Farman organisation, and some of their products reflected this relationship. Of particular importance in

the pre-war years to several fledgling air arms was the Maurice Farman M.F.7. This large, cumbersome framework biplane featured a pusher layout and was known as the '1913 type' due to the year that it first appeared in numbers. The distinctive layout of the M.F.7 included the elevator positioned on outriggers at the front of the aircraft – a formula much favoured by some early pioneers – and this led to the nickname 'Longhorn' being given to the type in Britain. Longhorns were already in service with the French and British military at the start of World War One, and they performed limited observation missions, being fairly typical of the rather primitive aircraft with which most air arms entered the First World War. Longhorns remained in front-line service principally until 1915, and they also performed valuable assistance as pilot trainers. In contrast, the M.F.11 (also a pre-war design) was a somewhat more advanced machine that did away with

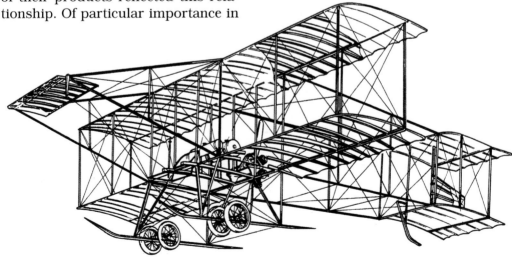

The Henry Farman III, the first true design of Henry Farman.

An evocative poster celebrating Henry Farman.

the M.F.7's cumbersome frontal elevator and featured a more conventional tail unit. Nicknamed 'Shorthorn' because of the simple short skid extensions at the front that served simply to prevent the aircraft from nosing over on bad landings, the M.F.11 provided valuable service as an armed reconnaissance aircraft that could drop bombs. It additionally had a machine gun for its observer. The crew nacelle was distinctively mounted between the aircraft's biplane wings, as opposed to the M.F.7's crew nacelle on the lower wing. Licence production took place in Britain of both the M.F.7 and M.F.11. In addition to these types, the Farman brothers created a series of biplane bombers and reconnaissance aircraft that gave valuable service to several Allied air arms during the war. Some of these were known as 'Horace' Farmans.

Specifications – Maurice Farman M.F.7 'Longhorn'

Wingspan	51 ft
Length	37 ft 3 in
Maximum speed	59 mph at sea level
Maximum take-off weight	1,885 lb
Armament	Various improvised weapons (when carried)
Engine	One Renault inline piston engine, of 70 hp (other options available)
Crew	Two

Dunne D.5 and D.8

Although aviation developments in Britain generally lagged behind those in France and the United States in the years after 1903, there were nevertheless some important pioneers who created a number of interesting concepts. It was actually an American, Samuel Cody, who made the first recognised manned aeroplane flight in Britain (although there is at least one other contender to this title), in 1908. At that time a now almost-forgotten British pioneer, John William Dunne, was experimenting with a novel concept for a tail-less, swept-wing inherently-stable biplane aircraft. Dunne's first aerial creations were built at H.M. Balloon Factory, Farnborough, near where Cody was to make his historic flight in 1908. Dunne at first secured some official interest and support for his experiments, one of the first pioneers in Britain to receive this distinction. His early experimentation with tail-less biplanes was not particularly successful, but he persevered and achieved more with his later work. Developed in 1909 was the Dunne

D.5, a swept-wing tail-less pusher biplane. Successful flights were achieved with this contraption in 1910, at Eastchurch in Kent. A single-seater with the fuselage pod on the lower wing, the D.5 featured control surfaces on the upper wings and vertical side surfaces at the wing ends between the wings. The aircraft was built by the British company Short Brothers – this early British aviation company later went on to make many much more famous aircraft of their own. The D.5 in fact reflected the excellent engineering quality of this pioneering company. It has been claimed that the D.5 was inherently-stable, flying straight and level without control inputs from the pilot – a feature that a number of early pioneers tried to achieve. It was later developed into the Gnome rotary-engined D.8, which flew in 1912/1913 with some success. This generated interest especially in the United States, where the Burgess company formed an alliance with Dunne to develop his designs into seaplanes. The subsequent Burgess-Dunne sea-

Dunne's swept-wing tail-less biplanes were the first V-shaped aircraft to fly, pre-dating the V-Bombers built in Britain in the 1950's, and anticipating the Northrop B-2A Spirit flying wing of the 1990's. This is the Dunne D.8.

John Dunne seated in the 'cockpit' of his Dunne D.5.

planes were built in very small numbers, possibly three being supplied to the fledgling U.S. Navy air arm. Dunne was in fact well ahead of his time with tail-less aircraft. In later years the Northrop company in particular developed 'flying wing' tail-less aircraft, which culminated during the 1990's in the superb Northrop B-2A Spirit 'stealth bomber'.

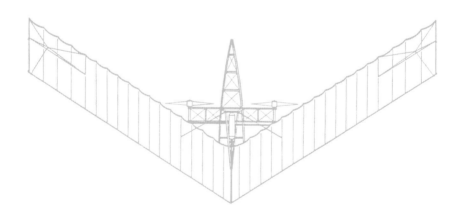

Specifications – Dunne D.5

Wingspan	46 ft
Length	of fuselage pod 18 ft
Maximum speed	approximately 55 mph at sea level
Engine	One Green inline piston engine, of 50 or 60 hp
Crew	One

Early Helicopter Pioneers

A helicopter is a very different flying machine to an aircraft, and the successful development of a viable helicopter layout proved just as elusive – if not more so – than that of creating a practical powered man-carrying aircraft. Although da Vinci had sketched possible 'helicopter' designs around 1500 (see page 25), one of his more ambitious concepts would only have 'cork-screwed' itself into the air without any control or means of moving forward. It was necessary for a lot of thought – and the invention of the internal combustion engine with its good power-to-weight ratio – before practical machines could be invented that were capable of controlled vertical lift-off using rotating surfaces. In the centuries following da Vinci, many inventors tried their hands, and in 1842 W.H. Phillips produced a steam-powered model 'helicopter' with rotating blades and blade tip 'jets'. By the early 1900's the general concepts of vertical flight were starting to be understood, even the thorny problem of moving forwards or backwards once vertical flight had been accomplished. The concept of cyclic pitch control to alter the pitch angle of the helicopter's rotor blades to achieve this, eventually became clear to the early helicopter pioneers. In France a number of inventors worked on the helicopter concept. They included the Breguet brothers Louis and Jacques. Together with Professor Charles Richet they produced the Breguet-Richet Gyroplane I – on 29 September 1907 this rose erratically into the air to become the first helicopter to lift a man off the ground, although it was steadied by four very brave onlookers on the ground. Better, on 13 November 1907, the French pioneer Paul Cornu lifted off, to the awe-inspiring height of one foot, in his twin-rotor 'flying bicycle' contraption – this was the first actual helicopter flight in history. Louis Breguet subsequently continued his pioneering work before and after World War One. The first helicopters that incorporated some form of cyclic pitch control were made by the Argentine the Marquis de Pescara, in Europe between 1919 and 1925. Other important work was carried out by Frenchman Etienne Oehmichen dur-

The Paul Cornu helicopter of 1907.

Left:
de Bothezatt:
In December 1922 this
single-seat helicopter
managed to make a
flight of 1 minute 40 seconds
in the United States.

Below:
Oehmichen: French pioneer
Etienne Oehmichen
achieved helicopter flight
with this four-rotor machine
in the early 1920's.

ing that period. However, it was not until the 1930's with pioneering machines in Germany and the United States that long-term success was achieved in helicopter development.

With multiple rotor blades
frantically thrashing, an early
helicopter undergoes indoor
flight testing.
This is almost certainly one
of de Pescara's experimental
helicopters in the early 1920's
(Photo: John Batchelor Collection).

Specifications – Paul Cornu helicopter

Rotor diameter	19 ft 8.25 in
Take-off Weight	573 lb
Important flight height	One foot
Important flight time	approximately 20 seconds
Engine	One Levavasseur Antoinette V-8 inline piston engine, of 24 hp
Crew	One

Curtiss Flying Boats

All the successful man-carrying powered aircraft of the early days of true manned flight were land-based, with either skid or wheel undercarriages. Several aviation pioneers, however, saw the benefit of operating aircraft from water, although it proved initially very difficult to design a suitable lower fuselage or float layout. The true father of powered water-borne flight was Frenchman Henri Fabre. In March 1910 in the south of France, his curious Hydravion was the first-ever aircraft, to successfully take-off from water and fly. In the United States, the great pioneer of water-borne aircraft was Glenn Curtiss, who had already gained success with the land-based 'June Bug' (see page 40). In addition to land-based aircraft, Curtiss experimented with aircraft for operation on water, and became the greatest early exponent of water-based aircraft. His first successful water-going aircraft flew in January 1911, and he subsequently created the Triad in 1911 which was a successful early amphibian (with both water-capable and conventional land undercarriage). In 1912 he evolved the first really successful flying-boat (his Flying-Boat No.2) with a developing boat-like lower fuselage hull shape. Important to the success of an aircraft on water is a 'stepped' (lower fuselage side-profile shape) hull, and boat keel-like cross-section. Curtiss refined these basic design requirements into many winning flying-boat designs in later years. His successful Model F series were amongst the first flying-boats for the U.S. Navy's fledgling air arm. Prior to the start of World War One, a Curtiss flying-boat was possibly the first ever aircraft to fly with an automatic pilot. Also highly successful was the slightly later HS flying-boat series, which proved well-suited to coastal patrol work and was one of the first mass-produced military flying-boats to serve in large numbers. Well over one thousand of the HS-1L and HS-2L models were built during World War

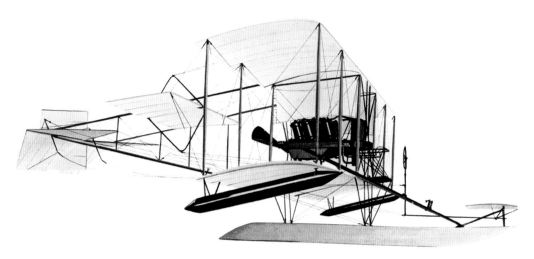

The Curtiss Triad of 1911 was a successful early amphibian, and helped to establish Curtiss at the forefront of water-borne aircraft development.

The Curtiss HL Series of flying-boats achieved much good service in military and civilian operation. This Canadian civil registered machine is mounted on a wheeled dolly for ease of handling on the ground out of the water.

One. Some of these continued to serve even after the war. Several operated in civil guise in Canada, where one pioneered 'bush' flying in remote outback areas, as the first commercial aircraft in Canada.

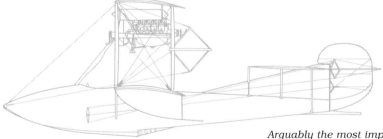

Arguably the most important early flying-boat was the Curtiss Model F, which was one of the first truly successful production flying-boats.

Specifications – Curtiss HS-2L

Wingspan	74 ft 1 in
Length	39 ft
Maximum speed	82.5 mph at sea level
Endurance	4 hr 30 min
Armament	Two 0.303 in machine guns,
	two 230 lb depth charges, or equivalent bombs
Service Ceiling	5,200 ft
Engine	One Liberty inline piston engine, of 360 or 400 hp
Crew	Two or three

Martin Sonora

Only a few years after the Wright brothers' first flights in December 1903, aircraft started to be used in conflicts around the world. Their influence in warfare was soon very important, and from small beginnings aircraft started to be used in a multiplicity of warlike roles. Commencing with simple observation missions, aircraft were soon fulfilling active combat roles. Quite possibly the first use of military aircraft in conflict was made by Italian military aviators against Turkish forces in a dispute for the control of Libya during October/November 1911. Before that time, in February 1911, aviators in the pay of the Mexican government had reconnoitred rebel positions during the Mexican Revolution. Later, a number of mercenary pilots flew for both sides in the continuing Mexican troubles. Two of these pilots became involved during 1913 in what is believed to be the world's first aerial dogfight, when they engaged each other unsuccessfully with pistols. Between May and August 1913, Frenchman Didier Masson together initially with a Mexican crew member made possibly the world's first genuine bombing missions in an aircraft specially modified as a bomber. During that time they unsuccessfully dropped home-made 18 inch long iron pipe bombs using a primitive bombsight aimed at Mexican government gunboats. The aircraft that Masson piloted was a Martin biplane. Powered by a 75 hp Curtiss engine driving a pusher propeller, the aircraft had a wingspan of approximately 50 feet, a range of some 100 miles, and it featured independent ailerons between its biplane wings. Known as the Martin Sonora, it was apparently named for the province in northern Mexico that was a rebel stronghold.

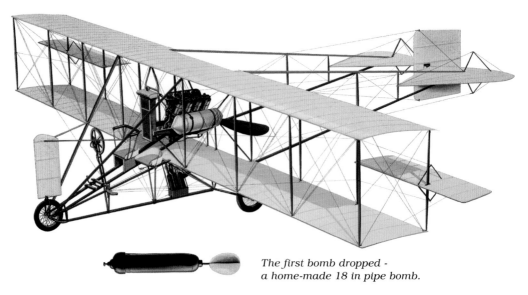

The first bomb dropped -
a home-made 18 in pipe bomb.

Few details of the Martin Sonora shown here, or its primitive bomb-release equipment are known.

Deperdussin Monocoque Racer

An aircraft company that helped to further aircraft design and manufacture was the short-lived Deperdussin aircraft company of Armand Deperdussin. This French-based organisation produced several increasingly innovative aircraft. Particular requirements were streamlined design and high speed. The best representation of these ideas was the Deperdussin Monocoque of 1912-1913, which introduced a whole new appearance to aircraft design, with a beautifully-streamlined fuselage and undercarriage arrangement. The Monocoque's fuselage was just that, a revolutionary monocoque structure made from tulip-wood strips glued over a removable jig to make a strong shell-like structure. The heavy framework of longerons and cross-pieces over which fabric was fixed on many contemporary aircraft was not needed by the Monocoque. Lateral control, however, was still by warping of the aircraft's monoplane wing. Deperdussin's successful Monocoque racers were the fastest aircraft prior to the outbreak of World War One, achieving many race wins and records. On 29 September 1913 at Reims, a Monocoque broke the world speed record at 126.67 mph – this record stood until 1920.

Specifications – Deperdussin Monocoque Racer

Wingspan	21 ft 9.75 in
Length	20 ft 0.15 in
Record-breaking speed	126.67 mph
Maximum take-off weight	approximately 1,349.2 lb
Engine	One Gnome 14-cyl rotary piston engine, of 160 hp
Crew	One

Bristol Scout

The earliest warplanes of the First World War were not the famous fighting machines that starred in the mid to late war period. They were instead capable if unspectacular types that would have been more at home in a pre-war racing meeting or air show, or performing unarmed scouting missions for a fledgling air arm. One of the first combat aircraft on the Allied side in World War One was just such a type, the Bristol Scout. The first Scout flew in February 1914, and two Scout B were sent to the Western Front shortly after the war started. They were followed by the first true production model, the Scout C, which was built for Britain's Royal Flying Corps and Royal Naval Air Service. Finally was the Scout D, again for both services, the last examples of which were delivered well into 1916. Production numbered 211 Scout C, and 160 Scout D, (these numbers are open to debate). Several engine options were available. Approximately 80 Scouts were sent to France for operational service there, and the type also served in the Middle East. Scouts performed their scouting missions with improvised weapons, and they were at first allocated piecemeal to operational units sometimes to escort more vulnerable types. The Scout in fact was a strong and capable aircraft with good handling qualities, and many were used as trainers. When later fitted with adequate armament when interrupter gear became available to allow forward-firing weapons, the Scout was a potentially useful, early combat aircraft. Before that time, in July 1915, Captain Lanoe G. Hawker was the first 'fighter pilot' to gain the Victoria Cross (Britain's highest military gallantry award), for successful air combat with several German aircraft in his Scout fitted with an angled outwards/forwards-firing gun. The Royal Naval Air Service used several Scouts for anti-Zeppelin operations from the seaplane carrier H.M.S. Vindex, from which they could take off, but not land back on.

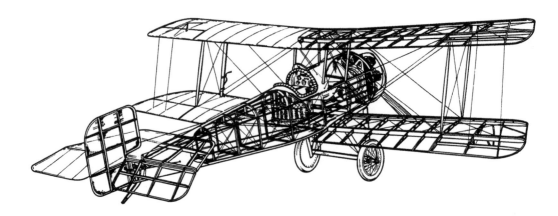

A Bristol Scout D pictured at Filton.

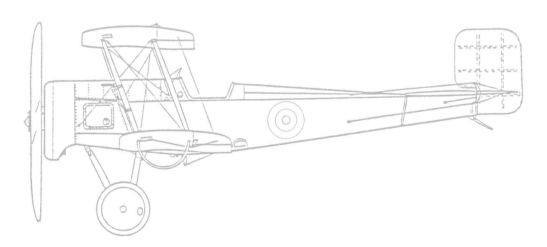

Specifications – Bristol Scout C

Wingspan	24 ft 7 in
Length	20 ft 8 in
Maximum speed	92.7 mph at sea level
Endurance	2 hr 30 min
Armament	Originally improvised weapons, later one 0.303 in machine gun, option of Ranken anti-Zeppelin darts
Engine	One Gnome or Le Rhone rotary engine, of 80 hp (other options available)
Crew	One

Morane-Saulnier Types L and N

Created by the Morane brothers in collaboration with their associate Raymond Saulnier in 1911, the French Morane-Saulnier company was one of many pioneering aviation organisations that grew out of the huge expansion of aircraft design and manufacturing that was starting to take place at that time. Most early Morane-Saulnier aircraft were monoplanes, and these attracted military as well as civil orders. In 1913 Morane-Saulnier started the development of a parasol-wing monoplane for observation use, and this grew into the Type L of 1914. There followed a number of related Morane-Saulnier types for French as well as British military use. In military service the Type L (which was sometimes known as the Morane Parasol) was mainly flown as a two-seater, with the observer touting improvised weapons for air fighting. However, the well-known French pilot Roland Garros, who had started his pre-war flying career with a Santos-Dumont Demoiselle, used a Type L fitted with crude interrupter gear to allow a fixed forward-firing machine gun to fire through the spinning propeller disc for rather more organised air combat. His interrupter gear, to stop bullets striking the propellers of his aircraft as they revolved, consisted of deflector plates attached to the propeller blades that could deflect oncoming bullets. Garros achieved some early success in April 1915 against German aircraft with this equipment, but he later landed behind enemy lines and was captured. This led to the Germans, with the help of Anthony Fokker, developing a more sophisticated interrupter synchroniser gear for use on their fighter aircraft. In June 1915, while flying a single-seat Type L, Flight Sub-Lieutenant R.A.J. Warneford of Britain's Royal Naval Air Service dropped small bombs onto a German Zeppelin. He was later awarded the Victoria Cross for successfully causing the Zeppelin to crash. Some 600 Type L were built, and the model was later developed into the improved Type LA and thence to the Type P of 1916.

The latter intro-

This Morane-Saulnier Type L was flown by Flight Sub-Lieutenant Warneford when he won the Victoria Cross for bringing down a German Zeppelin.

The Morane-Saulnier Type P two-seat observation parasol shown here was built for French and British service (Photo: Philippe Jalabert Collection).

duced a neat circular-section fuselage instead of the Type L's slab-sides, and ailerons instead of wing-warping. Most remarkable was the Morane-Saulnier Type N of 1914/1915, which was a purposeful single-seat monoplane fighter that resembled the Deperdussin Monocoque (see Page 55). The Type N was used in small numbers by British and French units, and also (like the Type L) by Britain's and France's ally, Russia.

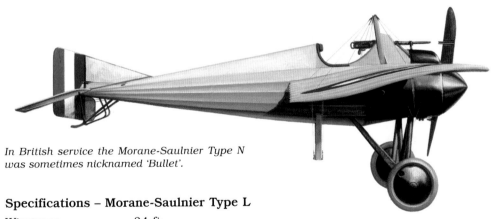

In British service the Morane-Saulnier Type N was sometimes nicknamed 'Bullet'.

Specifications – Morane-Saulnier Type L

Wingspan	34 ft
Length	20 ft 9 in
Maximum speed	76 mph at sea level
Maximum take-off weight	approximately 839 lb
Armament	Improvised armament of guns (usually small arms) and small bombs
Engine	One Le Rhone rotary piston engine, of 80 hp
Crew	Two, sometimes single pilot (especially R.N.A.S. service)

Voisin Type III

When World War One commenced in August 1914, one of the best-equipped military air arms in the world was France's Aviation Militaire. Amongst others it was operating Voisin biplane 'bombers', plus Blériot and Morane-Saulnier aircraft of various descriptions for reconnaissance or scouting (fighting) tasks. The Voisin brothers Gabriel and Charles were amongst France's true aviation pioneers (see pages 46-47), and by the start of World War One early examples of their biplane pusher series of primitive bombers were already in service. These included the Voisin I and II, but it was the Type III that deserves a particular place in history. Aerial bombing with an aircraft specially adapted for this task had been pioneered in 1913 (see Page 54), and the French were quick to launch bombing missions in the early days of the First World War. Despite being very basic and generally primitively-equipped warplanes compared

to the bomber types that came in subsequent years, some of these early French bombers were at least armed with free-mounted slow-firing Hotchkiss machine guns. On 5 October 1914 the world's first air-to-air victory by one aircraft over another in air combat was achieved by the Hotchkiss machine gun manned by Caporal Louis Quenault with Sergeant Joseph Frantz as pilot in a Voisin III (probably coded V 89). The unfortunate victim was a German-operated Aviatik B series reconnaissance aircraft. There were many versions of the basic and rather cumbersome Voisin bomber series; different sub-types were also created due to the re-positioning of the engine thrust line. Like many aircraft of its and subsequent times, the Voisin series achieved important foreign military sales, and some were licence-built in countries other than France. Due to there being a number of manufacturers who built Voisin bombers, it has

become difficult to identify exact specifications for given production blocks. Type III Voisins in fact are identified by two different sets of specifications, including a wingspan of 52 ft 6 in or 48 ft 4.25 in.

The first Dogfight

Joseph Frantz makes the first known kill in aerial combat, October 5th 1914.

Specifications – Voisin Type III

Wingspan	(see text)
Length	31 ft 6 in or 31 ft 2 in
Maximum speed	65 mph at sea level
Maximum take-off weight	3,020 lb
Armament	One free-mounted machine gun in some aircraft, various combinations of bombs up to some 132 lb
Engine	One Salmson (Canton-Unné Patent) 9M radial piston engine, of 120 or 130 hp
Crew	Two

Caudron G.3

Frenchmen Gaston and René Caudron had been building aircraft for several years prior to the appearance of the G.3 (or G.III) in 1913. Like several other pioneers at that time, they also ran a successful pilot training organisation. The immediate predecessor of the G.3 was the G.2, which saw some military service in the early part of World War One for training and observation. The first G.3 flew in May 1913, and an early export success was achieved with an order during 1913 from Chinese authorities for a batch of Caudron aircraft including some G.3 models. At the start of World War One the G.3 was in full production, and it duly served with several French units for reconnaissance and artillery spotting. Some were also used by the French for dropping small bombs, until more specialised types entered service. An export customer was Britain, and G.3 aircraft were also built in Britain. Britain's Royal Flying Corps and Royal Naval Air Service both used the type, principally for training but some British-operated examples were used in combat. Perhaps the most auspicious was the G.3 that was used in East Africa during the successful action to destroy the German light cruiser Königsberg. The G.3 principally involved in this action attacked the ship with bombs, but more successfully spotted for the guns of two British monitors which sank the German ship in July 1915. In addition to France and Britain, Russia and Italy (and also possibly Rumania) all used the G.3 in combat, where the type's good flying characteristics were appreciated – but against fighter opposition the type proved increasingly vulnerable. Most were eventually relegated to training duties. The American Expeditionary Force in France used the G.3 for training. Production totalled 2,450 in France, some 50 plus in Britain, and 250 in Italy. A twin-engined derivative of the G.3, the G.4, also gave valuable wartime service, mainly as a bomber. After World War One, 50 G.3 were built in Portugal, and many fledgling air arms including several in South America also used the type post-war. Some were employed for spectacular stunts by private pilots, including

A Caudron G.3 posed with its pilot on a French airfield in either 1916 or 1917. (Photo: Philippe Jalabert Collection).

hazardous flights under bridges. Frenchman Jules Védrines gained fame (and a money prize) for landing (actually crashing) a G.3 onto the roof of the famous department store Galeries Lafayette in Paris during January 1919.

Over the years a number of aviators have delighted in the idea of flying under bridges, including this Frenchman in a Caudron G.3 (Photo: Philippe Jalabert Collection).

Specifications – Caudron G.3

Wingspan	43 ft 11.5 in
Length	21 ft
Maximum speed	68.35 mph at sea level
Maximum take-off weight	1,565 lb
Endurance	4 hr
Armament	Various improvised guns, diverse combinations of small bombs
Engine	One Anzani radial piston engine, of 90 hp (other options available)
Crew	Two

Fokker Spider Series

One of Europe's celebrated aviation pioneers was Dutchman Anthony Fokker. Born in Java in the Dutch East Indies, Fokker commenced his aviation activities in Germany in 1910, and eventually built up one of Europe's premier aircraft design and manufacturing companies. Fokker began his aviation career as an aircraft engineering and pilot apprentice in Germany, and soon began to design and build his own aircraft. Initially unsuccessful, as with so many other early pioneers persistence eventually paid off for him. Setting up during 1911 at Johannisthal in Berlin's suburbs, one of European aviation's early centres of aviation, Fokker went on to build a number of attractive, heavily-braced monoplanes. Named Spin (Spider) after their web of bracing wires, these aircraft grew from the original fin/rudderless first aircraft of 1910, through a series of increasingly successful but basically similar aircraft including the fully-developed M

Series of monoplanes. With these machines, Fokker established the single-engine, tractor monoplane design layout that was to become a trademark of Fokker's fighters in the early to mid-World War One era. Fokker gained his own pilot's licence by flying one of his own aircraft (his second Spin) in May 1911, and his original Fokker company was set up in 1912. A factory was eventually established at Schwerin in northern Germany during 1913/1914. Like several other early aviation pioneers, he also ran an important pilot training school. One of the most significant military air arms at the commencement of the First World War was that of Germany, and as related in the following two pages on the Fokker E III, Fokker's E Series of monoplane fighters became highly important to the Germans as the First World War progressed. Fokker also played a considerable role in the development of 'interrupter' gear, to

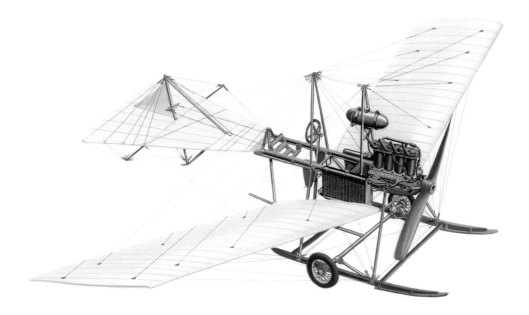

allow a machine gun to fire through the spinning disc of a propeller, and successfully patented his device in 1915.

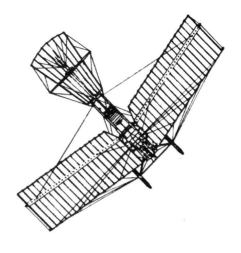

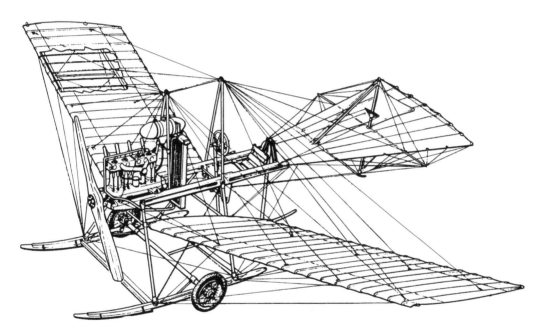

Specifications – Fokker Spin (Spider) III

Wingspan	36 ft
Length	25 ft 5 in
Maximum speed	55 mph at sea level
Maximum take-off weight	880 lb
Engine	One Argus inline piston engine, of 50 hp
Crew	One pilot, one passenger

Fokker E III

The 'E' series of early First World War-vintage Fokker fighters were amongst the first true monoplane military combat aircraft, and they advanced the technology of the then new but fast-developing art of aerial combat with their armament and the tactics used by their pilots. The original E I entered service in the summer of 1915, and importantly included an 'interrupter' mechanism that allowed the type's fuselage-mounted machine-gun to safely fire through the spinning disc of the aircraft's propeller. It was followed by several improved models including most famously the E III, which entered service in 1915/1916. This aircraft was one of the first-ever major fighter aircraft, and it gained for the Germans massive air superiority in late 1915 and early 1916. It helped to establish the so-called 'Fokker scourge', with its many Allied victims being 'Fokker fodder'. Some of the first-ever air combat manoeuvres for aerial dog-fighting were established by pilots of the 'E' or 'Eindecker' (monoplane) series Fokkers, including the well-known German ace Max Immelmann. The E III gained disproportionate success for its pilots (possibly no more than 150 were built), before the increasingly fast pace of combat aircraft development rendered it obsolete by newer types. Nevertheless, the 'E' series had by then established many of the ground rules for aerial combat, and warfare would never be

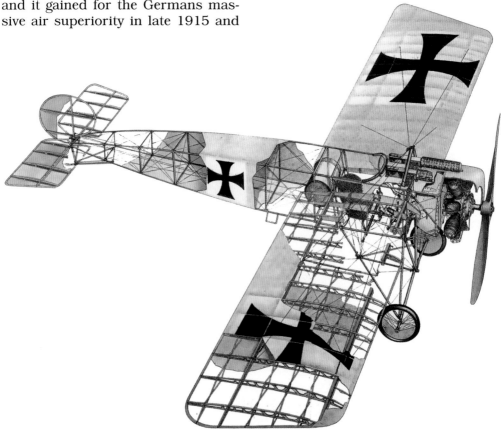

quite the same again. Aircraft hence-
forth were increasingly to play a central role in the conduct of war and the
way in which wars are fought.

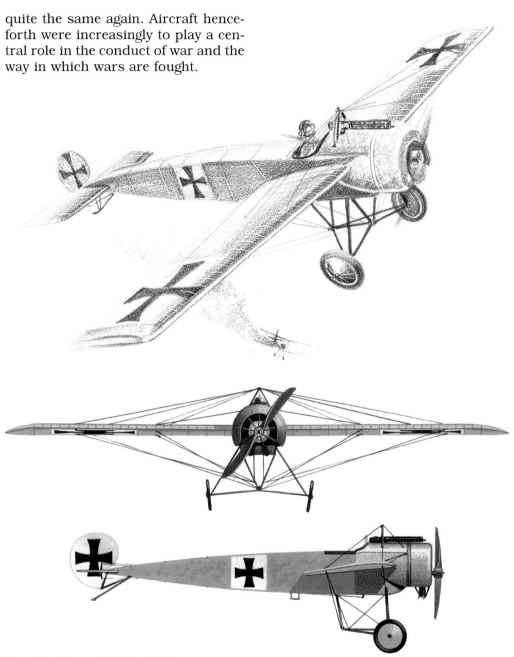

Specifications – Fokker E III

Wingspan	31 ft 2.75 in
Length	23 ft 7.5 in
Maximum speed	87 mph at sea level
Endurance	up to 2 hr 45 min
Armament	One 0.312 in machine gun
Engine	One Oberursel U I rotary engine, of 100 hp
Crew	One

Airco D.H.4

Many classic aircraft were produced during the First World War, but some of them were not the high-profile fighter aircraft of the well-known 'aces'. Arguably the best two-seat bomber of the conflict was the Airco D.H.4. Designed by Geoffrey de Havilland and produced by Airco (the Aircraft Manufacturing Company), the D.H.4 first flew in August 1916. A significant proportion of the production aircraft were equipped with various possible models of the excellent Rolls-Royce Eagle piston engine, although several other engine types were also tried. As a two-seat day-bomber the D.H.4 excelled in service with Britain's Royal Flying Corps and Royal Naval Air Service, commencing operations with the former in April 1917. Production of the D.H.4 was carried out by several manufacturers in Britain, and altogether 1,449 were produced. There were detail differences between the aircraft made by these manufacturers, some of the best being those built by Westland Aircraft. British-operated D.H.4 aircraft successfully operated as day-

bombers and for reconnaissance and many other duties. The accomplishments of the D.H.4 attracted American attention, and the type was selected for production in the United States for American military service. Three main manufacturers built the American D.H.4, including Dayton-Wright, Standard and Fisher Body. At least 4,844 D.H.4 were manufactured in the United States, and it was the only U.S.-manufactured British-designed aircraft that saw combat in the First World War. Significant numbers equipped American units flying in France in the final months of the war. American D.H.4 aircraft were powered by the ubiquitous 400 hp Liberty inline engine. Post-war the career of the D.H.4 continued, and surplus examples were also supplied to several fledgling air arms. Limited licence production took place in Belgium. Some of the American-built D.H.4 aircraft were converted for mail-carrying duties, the type becoming the most important aircraft to be

A substantial number of D.H.4 were built in the United States and called 'Liberty Planes'.
The type served with American forces in France during 1918 – the particular aircraft shown here
became famous for finding and saving a 'lost battalion' of troops.

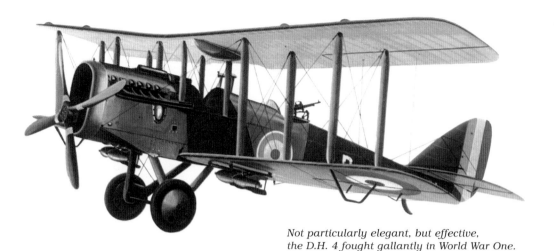

*Not particularly elegant, but effective,
the D.H. 4 fought gallantly in World War One.*

used on the growing air-carried mail delivery network in the United States until replaced by specially-designed mailplanes including the Douglas M-2 (see Pages 156-157). In Britain the D.H.4 also saw some passenger-carrying use in military and later civil operation in the form of the D.H.4A, with a special enclosed cabin for its two passengers.

*A brand new
de Havilland D.H.4
awaiting delivery.*

Specifications – Airco D.H.4 (Eagle VIII)

Wingspan	42 ft 4.75 in
Length	30 ft 8 in
Maximum speed	143 mph at sea level
Service Ceiling	22,000 ft
Endurance	3 hr 45 min
Armament	One or two 0.303 in machine guns fixed forward-firing, one or two 0.303 in flexible ring-mounted machine guns in rear cockpit, up to 460 lb of bombs, depth-charges or equivalent
Engine	One Rolls-Royce Eagle VIII inline piston engine, of 375 hp (other options available)
Crew	Two

Felixstowe F.2A

The big, impressive maritime patrol and anti-submarine Felixstowe flying boats were an important part of Britain's air defences during World War One. They were developed from various Curtiss flying-boat models that were originally ordered by the British Admiralty from the USA early in the war. As related on pages 52-53, American Glenn Curtiss was a pioneer of successful water-based aircraft, and by the First World War his company was producing increasingly large and ambitious flying-boats. One of these was the Curtiss-Wanamaker Model H America twin-engined flying-boat, which was designed to fly across the Atlantic Ocean to win a prize of £10,000 offered by the 'Daily Mail' newspaper in 1913. The planned flight was cancelled due to the start of World War One. However, the Curtiss-Wanamaker was the forerun-

ner of the Curtiss H-4 Small America and H-12 Large America flying-boats that were extensively used by Britain's Royal Naval Air Service during the war. Involved in the design of the Curtiss-Wanamaker America had been John Porte, a British aviator who during the war became an important personality in British flying-boat development, as well as serving in the R.N.A.S. Based at Felixstowe in Eastern England he improved on the basic Curtiss designs, specifically by redesigning the hull (fuselage), and a line of successful Felixstowe flying-boats ensued. They were named for the naval base at Felixstowe but were built by several manufacturers. The most famous was the Felixstowe F.2A, although the F.3 and F.5 also existed. Entering operational service in early 1918, these big, wooden-hull flying-

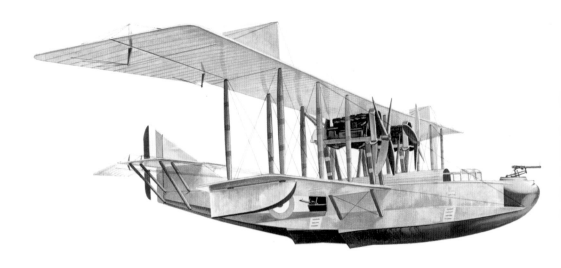

The Felixstowe flying-boats were large, impressive aircraft, and their classic lines are captured in this painting.

boats successfully hunted German U-boats in the North Sea, and were also useful as heavy fighters against German Zeppelins. Some operated from towed lighters out at sea.

Approximately 130 F.2A were built, and a Curtiss-manufactured derivative, the H-16 Large America, also served with the R.N.A.S.

Some of the most colourful aircraft to go to war were the Felixstowe F.2A flying-boats. The bright colours made them easier to find if they had to come down on the sea in an emergency. N4545 was one of the best known of them, and was appropriately based at Felixstowe.

Another example of a dazzle paint scheme for high visibilty.

Specifications – Felixstowe F.2A

Wingspan	95 ft 7.5 in
Length	46 ft 3 in
Maximum speed	95 mph at 2,000 ft
Endurance	6 hr
Service Ceiling	9,600 ft
Armament	Four to seven or more 0.303 in machine guns, two 230 lb bombs
Engine	Two Rolls-Royce Eagle VIII 12-cylinder 'V' inline piston engines, of 360 or 375 hp each
Crew	Usually four

Aviatik B Series

One of the most important military air arms in Europe at the start of World War One was that of Germany, operating aircraft of various different types together with an important selection of airships including Zeppelins. Amongst the aircraft in German service during the early part of the war were attractive two-seat biplane reconnaissance aircraft of the Aviatik series. The Aviatik company was established in 1910, and in addition to production in Germany it also had connections within Germany's main ally, the Austro-Hungarians, in the form of the Österreichische-Ungarische Flugzeugfabrik Aviatik concern. At the start of World War

One the Germans were already operating the basic Aviatik B I reconnaissance model, and eventually a series of B-model aircraft were produced by the German and the Austrian branches of the organisation. In some early production models the observer sat in the front seat, with the pilot to the rear, a fairly common arrangement at the time. Most if not all surviving examples had been relegated to training duties by the end of 1916. An Aviatik B I (presumably a German-built machine) is recognised by most historians as being the first-ever aircraft to be shot down in aerial combat, on 5 October 1914 over the Western Front (see pages 60-61).

Specifications – Österreichische-Aviatik B II (Series 32)

Wingspan	45 ft 11.25 in
Length	26 ft 3 in
Maximum speed	67.7 mph at sea level
Service Ceiling	8,202 ft
Endurance	4 hr
Armament	Various improvised guns, two 22 lb bombs
Engine	One Austro-Daimler inline piston engine, of 120 hp
Crew	Two

There were important differences between the German and Austrian-built Aviatik B Series aircraft – this is a German-built machine.

Boeing Model C

One of the most famous names in American aviation has been – and continues to be today – that of the Boeing company. Widely regarded as one of the world's most important aviation manufacturers, Boeing in fact was a latecomer to aviation production compared to other American pioneers such as the Wright brothers and Glenn Curtiss. William E. Boeing created the forerunner of today's massive Boeing organisation in 1916 (the Boeing name first appeared in 1917), and initially built small and attractive seaplanes for civil and military use. His first aircraft was the B & W (named for Boeing and Westervelt, also called the Model 1) of 1916. An early major military contract that Boeing obtained was for approximately 50 Boeing Model C two-seat biplane floatplane trainers for the U.S. Navy, under the general designation Boeing Model C. Delivered in 1918, these were not particularly successful due mainly to their comparatively unreliable engines. They were, however, the forerunners of the large number of mass-produced Boeing aircraft that ensued in the following decades. The designation C-L4-S (sometimes simply written CL-4S) has been used for specific models of the C-series aircraft. Boeing himself is said to have used a Model C derivative for a short time.

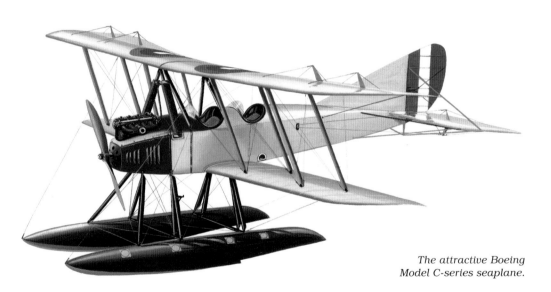

The attractive Boeing
Model C-series seaplane.

Specifications – Boeing Model C

Wingspan	43 ft 10 in
Length	27 ft
Maximum speed	72 mph at sea level
Service Ceiling	6,500 ft
Range	200 miles
Engine	One Hall-Scott A-7A inline piston engine, of 100 hp
Crew	Two

Gotha G Series

Amongst the most famous bombers of World War One, the Gotha G Series were effective if cumbersome comparatively long-range bombers that brought the war to Britain's home front during the later stages of the conflict. This only became possible with the development of bombers such as the Gothas that had the range to allow them to operate over England from German-held bases in Belgium. The German company Gotha (the Gothaer Waggonfabrik) came to the development of bombers during the war. Starting in 1914-1915, Gotha became associated with the 'G' classification of bombers then being developed, with the Gotha G I. This was followed by the different G II and G III models, which entered service in 1916. These were comparatively short range and short endurance bombers for tactical use above the battlefield, but with the G IV of 1917 the emphasis switched to designs that could perform longer-range missions. The G IV entered service during the spring of 1917, and was soon involved in operations over England. Hitherto these had been principally carried out

by German airships, in a sporadic but deadly manner. The Gotha bombers transformed the effectiveness of this campaign, and began raids on southern England on 25 May 1917. They were at once deadly, with significant civilian casualties. A particularly notorious daylight raid on London, on 13 June 1917, caused considerable public outrage and fear, and led to British fighter squadrons being re-assigned specifically to air defence missions to prevent the Gothas from getting through to the capital. A number of British aircraft, including examples of the Sopwith Pup (see pages 86-87) were so assigned. The Gotha G IV was followed into production by the G V, which soon became involved in night raids over England later in 1917. Several versions of the G V were built, late models being fitted with additional forward undercarriage wheels to prevent the aircraft from nosing over on landing. In addition, several other G series Gothas were later developed. Approximately 230 G IV were manufactured, and this model plus the G V represented the drift of

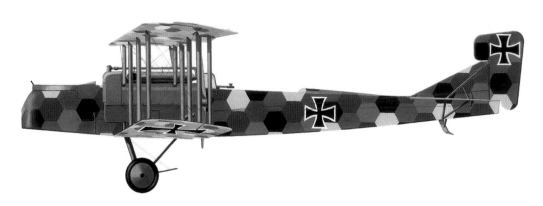

The Gotha G V was the ultimate expression of the German's 'G' Series of bombers.

The Gotha series of pusher-engined bombers became infamous during World War One for their raids on civilian targets.

aerial warfare into the strategic realm of deliberately targeting civilians in their own homes – a reality that became even more marked much lat-er in Spain during the Spanish Civil War, and thence in the Second World War.

The Gotha G IV introduced devastating bomber raids on southern England in May 1917.

Specifications – Gotha G V

Wingspan	77 ft 9 in
Length	40 ft 8 in
Maximum speed	87 mph at sea level
Range	approximately 522 miles
Service Ceiling	21,325 ft
Armament	Two 0.312 in machine guns, bomb load of approximately 661 to 1,102 lb dictated by mission requirements
Engine	Two Mercedes D IVa inline piston engines, of 260 hp each
Crew	Three

Friedrichshafen G Series

The German aircraft company Friedrichshafen (based, not surprisingly, in the vacinity of Friedrichshafen in southern Germany on Lake Constance) was well-known during the First World War as the designer and manufacturer of a series of successful seaplanes for German naval aviation use. However, the company also became involved in the creation of a series of land-based biplane bomber aircraft under the 'G' classification. These began in 1914 with the twin-engined G I, and thence to the G II (FF 38) of 1916. The latter was a large, twin-engined pusher two-bay biplane that established Friedrichshafen alongside A.E.G., Gotha and Zeppelin-Staaken as one of the German producers of large, comparatively long-range bombers for service during the war. The Friedrichshafen company actually had important links with the Zeppelin concern in its own right. The most notable of the G-model bombers from Friedrichshafen was the G III, known to the company as the FF 45. In service from 1917 to the end of the war, the G III was again a twin-engined biplane pusher bomber, but with three-bay wings. It was in service principally over the Western Front, including many night attacks. It operated at the same time as the later G Series Gotha bombers (see the preceding two pages), the chief difference in employment of these two types being the greater use of the Gotha bombers for longer-range operations over southern England. However, the Friedrichshafens saw considerable employment and were also used for air raids on Paris. Some 338 examples of the G III and the differently-tailed G IIIa are thought to have been built. Bombs were carried both internally, as well as externally beneath the wings. Further developments led to the revised Friedrichshafen G IV series and the G V of 1918. Some of the G IV models employed a twin-engine tractor rather than the pusher power plant layout usually employed on Friedrichshafen's bombers. After the war, some Friedrichshafen aircraft were used by civil operators, including at least one converted example of the large bombers.

The Friedrichshafen G III.

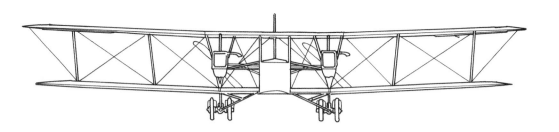

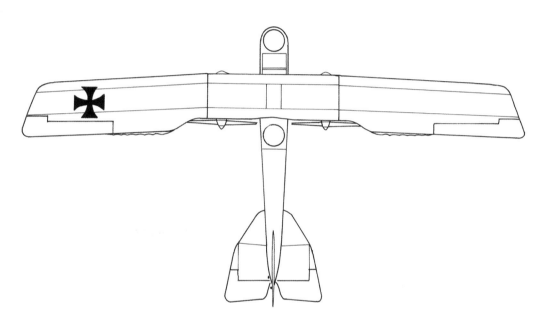

The line drawings show the Friedrichshafen G II, predecessor of the Friedrichshafen G III.

Specifications – Friedrichshafen G III

Wingspan	77 ft 9 in
Length	42 ft 2 in
Maximum speed	87.6 mph at 3,281 ft
Endurance	5 hr
Service Ceiling	14,797 ft
Armament	Two or three 0.312 in machine guns, total bomb load of some 3,307 lb
Engine	Two Mercedes D IVa inline piston engines, of 260 hp each
Crew	Three

Junkers J 1

In 1910 the German Hugo Junkers, who was to become one of aviation's great manufacturers in the following decades, patented a design layout consisting of a thick section wing. Further development work led to the breakthrough of the Junkers J 1, the world's first significant all-metal aircraft. Previous to the J 1, at least one metal aircraft had existed in France, but had not been further developed in the way that the J 1 subsequently was. The J 1 first flew on 12 December 1915, powered by a 120 hp Mercedes D II piston engine. It achieved some 106 mph despite its rather heavy structure, and rejoiced in the nickname 'Blechesel' (Tin Donkey). The J 1 was developed into the J 2 single-seat fighter monoplane of 1916, and a line of related derivatives followed.

The most important of these was the J 9 of March 1918, which became the Junkers D I in German military service. Approximately 41 examples of the D I appear to have been made before the end of World War One, and in 1918 they were the world's first all-metal front-line fighter aircraft. A further development was the Junkers J 10, which was a two-seat development of the D I and other models, and had the German military designation CL I. It was an all-metal escort fighter and ground attack aircraft that served in small numbers near to the end of the war.

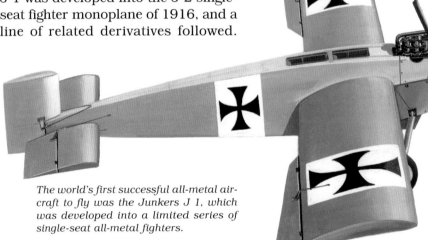

The world's first successful all-metal aircraft to fly was the Junkers J 1, which was developed into a limited series of single-seat all-metal fighters.

Specifications – Junkers D I (J 9)

Wingspan	29 ft 6.5 in
Length	23 ft 9.5 in
Maximum speed	140 mph at sea level
Service Ceiling	19,685 ft
Endurance	1 hr 30 min
Armament	Two 0.312 in machine guns
Engine	One BMW IIIa inline piston engine, of 185 hp (other options available)
Crew	One

Junkers J 4 (J I)

At roughly the same time that Junkers was developing the single-seat all-metal fighter monoplanes based on the original J 1 (see previous page), work was also progressing on a two-seat all-metal biplane design. It was intended that this larger aircraft would be used as an escort fighter and ground-attack airplane for close-support fighting immediately over the trenches on the battlefield. This was a particularly hazardous task, and the all-metal layout favoured by Junkers promised increased protection for aircrew and aeroplane. Under the Junkers designation J 4, development was carried out during 1917. In a leap of faith by the German military authorities, this unconventional (for its time) aircraft that was years ahead of its time was ordered into production, and the first series examples came off the production line in the latter part of 1917. The

J I entered front-line service in early 1918, as the world's first all-metal aircraft to enter operational service. Production appears to have comprised 227 examples. An alliance was formed between Junkers and the Dutch aviation pioneer Anthony Fokker to manufacture the J I, but this arrangement apparently did not succeed. However, the operational J I was generally well-liked by its aircrews, particularly as the whole forward fuselage containing the engine, fuel and crew compartments was an armoured structure. The appropriate nickname 'Möbelwagen' (Furniture Van) seems to have been given to the J I to celebrate its practical if sluggish ruggedness. The corrugated sheet metal skinning of significant areas of the J I's structure was a precursor of the same construction used by Junkers on some of its products in subsequent years.

Specifications – Junkers J I (J 4)

Wingspan	52 ft 6 in
Length	29 ft 10.25 in
Maximum speed	96.3 mph at sea level
Range	193 miles
Endurance	2 hr
Armament	Three 0.312 in machine guns (two fixed forward-firing, one flexible ring-mounted)
Engine	One Benz Bz IV inline piston engine, of 200 hp
Crew	Two

Fokker Dr I

The Fokker Dr I 'Dreidecker' (tri-plane) was a very successful fighter from the era when air aces became celebrities in their own right, and it was made famous by the exploits of the so-called 'Red Baron', actually Manfred Freiherr von Richthofen. Inspired in part by the earlier British-designed Sopwith Triplane, Fokker produced the Dr I (originally called the F I) from the summer of 1917, and some 320 are believed to have been built. The evolution of the Fokker Dr I showed just how quickly aircraft design and usage had developed in the comparatively short time since the Wright Brothers had made their historic first controlled powered flight less than 14 years before. Agile and flown by skilled pilots on the German side, the Dr I originally entered service in August/September 1917 and was produced some way into 1918. By that time, however, it had become outclassed by newer and more capable Allied fighter aircraft. Flown most famously by von Richthofen's celebrated 'Flying Circus', the highly manoeuvrable Dr I was the mount of several well known German aces in addition to the 'Red Baron' himself, including Werner Voss, and Hermann Göring (who was later the German Luftwaffe chief during World War Two). Today the Fokker Dr I has become one of the best-known of the early combat aircraft from the first century of powered flight. Equally legendary are the exploits of the men who flew this remarkable little machine, from a time when fighter pilots were often seen by the public as 'knights of the air'.

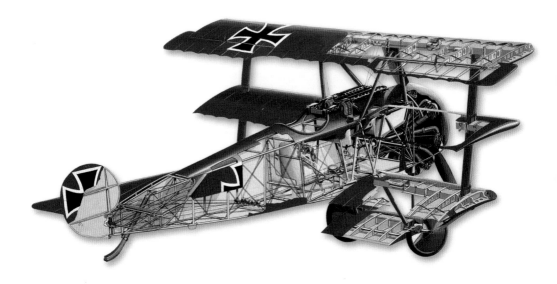

Von Richthofen, 1917

Shows the top and bottom plan view of Dr I.

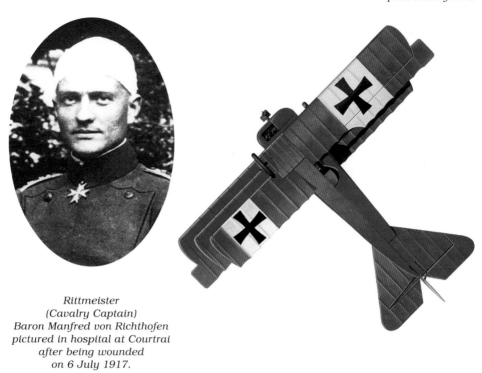

Rittmeister (Cavalry Captain) Baron Manfred von Richthofen pictured in hospital at Courtrai after being wounded on 6 July 1917.

Photograph shows the Fokker Dr I at Rhinebeck, N.Y. with the Cole Palen Flying Circus.

Specifications – Fokker Dr I

Wingspan	23 ft 7.5 in
Length	18 ft 11.25 in
Maximum speed	103 mph at 13,125 ft
Endurance	1 hr 30 min
Armament	Two 0.312 in machine guns
Engine	One Oberursel Ur II or Le Rhone rotary engine, of 110 hp
Crew	One

Avro 504

Without doubt one of the classic aircraft of its time, the Avro 504 was produced in greater numbers than any other British type of the First World War era, and its longevity in service made it one of the best-known aircraft types of the 1920's as well. The first Avro 504 flew in July 1913, and a small number had been ordered for the British military prior to the start of World War One. The type saw limited combat activity on the Continent after the war had commenced. The Royal Naval Air Service put several to good use on 21 November 1914, by performing what has been claimed to have been the world's first-ever properly organised bombing mission, when they raided airship sheds at Friedrichshafen in southern Germany on Lake Constance. An Avro 504 had the unhappy distinction of being the first British military aircraft to be shot down during the war, on 22 August 1914. Following construction of a number of basic two-seat Avro 504, the two-seat Avro 504A model entered production and was built in significant numbers, with most being used as trainers. The 504B was an R.N.A.S. version employed principally for training, and the 504C was a single-seater used by the

R.N.A.S. for reconnaissance missions, the additional fuel (carried in the area where the observer normally sat) giving eight hours endurance. Anti-Zeppelin work was also carried out by the 504C, some carrying a Lewis machine gun on their upper wing inclined at an angle of around 45 degrees. A variety of other 504 models ensued, including a one-off 504H that was used in early development work for catapult-assisted take-offs from aircraft-carrying ships. Particularly important was the 504J from the autumn of 1916, which established the type as a significant ab initio trainer (hitherto it had been used mainly as an advanced trainer), and set out much of the foundations for pilot flying training that held good for many years to come. The final main World War One production model was the 504K, with an engine mounting capable of taking any of the then available rotary engines. Although mainly used for training, a single-seat 'K' model was developed for Home Defence in England against German air raids. Postwar, many surplus

The classic lines of the Avro 504, one of aviation's great aircraft.

Some Australian Avro 504 aircraft, like this example, were powered by the Sunbeam Dyak engine giving a completely different nose shape.

504 aircraft found their way into civilian hands, for a variety of uses including pilot training, joy-riding and 'barnstorming'. Large numbers served with foreign air arms around the world, and included licence production in several countries. A large number of copies were built in the Soviet-run Russia as the U-1, powered by a copied rotary engine. Production was resurrected in Britain during the 1920's, as the Avro 504N trainer with many improvements including a revised undercarriage and a 160 hp Armstrong Siddeley Lynx radial engine. Other revisions led to several additional models, including the Avro 536 with a widened fuselage able to seat a pilot and four passengers. Over 10,000 Avro 504s of all types were eventually built.

Many Avro 504 aircraft were used by civilian owners during the 1920's, like this colourful example from the Cornwall Aviation Co.

Specifications – Avro 504K

Wingspan	36 ft
Length	29 ft 5 in
Maximum speed	95 mph at sea level
Endurance	3 hr
Service Ceiling	16,000 ft
Armament	None in trainer 504K, one 0.303 in machine gun in Home Defence 504K
Engine	One Le Rhone rotary piston engine, of 110 hp (other options available)
Crew	Two (one in Home Defence 504K fighter)

Short Type 184

The use of air-launched torpedoes against enemy shipping found its greatest expression during the Second World War, but this form of air-to-surface attack was pioneered years earlier before World War One. The first successful torpedo drop from an aircraft is believed to have been made as early as 1911 (from a Farman biplane). In Britain, the first successful torpedo launch was made by a Short Folder in July 1914. A product of the famous early British aircraft company of the Short brothers, the Folder seaplane was unique in being the first British aircraft to feature folding wings (a useful attribute for utilisation in particular in the confined spaces available aboard warships). The relative success of the Folder led to the requirement for the Royal Naval Air Service to operate a dedicated tor-pedo-carrying floatplane, and this evolved as the Short Type 184. The first example was completed early in 1915, and the type went on to be made in large numbers (well over 650 are believed to have been built, of several sub-types) by a number of companies including another important British pioneer, Westland. The war record of the Short 184 started spectacularly. On 12 August 1915, during the Dardanelles campaign against Turkey, a Short 184 operating from the seaplane carrier H.M.S. Ben-my-Chree was the first aircraft in the world to sink an enemy ship with a torpedo. Five days after, two more ships were destroyed by aircraft from the same carrier. The following year, a Short 184 was the only aircraft to play a part in the great naval Battle of Jutland. Despite these important actions the

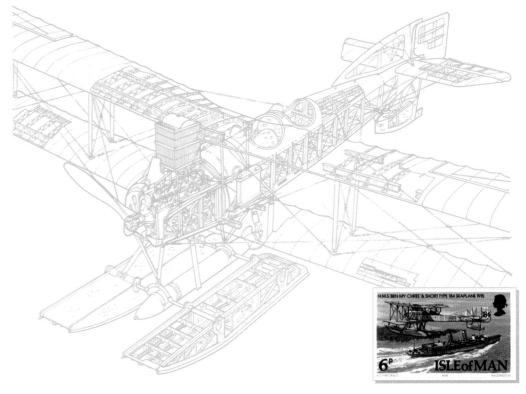

*The Short Folder in
1914 was the first aircraft in Britain to successfully launch a torpedo. It was the
start of an excellent family of Short seaplanes.*

Short 184 was generally of poor performance, particularly in hot climates, and sometimes had trouble taking off. Nonetheless, the type was used extensively in several war theatres for patrol work and as a bomber or reconnaissance aircraft, and spotting for ships' guns. Some remained in service after the war. An important derivative based on the Short 184 was the land-based Short Bomber, which featured a conventional undercarriage and was used as a bomber in France from late 1916 into 1917.

*These two photographs show the remains of a Westland-built Short 184 that are displayed at the
Fleet Air Arm Museum at R.N.A.S. Yeovilton in Somerset, southern England (Photos: John Batchelor).*

Specifications – Short Type 184

Wingspan	63 ft 6.25 in
Length	40 ft 7.5 in
Maximum speed	88.5 mph at 2,000 ft
Endurance	2 hr 45 min
Service Ceiling	9,000 ft
Armament	One 0.303 in machine gun, one 14 in torpedo, various combinations of bombs such as four 100 lb
Engine	One Sunbeam Maori piston engine, of 260 hp (other options available)
Crew	Two

Sopwith Pup

Although known officially as the Sopwith Scout (not to be confused with the Bristol Scout, pages 56-57), the name 'Pup' was more relevantly applied to this diminutive fighter which served so well with Britain's Royal Flying Corps and especially the Royal Naval Air Service. The first Pup flew in or slightly before February 1916, and the type entered service during September 1916 (although a single example had been in France several months before). The Pup developed an excellent combat record, and was easily the match for most German fighters of the period. Between September 1916 and mid-1917 it was one of the chief fighters on the Allied side. Pups were especially liked by their pilots – despite their relatively low-powered rotary engine they were easy to fly, manoeu-

vrable, and were an excellent gun platform. Altogether 1,770 were built, by several manufacturers in Britain. Some Pups were fitted with inflatable air bags for emergency landings on the sea when they were employed to protect merchant shipping or to escort seaplane reconnaissance aircraft. Pups were also used in highly important experiments to establish a presence of combat aircraft at sea. This included flying off Pups from specially constructed platforms on top of the gun turrets of warships (although there was no provision for the Pup to land back on board these types of ships). However, in August 1917 Squadron Commander E.H. Dunning, R.N.A.S., succeeded in landing a Pup onto the deck of the early aircraft carrier H.M.S. Furious. This was a hazardous task – none of

today's techniques and equipment for aircraft carrier operations existed at that time, and the deck of the Furious was forward of the ship's bridge, and thus difficult to manoeuvre onto. Dunning's first successful landing was on 2 August 1917, but he was killed on a later attempt trying to emulate the feat. In 1918 Furious was fitted with a proper landing after-deck. Several Pups were thereafter used to trial the methods for safe deck landing, and were fitted with wooden skids for this purpose. The British company Beardmore developed a special carrier-capable Pup derivative, the W.B. III, with folding wings and a very early example of a 'retractable' undercarriage. Serial numbers were allocated for 100 of these aircraft. As a part of their excellent combat record, Pups also served on Home Defence duties against German air raids over England from 1917 onwards.

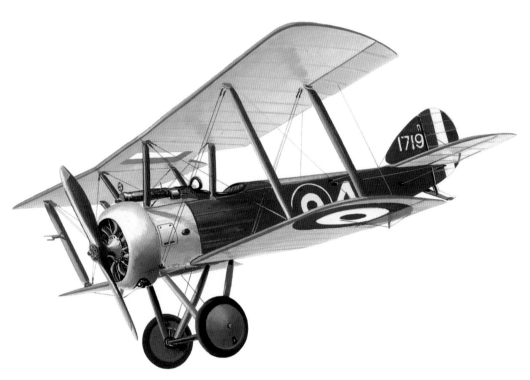

Specifications – Sopwith Pup

Wingspan	26 ft 6 in
Length	19 ft 3.75 in
Maximum speed	111.5 mph at sea level
Endurance	3 hr
Armament	One 0.303 in machine gun, up to 100 lb of bombs carried externally
Engine	One Le Rhone rotary engine, of 80 hp
Crew	One

Handley Page O/100 and O/400

The most famous of Britain's World War One bombers, the Handley Page O/100 and O/400 series originated from an Admiralty requirement of December 1914 for a patrol bomber. The aircraft that resulted attracted the nickname 'bloody paralyser' from Naval officers in describing the way they wanted the new aircraft to take the war to the enemy. The first O/100 successfully flew in December 1915, and was the largest aircraft built in Britain up to that time. First deliveries of operational aircraft to Britain's Royal Naval Air Service began in late 1916, and operations began in March/April 1917. Night raids were included in the schedule – the use of these aircraft represented the beginnings of true strategic bombing by British forces, when industrial centres in Germany were attacked. Development of the O/100, with a revised fuel system, relocated fuel tanks plus other changes led to the celebrated O/400. A prototype config-

uration for the O/400 was flown in autumn 1917, and production aircraft appeared in numbers in the spring of 1918. O/400s were employed in important numbers in the last three months of the war. By then the Royal Air Force was in existence, and a special strategic bomber force, the Independent Force, was in being. In September 1918 the R.A.F.'s O/400s began using a large (for those days) 1,650 lb bomb. The O/400 was also built in the United States, by Standard. The first of these flew in July 1918, and 107 are believed to have been built there. In total, 46 production O/100 were built, and approximately 400 (possibly more) O/400 in Britain. Some converted O/400 were used post-war as makeshift airliners. Further military development created the V/1500, the R.A.F.'s first four-engined front-line heavy bomber. This was intended to be the next major bomber for the Independent Force, able to raid Berlin

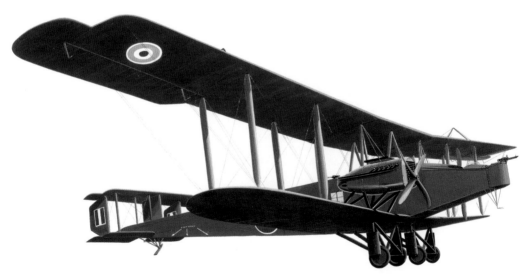

The Handley Page O/100 and O/400 represented an important leap forward in bombing capability when they entered service. The O/400 remained in service until late 1919.

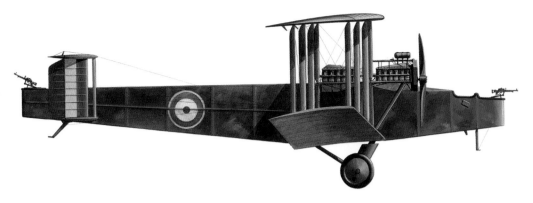

The Handley Page V/1500 was too late to see action in World War One, but it was an important step in the evolution of the heavy bomber in Britain. It even had the innovation of a rear gunner.

from bases in eastern England. The prototype flew in May 1918, but only a handful had reached the R.A.F. by the end of the war.

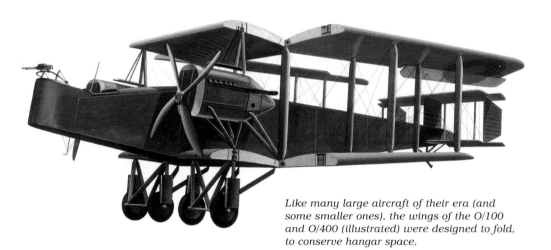

Like many large aircraft of their era (and some smaller ones), the wings of the O/100 and O/400 (illustrated) were designed to fold, to conserve hangar space.

Specifications – Handley Page O/400

Wingspan	100 ft
Length	62 ft 10.25 in
Maximum speed	97.5 mph at sea level
Endurance	8 hr
Maximum take-off weight	13,360 lb
Service Ceiling	8,500 ft
Armament	Up to five 0.303 in machine guns, bomb load of various bomb combinations, such as sixteen 112 lb, one 1,650 lb, etc.
Engine	Two Rolls-Royce Eagle VIII inline piston engines, of 360 hp each (other options available)
Crew	Three to five

Sopwith 1½ Strutter

The Sopwith 1½ Strutter has a number of claims to fame, in addition to enjoying an unusual name. It was one of the first - if not actually the first - major front-line production aircraft from the famous British Sopwith company. More significantly, it introduced from the first production aircraft onwards an 'interrupter' synchronisation gear as the first British aircraft to be so equipped – this allowed it to have a forward-firing machine gun that could safely fire bullets through the spinning disc of its propeller. The peculiar name of the aircraft is said to have derived from its unusual cabane struts arrangement. The Strutter was one of the first multi-role aircraft, being able to operate as a two-seat fighter-reconnaissance aircraft, while other Strutters were built for single-seat bombing missions. The Strutter in fact helped to develop the tactics of the two-seat fighter-reconnaissance aircraft type that were so effectively performed by the Bristol F.2B Fighter (see the following two pages). The

first 1½ Strutter flew in late 1915, and initial deliveries were made, to Britain's Royal Naval Air Service, in the early spring of 1916. The type subsequently operated successfully with the R.N.A.S. and the Royal Flying Corps, and performed a number of important bombing missions (including what are sometimes seen as the first strategic bombing raids, against German industrial centres). Production in Britain included some 1,513 examples by several manufacturers. Up to possibly 4,500 are believed to have been built in France, again by various different companies. 1½ Strutters served in significant numbers not just with British but also French units, and the Russian and Belgian air arms also operated the type. The American Expeditionary Force in France additionally flew the 1½ Strutter, mainly but not exclusively for training. Naval 1½ Strutters were principally land-based, but important numbers also went to sea aboard some of the first aircraft carriers and specially-converted ships of

This painting shows the classic two-seat fighter-reconnaissance layout of some of the 1½ Strutter models, with a forward-firing synchronised Vickers machine gun.

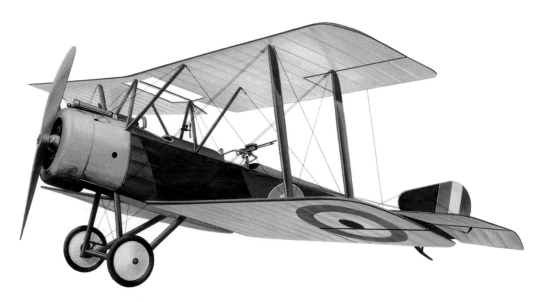

other types. Although mainly operated over the Western Front, 1½ Strutters also flew on other war fronts with considerable success. The type established a very good war record, and was eventually replaced in some units by the excellent Sopwith Camel – a type that has tended to overshadow

the exploits of the generally well-liked 1½ Strutter.

The somewhat unusual cabane struts arrangement above the fuselage is claimed to have given the 1½ Strutter its strange name. This example was preserved in Belgium (Photo: John Batchelor).

Specifications – Sopwith 1½ Strutter (two-seater fighter-reconnaissance)

Wingspan	33 ft 6 in
Length	25 ft 3 in
Maximum speed	106 mph at sea level
Service Ceiling	approximately 13,000 ft
Endurance	4 hr 15 min
Armament	Two 0.303 in machine guns (one fixed forward-firing, one flexible ring-mounted), two 65 lb bombs or 12 smaller bombs
Engine	One Clerget 9 Z rotary piston engine, of 110 hp (other options available)
Crew	Two

Bristol F.2B Fighter

The highly-successful F.2 series of fighter-reconnaissance aircraft originated from a need to replace increasingly obsolete types such as the B.E.2 with a more powerful and capable aircraft for reconnaissance and artillery-spotting. Originally a Beardmore-powered biplane called the Bristol R.2A was conceived in 1916. However, an excellent new engine, the Rolls-Royce Falcon inline engine was just becoming available. Redesigned and fitted with a Falcon engine, the R.2A grew into a multi-purpose aircraft with fighter-performance that became the F.2 two-seat fighter-reconnaissance series. The Falcon-powered first prototype flew in September 1916, and deliveries of production examples for the Royal Flying Corps began that December. Unfortunately initial combat experience in 1917 was disastrous, because the aircraft were flown primarily to allow the second crew member to operate his Scarff ring-mounted Lewis machine gun against attacking fighters. When the Fighter was later flown like a true fighter, using its forward-firing synchronised machine gun as main armament and allowing the gunner to cover the aircraft's rear, the F.2A and subsequent F.2B proved to be excellent two-seat multi-role fighters. Slight re-design of the F.2A led to the widely-built F.2B, which became the R.F.C.'s standard two-seat fighter aircraft. Most of the subsequent production aircraft were powered by the Rolls-Royce Falcon III inline, the aircraft's almost-circular radiator in the nose giving the erroneous appearance of a radial-engined aircraft. So many F.2B Fighters were ordered that demand outstripped the supply of Falcon engines, and several alternative power plants were tried. Approximately 3,101 Fighters had been built by the start of 1919, and well over five thousand of all types are believed eventually to have been manufactured. Operationally the F.2B was very successful as a fighter, ground-attack, reconnaissance and night fighter platform in several theatres of war. The Canadian pilot A.E. McKeever, with several different gunners, achieved 31 aerial victories – an excellent record for a two-seat fighter pilot. After World War One the 'Brisfit', as it was affectionately

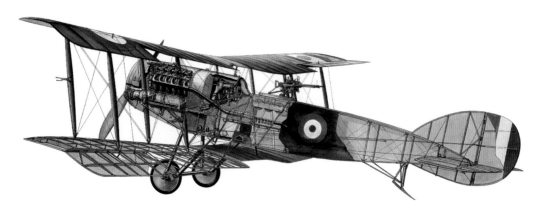

Cutaway of the Bristol F.2B Fighter.

Prince Albert of Belgium seated in his personal Bristol Fighter, specially converted for VIP use and claimed to be the first-ever Royal aeroplane transport. Photo dated 1921.

known, continued in RAF service until 1932, with production continuing after the war plus reconditioning of wartime veterans. 'Brisfits' also flew with and were produced in various other countries – although manufacture in the United States faltered due to the installation of an unsuitable Liberty engine type.

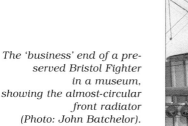

The 'business' end of a preserved Bristol Fighter in a museum, showing the almost-circular front radiator (Photo: John Batchelor).

Specifications – Bristol F.2B Fighter

Wingspan	39 ft 3 in
Length	25 ft 10 in
Maximum speed	123 mph at 4,000 ft
Service Ceiling	21,500 ft
Endurance	3 hr
Armament	Two 0.303 in machine guns (one fixed forward-firing, one flexible ring-mounted), up to twelve 20 lb fragmentation bombs
Engine	One Rolls-Royce Falcon III inline piston engine, of 275 hp (other options available)
Crew	Two

B.E.2 Series

The birthplace of aviation in Britain can rightly be seen as Farnborough in Hampshire, southern England. It was there that the American Samuel Cody had made his famous first flight in Britain during 1908 (see pages 48-49). In later years the Royal Aircraft Factory was established there as a successor to H.M. Balloon Factory. The Royal Aircraft Factory designed and produced a number of aircraft that were used by British forces during the First World War, including the B.E.2 series of observation aircraft, and the excellent S.E.5a fighter (see Pages 102-103). The very first B.E. aircraft (B.E. = Blériot Experimental) was built in 1911 from the wreck of a crashed Voisin. This led on to the B.E.2 of 1912, which was a neat tractor biplane that was followed by a series of similar B.E.2 models. These aircraft were mainly for observation purposes, and were built to be stable, two-seaters ideal for the reconnaissance role. The first British aircraft that was rushed to France on the outbreak of the First World War in

August 1914 was a B.E.2a of No.2 Squadron, Royal Flying Corps. In 1914 the B.E.2b variant was introduced, but this was another unremarkable, low-performance but stable unarmed observation model like the B.E.2 and B.E.2a. Some improvements in the series were introduced on the B.E.2c of 1914, including ailerons as standard for lateral control. The B.E.2c was another example of a flying machine that was designed to be inherently stable, but unfortunately this sort of admirable flying characteristic was not practical in the vicious, bloody air war that developed as World War One progressed. Any aircraft, including the B.E.2 series, that were low powered and could not rapidly manoeuvre their way out of trouble were doomed, and B.E.2 series aircraft were a significant part of the 'Fokker fodder' losses of late 1915 to early 1916 – and were little better off at any other time. Nonetheless, large numbers of B.E.2 type aircraft were ordered for the British services, and the breed was

C7086 was the serial number allocated to a B.E.2e built by Barclay Curle.

Serial number 6478 was a Daimler-built B.E.12 fighter (Photo: Philippe Jalabert Collection)

still being flown (albeit mainly as a trainer) in 1918. However, for Home Defence duties the B.E.2 proved to be slightly more useful, and five German airships were brought down by specially-configured B.E.2c aircraft. The B.E.2e of 1916 introduced several improvements, but its observer was once more sat in the front cockpit where he could do little to defend the hapless aircraft. In an effort to protect the B.E.2 in combat, the bizarre idea was born to develop the B.E.2 into a fighter, leading to the single-seat B.E.12. The type entered combat in July-August 1916, but was a hopeless fighter due to its ponderous stability, and it could not be manoeuvred quickly enough – many were later used for light bombing, although a B.E.12 did manage to shoot down a Zeppelin in June 1917. 1,793 B.E. models (2a, 2b, 2c, and 2d) were built, plus at least 1,801 B.E.2e, and approximately 583 B.E.12. The failure of the B.E.2 in combat created a considerable scandal in Britain.

Specifications – B.E.2e

Wingspan	40 ft 9 in
Length	27 ft 3 in
Maximum speed	90 mph at sea level
Service Ceiling	9,000 ft
Endurance	4 hr
Armament	One 0.303 in machine gun, manually carried from one fixing to another, various light bombs
Engine	One R.A.F.1a inline piston engine, of 90 hp (other options available)
Crew	Two

Halberstadt CL II

As tactics and weapons evolved during the First World War, so aircraft were devised for specific roles that had probably not been thought of before the war. In German military service, the rather fragile B-model observation aircraft that were in service at the start of the conflict were eventually replaced by more competent and warlike reconnaissance aircraft able to much more capably defend themselves. Eventually a series of C-model armed two-seat reconnaissance aircraft evolved, which expanded into large aircraft that needed some protection themselves. The smaller two-seat CL Series was therefore evolved to escort these C-model machines, and to perform other duties such as ground attack tasks. Amongst the best in this class were the Halberstadt CL aircraft, the CL II and CL IV proving to be very capable fighting machines. The CL II entered service in 1917, and was a rugged two-seater bristling with small bombs and grenades in racks on the outer fuselage sides which could be dropped over the side by the observer/gunner. The two crew members shared a com-

mon cockpit opening, the observer being fitted out with a gun ring for a free firing machine gun in addition to the type's fixed forward-firing synchronised armament. All this made the Halberstadt very well armed, and the CL II soon proved to be highly capable for ground attack duties. In September 1917 a formation of CL IIs effectively attacked Allied ground forces crossing the Somme river, and successfully supported a German counter-attack during the Battle of Cambrai that November. Some examples of the CL IIa were built with a 185 hp BMW IIIa power plant in a revised nose. The shorter CL IV, again with altered nose contours plus a redesigned tail, played an important part supporting the major German spring offensive that began in March 1918. These strong and comparatively powerful aircraft proved the worth of the two-seat ground-attack concept in the context of the First World War, although they were less effective when faced by well-flown Allied single-seat fighters. Some were used later in the war for night attack duties.

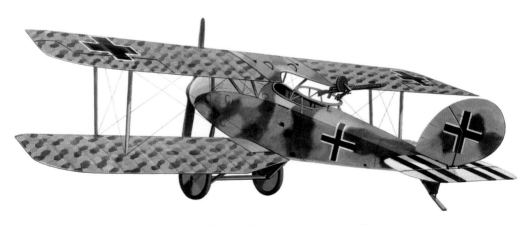

Note the intricate 'lozenge' style camouflage on the wings,
as applied to examples of the Halberstadt CL series.

The Halberstadt CL II series were strong, capable ground-attack aircraft. (Photo: Hans Meier Collection).

The Halberstadt CL IV featured altered nose contours.

Specifications – Halberstadt CL II

Wingspan	35 ft 4 in
Length	23 ft 11.5 in
Maximum speed	102.5 mph at 16,405 ft
Service Ceiling	approximately 16,732 ft
Endurance	3 hr
Armament	One or two 0.312 in machine guns fixed forward-firing, one 0.312 in machine gun flexible ring-mounted, various small bombs and grenades
Engine	One Mercedes D III inline piston engine, of 160 hp
Crew	Two

Sopwith Camel

Amongst the first of the truly classic combat aircraft from the first century of flight was the famous British designed and built Sopwith Camel. One of the principal Allied fighters of the First World War, the Camel combined agility and firepower to bring it great success in aerial combat, although it was a demanding aircraft to fly. Allied-operated Camels are claimed to have achieved well over 3,000 aerial victories during their period in combat during World War One, and several of the Allies' top air aces flew the Camel, including the Canadians Raymond Collishaw (second on the British Empire World War One aces list) and William Barker. The original design took shape in 1916 and Camels started to reach front-line units in numbers during July 1917 – the type served with distinction from then until the war's end. 5,490 Camels were ordered – a massive total at the time – and a navalised version with a single machine-gun and other changes also existed as the 2F.1 Camel. In addition to British-operated aircraft, the Camel served successfully with several other air arms. Without doubt the Sopwith Camel was one of the first great military aircraft to be created and manufactured by Britain's then-growing aircraft industry. The type remains today almost as well-known as the legendary Spitfire as one of the truly great aircraft from Britain's once large and proud aircraft industry.

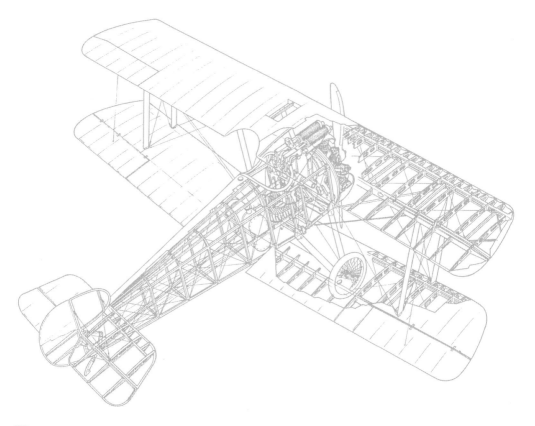

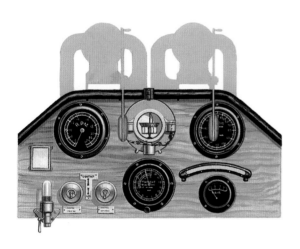

Stamp issued by
Great Britain, 1968.

Illustration showing the cockpit
controls of the Sopwith Camel.
Note breeches for the twin .303 in
machine guns.

Specifications – Sopwith F.1 Camel

Wingspan	28 ft
Length	18 ft 9 in
Maximum speed	115 mph at 6,500 ft
Endurance	2 hr 30 min
Armament	Two 0.303 in machine guns, up to 100 lb of bombs carried externally
Engine	One Clerget 9 B rotary engine, of 130 hp (other options available)
Crew	One

SPAD S.XIII

The SPAD S.XIII was the culmination of a highly-successful series of First World War fighters from the French company Société Anonyme pour l'Aviation et ses Dérivés (SPAD). These aircraft employed an excellent new engine type, the Hispano-Suiza 8-series inline piston engine which possessed much more development potential that the common rotary engines then in widespread use, and was a predecessor of the inline piston engines that saw such widespread use in the decades that followed. The direct production predecessor to the SPAD S.XIII was the S.VII, the prototype of which flew in April 1916. This proved to be a classic fighter, possessing great strength, speed and stability, and it was built in large numbers (possibly as high as 5,600). Continuing development led to the S.XIII, which first flew in April 1917. This rugged and successful fighter was also built in considerable numbers (approximately 8,472), and it was extensively used by the air arms of several countries including France and the United States. Several high-scoring air aces flew SPAD fighters, including the famous French aces René Fonck and Georges Guynemer. Edward Rickenbacker, the highest-scoring American ace of the First World War, flew

John Batchelor with SPAD S.XIII getting technical details, Musée de Air, France.

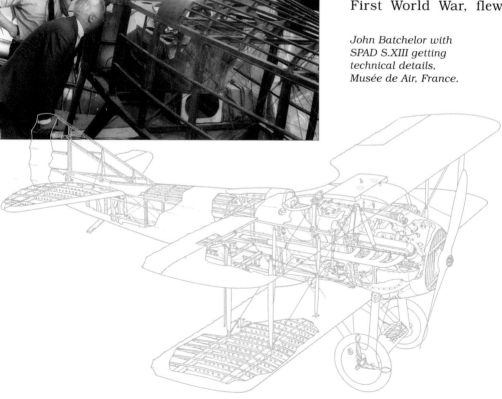

Photograph sent to John Batchelor from Ray Brooks showing him and his crew by his SPAD S.XIII in France, 1918. He served with the 22nd Aero Squadron in the A.E.F.

the SPAD S.XIII and gained a total of 26 aerial victories. Overall the SPAD fighters are regarded with particular affection by the French, because they were amongst the first classic military aircraft that were produced by France's dynamic aircraft industry. Both the SPAD S.VII and the S.XIII are recognised as being true classics from the First World War.

ANTIGUA & BARBUDA

Spad VII $1.50

The stamp issued by Antigua and Barbuda, 1985.

Specifications – SPAD S.XIIIC.1

Wingspan	26 ft 11 in
Length	20 ft 8 in
Maximum speed	135 mph at 6,562 ft
Endurance	2 hr
Armament	Two 0.303 in machine guns
Engine	One Hispano-Suiza 8 Be piston engine, of 235 hp
Crew	One

S.E.5a

During the later stages of the First World War, two British fighters stand out for being particularly responsible for the eventual Allied success in the air war that contributed to final victory in November 1918. These were the Sopwith Camel and the S.E.5a. The S.E.5a was a product of a design team at the Royal Aircraft Factory, Farnborough, in southern England. This factory had already been responsible for the B.E.2 series of observation aircraft (see pages 94-95), and the S.E.5a design came about to make the best use of a potentially high-performance new Hispano-Suiza engine under development in 1915. The prototype S.E.5 (S.E. = Scout Experimental) first flew in late 1916, and initial production S.E.5 aircraft reached No.56 Squadron, Royal Flying Corps, in March 1917. They went into combat the following month, and soon showed that the type's firepower and strength were likely to make it into a very successful fighter. Production problems with the Hispano-Suiza engine intended for the S.E.5 soon led to production delays, however.

Eventually Hispano-Suiza engines with the problems ironed-out started to become available, plus British-built Wolseley Viper power plants which were based on the Hispano-Suiza engine. A slightly improved model, the S.E.5a, soon became the main production variant of the fighter, with a number of alterations over the original S.E.5. The first S.E.5a was delivered to No.56 Squadron in June 1917. The S.E.5a soon established an excellent reputation as being a strong, stable fighting machine that could take on the best of the German fighters then available, including the superb Fokker D VII. Several of the Allies' top-scoring air aces of the First World War flew the S.E.5a, including James McCudden, Edward 'Mick' Mannock, and the highest scorer of all, the Canadian William Avery Bishop. Some S.E.5a aircraft were also used for ground-attack duties. Most flew over the Western Front, but a number were issued to units on other war fronts. Intended production by Curtiss in the United States ran to only one example due to the ending of the war, but a num-

B4863 was a well-known S.E.5a, because it was flown by the famous ace Captain James McCudden of No.56 Squadron, Royal Flying Corps.

cessful though it was, the type did not continue in service for long after the end of the war. A number did nevertheless come into private hands following the conflict, with several being used for aerial skywriting.

ber were built in the United States from parts supplied by Britain. Altogether, 5,205 S.E.5 and S.E.5a were built in Britain. However, suc-

Specifications – S.E.5a

Wingspan	26 ft 7.5 in
Length	20 ft 11 in
Maximum speed	137.8 mph at sea level
Endurance	2 hr 30 min
Armament	Two forward-firing 0.303 in machine guns (one mounted above the upper wing), up to four 25 lb bombs carried externally
Engine	One Wolseley W.4A Viper inline piston engine, of 200 hp (other options available)
Crew	One

Breguet 14

One of the great names in early aviation was that of Frenchman Louis Breguet. As related on pages 50-51, Breguet was an early pioneer of helicopter flight. However, he is far better known for his work on aircraft, his Breguet company having been established in 1911. Over the years Breguet was to create many classic aircraft, and the Breguet name existed into the early 1990's. One of Breguet's first classic designs, and one of the finest French military aircraft of all time, was the Breguet 14. In fact, the Breguet 14 was one of the most outstanding aircraft of its era. First flown in November 1916, the Breguet 14 was a strong, powerful and adaptable tractor biplane, characterised throughout its production life by its big, squared-off front end and prominent cowling side louvers. The design was immediately successful, and proved to be one of France's principal combat aircraft in the later stages of World War One. Indeed, it remained in service with the French right up to 1932. The Breguet 14

served in two main roles during the war, for armed reconnaissance and artillery-spotting (14A2), and as a dedicated light bomber (14B2). In that sense it was roughly equivalent to Britain's D.H.4 and D.H.9a. The initial production examples entered service in the summer of 1917. Some debate has existed amongst historians as to how many Breguet 14 aircraft were built, but the best estimates come to at least 8,000 examples and probably more were built during and after the war. Several manufacturers were involved in this large-scale enterprise, and there were a number of different versions and sub-types during the production run. These included an air ambulance model (14S), with provision within the fuselage for casualties to be carried. Breguet 14s served in many theatres of the First World War air war as well as over the Western Front (including night bombing). The American Expeditionary Force in France also used the type in combat and for training (including some Fiat-

The colour drawing shows an example of the Breguet 14 in American service.

Good air-to-air photographs from the First World War period are rare.
This excellent photograph shows an American-operated Breguet 14 in flight.

engined examples), as did Belgium. Post-war, the Breguet 14 continued in wide-scale service, and was especially used in the French overseas colonies where local fighting was taking place. The design also saw very widespread service in a multitude of air arms world-wide, including those of some newly-created countries, and fledgling armed forces. The Breguet 14 was additionally widely used after the war by civil operators, in the hands of several long-distance pioneering aviators, but most notably as a converted passenger and mail carrier on the development of a large number of post-war civil air routes.

Specifications – Breguet 14B2

Wingspan	47 ft 1.5 in
Length	29 ft 1.25 in
Maximum speed	110 mph at sea level
Endurance	2 hr 45 min
Service Ceiling	19,029 ft
Armament	Three 0.303 in machine guns (one fixed forward-firing, two flexible ring-mounted), up to some 564 lb of bombs or equivalent
Engine	One Renault 12 Fe or Fcx inline piston engine, of 300 hp (other options available)
Crew	Two

Nieuport 11 and 17

Originally founded in France by Edouard de Niéport in 1910, a change of name gave us the famous Nieuport company and a title that became synonymous with small, superlative fighter aircraft in World War One. The best of these, the Nieuport 17, had its origins in the Nieuport 11 fighter. This in turn was based upon a pre-First World War Nieuport racer design, that had been created to compete in a famous race, the Gordon Bennett cup. This race did not take place in 1914 due to the start of the war, but the potential of the little Nieuport had been recognised and it was developed into a series of highly successful fighters that started with the Nieuport 11 Bébé. Aircraft of the whole series were unusual in having a sesquiplane biplane layout, the lower wing being a much smaller structure than the upper wing which was connected to it by a distinctive 'V' interplane strut arrangement. All the Type 11 and 17 series were relatively small, powered by a comparatively low-powered rotary engine but were fast-climbing and highly manoeuvrable. The Nieuport 11 entered service in 1915, and was used by French, British and Belgian fighter units. Its upper wing-mounted machine gun gave it a reasonable forward firepower, and it gained a measure of air superiority over the Western Front. It took on the Fokker 'E' series fighters that had hitherto been so successful against Allied aircraft. Further development led to the Type 16 and thence to the classic Nieuport 17. This featured slightly increased area wings and other improvements, including a synchronised machine gun on some aircraft. In service from the spring and early summer of 1916, the plucky Nieuport 17 continued to take on the best of the German fighters over the Western Front. Britain's Royal Naval Air Service knew the type as the Nieuport Scout. A number of famous fighter aces flew the Nieuport 17, including the celebrated Frenchman Charles Nungesser. The Canadian William Avery Bishop, who went on to

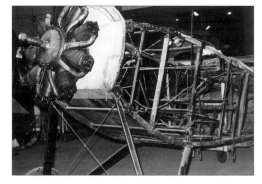

The photographs show constructional details of a preserved Nieuport Scout badly in need of restoration.

become one of the Allies' top-scoring pilots, flew the Nieuport 17 for a part of his career. The basic Nieuport 17 design was further refined and developed in a number of succeeding models. These included the Types 21 and 23, and thence to the Type 24 and finally the Type 27. In general the Nieuport fighters saw comparatively widespread use by several air forces, and the Americans used some models for training. Examples of the Types 16 and 17 were fitted with Le Prieur rockets for shooting down enemy balloons.

The colour drawings show two French-operated Nieuport 17 fighters.

Specifications – Nieuport 11

Wingspan	24 ft 9.25 in
Length	19 ft 0.33 in
Maximum speed	97 mph at sea level
Endurance	2 hr 30 min
Armament	One 0.303 in machine gun
Engine	One Le Rhone 9 C rotary piston engine, of 80 hp
Crew	One

Nieuport 28

Although the Nieuport 11 and 17 series fighters and their derivatives had proven to be successful in aerial combat, the sesquiplane layout of these aircraft with 'V' interplane struts contained little further future development potential. For its next fighter design, Nieuport therefore looked to a more conventional layout, and from this the Nieuport 28 was born. Larger, more powerful, and of a much more conventional layout with a lower wing of 'normal' proportions relative to the upper wing, and conventional interplane struts, the Nieuport 28 was a very different machine to the Nieuport 11 and 17 series in almost every respect. Unfortunately, it was also not the fighter that the smaller Nieuports had proven in battle to be. The first aircraft flew in June 1917, but comparative trials with several early prototype examples later in the year led to some tinkering with the design (particularly the wing layout and dihedral). It was not until the early spring of 1918 that deliveries of production aircraft began in earnest, and in the event only one operator really made any satisfactory use of the Nieuport 28. This was the American Expeditionary Force in France. The Americans ordered the type in January 1918 when faced with a potential shortage of front-line fighters, and subsequently obtained some 297 of these aircraft to equip several fighter squadrons. The Nieuport 28 entered full front-line operational status with the Americans in April 1918 (the 95th Aero Squadron received the first aircraft in March), but the type proved to be troublesome in service. One problem was its Gnome Monosoupape engine, which was not a particularly reliable power plant. Other difficulties were encountered with the Nieuport 28's upper wing. On recovery from a steep dive this sometimes shed its leading edge, resulting in the upper surface fabric covering (and forward plywood covered section) being ripped back as the leading edge pulled free and upwards. Indeed, the previous Nieuport 11 and

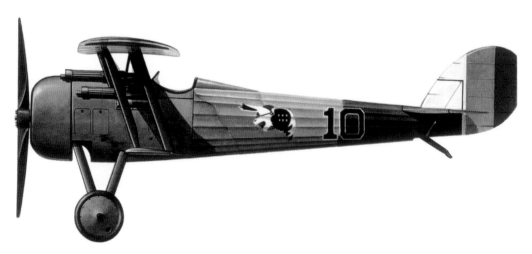

The United States was the principal user of the Nieuport 28.

17 series had also suffered from wing problems, but in a different form. On these types the small lower wing with its single spar construction had tended to fail on some aircraft under stress. The Nieuport 28, despite its upper wing failure problems, was reasonably well liked by the Americans who flew it. Several American aces, such as Douglas Campbell and Edward Rickenbacker, successfully piloted the type. Later in the summer of 1918 the Americans did, however, rather gladly start to replace their Nieuports with the much better SPAD S.XIII. Nonetheless, some Nieuport 28 were later taken to the United States, and several were used by the U.S. Navy aboard ships. Very limited use of the Nieuport 28 was also made by a small number of other armed forces.

Specifications – Nieuport 28C.1

Wingspan	26 ft 9 in
Length	21 ft
Maximum speed	122 mph at sea level
Endurance	approximately 2 hr
Armament	Two 0.303 in machine guns
Engine	One Gnome Monosoupape 9 N rotary piston engine, of 160 hp
Crew	One

Hansa Brandenburg D1

One of the great names in German aircraft design and manufacture was Ernst Heinkel. Although he is famous for the aircraft that bore his name that flew during the 1930's and served in World War Two, Heinkel was already a well-established aircraft designer prior to that time. During World War One he was an active aircraft designer, notably of the Hansa-Brandenburg D I fighter biplane. This type became an important combat aircraft for the air component of the Austro-Hungarian armed forces. The D I grew out of the need for a modern single-seat fighter for the Austro-Hungarian forces, and design work was carried out during 1916. The first production aircraft started to reach Austro-Hungarian units in the autumn and early winter of 1916. The D I was in reality an ungainly-looking fighter, whose single machine gun was mounted in a 'coffin' atop the upper wing because no interrupter gear was fitted, and so it had to fire outside the arc of the aircraft's propeller. The aircraft was unusual for its interplane struts arrangement, which gave it the

nickname 'star-strutter' and did away with the need for the bracing wires between the biplane wings that were otherwise a common feature of World War One aircraft. Production of the D I was carried out by Hansa-Brandenburg as well as the Austrian company Phönix. Hansa-Brandenburg built approximately 50, while Phönix constructed 48, although some contemporary sources claim that 122 were ordered in total. They served in Austro-Hungarian front-line units until the autumn or early winter of 1917, and thereafter in training and other second-line organisations. The D I was flown by several of the top First World War Austro-Hungarian fighter pilots, including Julius Arigi and Godwin Brumowski, although the D I was not a terribly easy aircraft to fly and some of the Phönix built machines featured tailplane alterations to improve handling. Nevertheless the D I served as the basis for the considerably re-

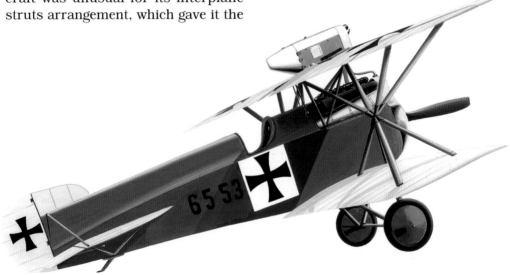

worked and more successful
Phönix D series of fighters.

*The top-scoring Austro-Hungarian air ace
in World War One was Hauptmann
Godwin Brumowski, with some
40 victories. He is seen here, seated
in the cockpit of his Hansa-Brandenburg
D I numbered 65.53. Sadly he was killed
in an air crash at Schiphol airport in
Holland during 1936.*

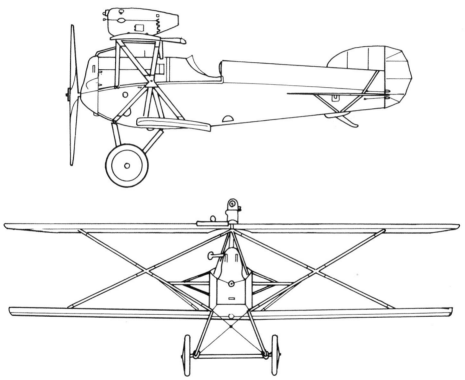

Specifications – Hansa-Brandenburg D I

Wingspan	27 ft 10.66 in
Length	20 ft 8.5 in
Maximum speed	116.5 mph at sea level
Endurance	approximately 2 hr 30 min
Armament	One 0.315 in machine gun
Engine	One Austro-Daimler inline piston engine, of 185 hp (160 hp also available)
Crew	One

Albatros B and C Series

One of the principal types equipping the German military air arm when World War One broke out was the elegant Albatros B I unarmed observation aircraft. The celebrated German Albatros company had been created in 1909 at Berlin-Johannisthal, and had commenced production of the B Series prior to the start of the war, thanks to collaboration with the well-known designer Ernst Heinkel. These aircraft were contemporary with the Aviatik B Series aircraft described on page 72. However, unlike the Aviatiks, the Albatros B-model aircraft evolved into a long and successful line of two-seat reconnaissance and general purpose aircraft for the German forces. Early combat experience confirmed that some form of arma-

ment would be useful, and this led to the B II with provision for the aircraft's observer (who sat in front of the pilot) to be armed with a rudimentary form of defence. Further evolution led to the B III with its distinctively changed vertical tail surfaces and other improvements. In addition to German service, some B-model Albatros also served for Austro-Hungarian forces. With the introduction of the 'C' Series of more powerful, armed reconnaissance/general purpose aircraft by the Germans in 1915, the B-model Albatros were generally relegated to liaison and training roles. The first Albatros C-model was the C I, and this was the commencement of a long line of Albatros C Series reconnaissance and general purpose aircraft that extended

Above: The Albatros B II was an elegant aircraft, but soon became unsuited to the increasingly aggressive aerial fighting of the First World War.

Right: An early Albatros B I in what appears to be the type's original form (Photo: John Batchelor Collection).

The Albatros C I introduced formal armament for the observer, who now occupied the rear seat. Note the radiator installation on the side of the fuselage beside the pilot (Photo: Hans Meier Collection).

to the C XV of 1918. The original C I resembled some B-model aircraft (although there had been a number of variations even in the B Series production), but it significantly introduced armament in the form of a flexible-mounted machine gun for the observer. The seating arrangement was also changed, with the pilot sitting up front, and the observer in the rear seat where his machine gun would have greater effect. With the introduction of more powerful engines and thus enhanced performance compared to those of the B-model line, the C Series proved popular with their two-man crews. Licence production ensued with several manufacturers, and some were also built in Austria-Hungary. Additional armament was added in later C-models of a fixed, forward-firing synchronised machine gun, and some aircraft also carried radio equipment for artillery spotting. Further developments also created various different engine and design configurations, although some of these aircraft illustrated the trend towards larger C-model aircraft that eventually led to the introduction in German service of the lighter and smaller CL Series of two-seat escort fighter/ground attack aircraft. The Albatros C XII of late 1917/early 1918 introduced a streamlined 'cigar-shaped' fuselage and tail surfaces more often associated with the Albatros single-seat fighters.

Specifications – Albatros C I

Wingspan	42 ft 3.75 in
Length	25 ft 9 in
Maximum speed	87 mph at sea level
Service Ceiling	9,843 ft
Endurance	2 hr 30 min
Armament	One 0.312 in machine gun in rear cockpit, various improvised bombs or grenades
Engine	One Mercedes D III inline piston engine, of 160 hp (other options available)
Crew	Two

Albatros D III and D V/Va

As described on the previous two Pages, the German company Albatros developed an accomplished line of two-seat observation/general purpose aircraft types during World War One. However, the company is best remembered for its related and famous family of 'D' Series fighters that appeared in the summer of 1916. The first of these, the D I, is believed to have first flown in August 1916. Some of the wing design features were taken from the C-model aircraft (albeit smaller), but the type's fuselage was a neat, streamlined shape for one occupant only. Power was provided by the ubiquitous 160 hp Mercedes D III, giving the new fighter a comparatively good performance and the ability to carry two fixed forward-firing synchronised machine guns. When it entered service later in 1916 the Allies had gained air superiority over the Western Front,

with the Nieuports in particular having gained the upper hand following the 'Fokker scourge' of late 1915 and early 1916. The new Albatros fighter at once made an impact, and started to redress the balance towards the Germans. The Albatros D II was a developed version of the D I, in which the clumsy fuselage side radiators of the latter were removed to the upper wing centre section. Further development led to the famous D III, which was intended to be far more manoeuvrable. This resulted in the adaptation, in similar style to the Nieuport 11 and 17 aircraft (see pages 106-107), of a small lower wing with a single spar, and 'V' shaped interplane struts. The

in the summer of 1917. However, these later Albatros aircraft did not have such an edge over Allied fighters, especially the Sopwith Camel and S.E.5a when those types started to be available in quantity. Over 1,000 were in service by May 1918, but they faced structural failures of the lower wing (as also found by the similar Nieuports). To circumvent the Armistice regulations imposed by the Allies after the war ended, the Albatros fighters were re-designated as 'L' type aircraft.

upper wing was altered and staggered relative to the lower. This new fighter entered service in early 1917 and was an immediate success. An even more refined design was the D V/D Va, which introduced a beautifully-streamlined fuselage shape that resembled a monocoque structure. The type entered service in numbers

The Albatros D V/Va series were the best-looking of the Albatros fighters, and were the finest expression of the 'cigar-shaped' fuselage that was so distinctive of later Albatros aircraft.

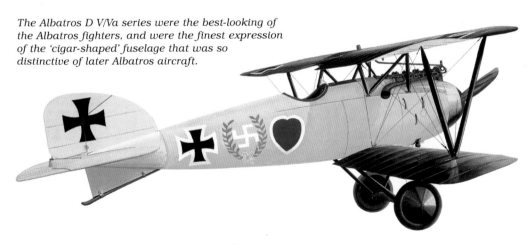

Specifications – Albatros D V/Va

Wingspan	29 ft 8.25 in
Length	24 ft 0.5 in
Maximum speed	115.6 mph at 3,281 ft
Service Ceiling	18,701 ft
Endurance	2 hr
Armament	Two fixed forward-firing 0.312 in machine guns
Engine	One Mercedes D IIIa inline piston engine, of 180-200 hp (other options available)
Crew	One

Fokker D VII

Fokker's 'E' Series of monoplane fighters had caused many problems for the Allies in late 1915 and early 1916, until superior fighters were brought into service on the Allied side. Similarly the trim little Fokker Dr I Triplane had gained a measure of success, especially in the hands of experienced or gifted pilots. Fokker worked on a wide range of fighter projects later in the war, including the neat biplane V 11 of late 1917. With some modifications this design won a significant fighter competition in the early weeks of 1918 to find a new fighter type for German military service. It so outclassed its opposition that it was ordered into immediate production, and even the Albatros company – whose D V fighter was a major rival – was ordered to build the excellent new Fokker fighter. As the Fokker D VII, this new aircraft made

an immediate mark when it entered service in April/May 1918. Few of the Allies' fighters were able to combat it with ease, and it is generally regarded as Germany's best fighter of World War One. Only when the Sopwith Snipe (see pages 130-131) came along did the Allies have an aircraft that was definitely superior to the D VII, although well-flown Sopwith Camels, SPAD S.XIII and S.E.5a could match the German fighter. The D VII was strong and particularly manoeuvrable at high altitudes, and its ubiquitous 160 hp Mercedes D III was adequate – some, however, were powered by a 185 hp BMW engine that considerably improved performance, and these were much prized by their pilots. Some 760 D VII are believed to have been taken on charge by the German military before the end of the war, although total production was probably higher than this. So successful was the D VII that

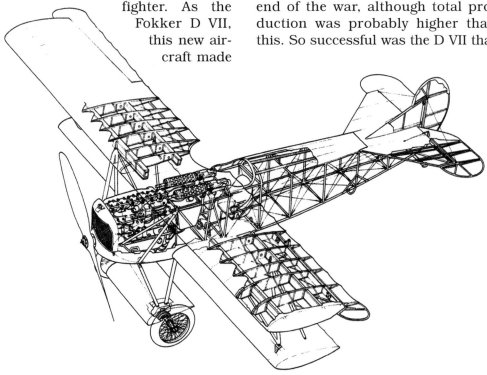

the victorious Allies at the end of World War One demanded that all surviving D VII must be surrendered – a demand that was not made for any other German fighter type. This 'accolade' prevented Anthony Fokker from being able to build the type in Germany after the war, or indeed to continue his aviation activities on anything like the scale that he had been able to achieve during the conflict. He therefore famously smuggled several hundred engines, whole aircraft and other parts of his aviation concerns out of Germany and into his native Holland, where he re-established his aircraft company in 1919. Post-war the D VII saw Dutch military service, and other air arms used the type including Switzerland and

The Fokker D VII was a strong, manoeuvrable fighter with what were effectively cantilever wings and a welded steel tube fuselage structure (Photo: John Batchelor).

Belgium (which flew a two-seat variant).

Individualised colour schemes were worn by many German-operated fighters during World War One. This Fokker D VII was flown by Josef Mai of Jasta 5.

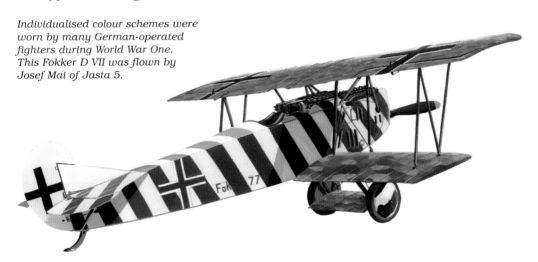

Specifications – Fokker D VII

Wingspan	29 ft 2.5 in
Length	22 ft 9.5 in
Maximum speed	124.3 mph at 3,281 ft
Service Ceiling	22,966 ft
Endurance	1 hr 30 min
Armament	Two fixed forward-firing 0.312 in machine guns
Engine	One BMW IIIa inline piston engine, of 185 hp (other options available)
Crew	One

Fokker D VIII

A somewhat strange mixture of advanced features and those fast becoming outmoded, the Fokker D VIII had a very brief combat history. It arose out of a successful design, the Fokker V 26 (and associated V 28), which performed well in the second German fighter competition which was held in May 1918 (the first competition was won by the Fokker D VII, as described on the preceding two Pages). The V 26 was a parasol-wing monoplane with (for its time) an advanced cantilever wing structure, but it nonetheless reverted to features seen on the by-then outmoded Fokker Dr I such as a rotary engine. At first the new fighter received an 'E' for 'Eindecker' (monoplane) designation, E V, to follow on from the E IV of 1916. Like the Fokker D VII, the production aircraft had a strong air-frame, the core of which was a welded steel tube structure. The cantilever wing, however, caused problems. Initial aircraft that went into service from about August 1918 suffered a number of catastrophic wing failures. Production is said to have been temporarily suspended until the source of the problem was identified. It is possible that official intervention in the design of the wing had led to unnecessary modifications that caused the wing to fail, although poor workmanship by sub-contractors has also been blamed. When production resumed in the autumn of 1918 after the difficulties had apparently been ironed out, the original wing design was used. The type had by then been re-designated as the D VIII. Deliveries to front-line units followed as soon as possible in October 1918, but it is

Very few Fokker D VIII had the opportunity to fly in combat for any length of time before the First World War ended. Amongst them were the aircraft assigned to Jasta 6.

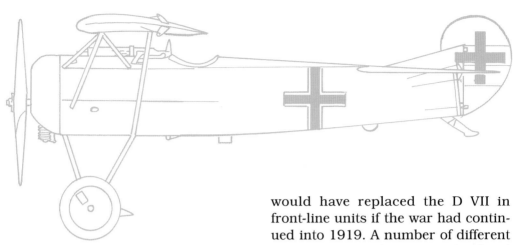

probable that only small numbers reached the Western Front – where they had little time to prove that they were capable fighters. It has sometimes been claimed that the D VIII would have replaced the D VII in front-line units if the war had continued into 1919. A number of different rotary engine options were tried out in the D VIII airframe. Post-war the D VIII saw some service use in Holland following Fokker's relocation to that country from Germany, while others served with Polish forces.

Specifications – Fokker D VIII

Wingspan	27 ft 4.75 in
Length	19 ft 2.25 in
Maximum speed	126.8 mph at sea level
Service Ceiling	20,669 ft
Endurance	1 hr 30 min
Armament	Two fixed forward-firing 0.312 in machine guns
Engine	One Oberursel UR II rotary engine, of 110 hp (other options available)
Crew	One

Caproni Ca.1 and Ca.3 Series

It is often forgotten that during World War One, Italy fought bravely and successfully on the side of the Allies, principally against Austro-Hungarian forces. As with other major European countries, an indigenous aircraft industry had started to evolve in Italy prior to the start of World War One. Several aircraft types of Italian design and manufacture were produced during the First World War, notably the neat S.V.A. reconnaissance/light bomber series (see Pages 128-129) and various Caproni bombers, but considerable licenced production of aircraft from other countries was also undertaken by Italian companies. Italy was one of the pioneers of long-range bombing, and possessed a fleet of large long-range bombers able to fly strategic missions earlier than several of the other main protagonists in World War One. In 1908 a true pioneer of Italy's aircraft industry was created, this being the Caproni company of Count Gianni Caproni. One of Caproni's great contributions to military aviation was a series of large bombers that were built during and after World War One. In 1913/1914 these began with the Ca.30, which set the design layout for all those machines that followed. This consist-

ed of a cabin/fuselage pod with a pusher engine at its rear, between large biplane wings; twin fuselages extended back from the wings, ending with a three piece vertical tail configuration, and a tractor engine layout at their forward ends. Although apparently ungainly, the production models of these four-crew contraptions nevertheless carried out important bombing raids following the Italian declaration of war against the Austro-Hungarian Empire in May 1915. First in widespread use was the Ca.31 (military designation Ca.1), and approximately 166 of these aircraft were built. They were in action against Austro-Hungarian targets in August 1915. The Ca.1 was followed

An excellent period photograph, showing to advantage the ungainly appearance of the Ca.1, Ca.2 and Ca.3 Caproni bombers.

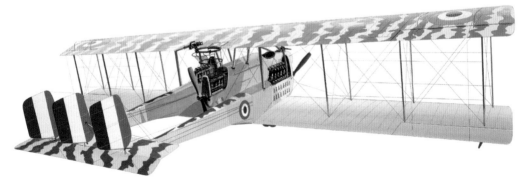

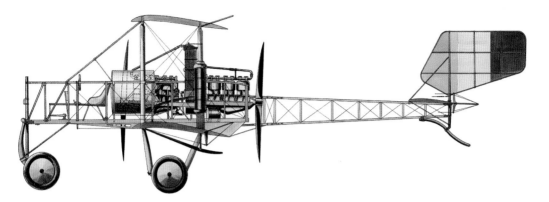

by the Ca.32 (Ca.2, built in small numbers), and the more powerful Ca.33 (Ca.3). Well over 250 of the latter are believed to have been built in Italy. They were particularly notorious for the exposed and very hazardous position of the rear gunner, in a precarious site near the pusher engine's propeller at the rear end of the fuselage pod. The Ca.3 served widely with Italian units, and the type was also operated by the French. Licence production additionally took place in France. A number of related versions also existed, while some of the Italian-operated machines were flown from French bases against German targets.

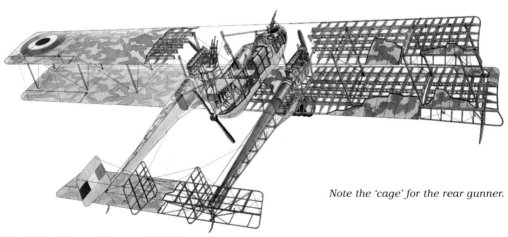

Note the 'cage' for the rear gunner.

Specifications – Caproni Ca.3

Wingspan	72 ft 10 in
Length	35 ft 9.25 in
Maximum speed	87 mph at sea level
Range	approximately 280 miles
Service Ceiling	13,452 ft
Armament	Two or four 0.303 in machine guns, up to some 992 lb of bombs or equivalent
Engine	Three Isotta-Fraschini V.4B inline piston engines, of 150 hp each
Crew	Four

Vickers Vimy

One of the most celebrated aviation achievements was the first-ever non-stop crossing of the Atlantic Ocean by an aircraft. This feat was achieved in a specially-prepared Vickers Vimy by two British aviators, John Alcock and Arthur Whitten Brown. Taking off during 14 June 1919, from a field near St. John's, Newfoundland (now a part of Canada), these two intrepid airmen travelled across the Atlantic, covering some 1,890 miles (3,042 km) and landing (rather heavily) dur-

ing the morning of 15 June at Clifden in Ireland. During 1913 the British newspaper, the 'Daily Mail', had offered a prize of £10,000 to the first aviator to achieve such a feat, and Alcock and Brown were duly presented with this prize. In addition, a different Vimy was flown on an equally trail-blazing flight in stages during November-December 1919 by an Australian crew from England to Australia, the first such actual flight. The Vickers Vimy itself had been

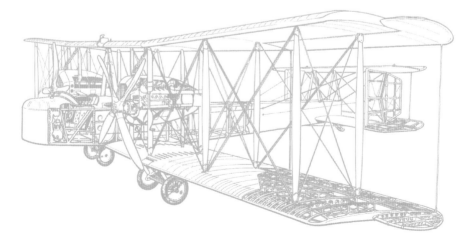

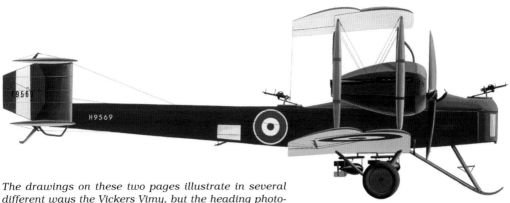

The drawings on these two pages illustrate in several different ways the Vickers Vimy, but the heading photograph on the opposite page is one of aviation's great historical images. It shows the Vimy of Alcock and Brown, shortly after take-off in Newfoundland, on its way into the grey June 1919 sky and the first-ever non-stop crossing of the Atlantic Ocean by an aircraft (Photo: Vickers Ltd.).

designed as a strategic bomber following a requirement of July 1917 for an aircraft able to bomb German industrial centres and other strategic targets. It was a direct contemporary of the Handley Page V/1500 (see Pages 88-89), and like the V/1500 it came along too late to serve in World War One. The prototype first flew in November 1917, and most production aircraft were fitted with the highly successful Rolls-Royce Eagle inline engine as the Vimy Mk.IV. Operational deliveries to the Royal Air Force began in summer 1919, the Vimy subsequently serving in Britain and the Middle East. The type was finally retired in 1933, total production being approximately 230. Some were employed as trainers later in their careers, and the Vimys in the Middle East were re-engined with radials when their inline engines finally succumbed to the sand and high temperatures. An important derivative was the Vimy Commercial. The prototype flew in April 1919, and 43 production examples were built, with a bulbous fuselage able to house up to ten passengers. 40 of these were bought by China. There was also an R.A.F. ambulance derivative, and a military transport named Vernon of which some 55 were manufactured. Historians disagree on the wingspan of the Eagle-powered Vimy, the figure given here being one option.

Specifications – Vickers Vimy Mk.IV

Wingspan	68 ft 1 in
Length	43 ft 6.5 in
Maximum speed	103 mph at sea level
Service Ceiling	7,000 ft
Range	900 miles
Armament	Two to four 0.303 in machine guns flexible ring-mounted, up to some 2,476 lb of bombs
Engine	Two Rolls-Royce Eagle VIII inline piston engines, of 360 hp (other options available)
Crew	Three or four

Curtiss NC-4

Forever associated with the first-ever Atlantic crossing of any description by a heavier-then-air craft, the Curtiss NC-4 was one of four similar flying-boats designed in 1917 by Curtiss in association with the U.S. Navy. The original intentions for this design had included roles such as long-range maritime patrol, but from the start their designers appear to have had their minds additionally on the possibility of an Atlantic Ocean crossing. The first of the four, known as the NC-1 flew in October 1918, but the other three did not fly until 1919, their warlike role by then having been negated. Some detail modification was carried out on the four 'boats, including alterations to their engine layouts – an original design concept had called for three engines, but eventually four were fitted. The transatlantic flight attempt grew into a fantastic logistical effort, in which the U.S. Navy left nothing to chance. Once the route had been decided upon, planning went ahead to provide well

over 50 major naval warships plus others spaced out to cover the route, in the event of catastrophe or the need for assistance. Three of the four NC craft made the transatlantic attempt (NC-1, NC-3, and NC-4). They left Trepassey Bay, Newfoundland, on 16 May 1919, bound for Horta in the Azores. Only the NC-4 reached this destination by air, on 17 May, the other two coming down in the sea although the NC-3 was able to taxi on the water to Ponta Delgada. However, the NC-4, commanded by Lieutenant-Commander A.C. Read, not only safely reached Horta, but from there flew on to Ponta Delgada on 20 May, and thence to Lisbon in Portugal on 27 May to complete the first-ever aircraft crossing of the Atlantic – albeit in stages. Eventually Read continued on to Plymouth, southern England, on 31 May. He and his crew subsequently made a triumphant return to the United States. The total flight time for this epic from the original start point in the U.S.A. had been 53 hours and

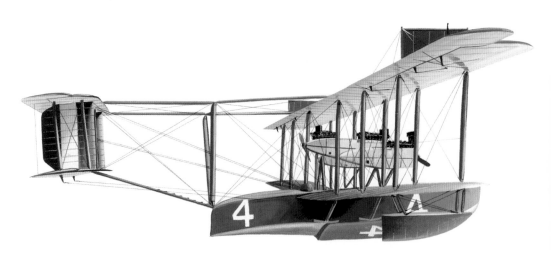

The illustration shows the Curtiss NC-4 of Read and his crew.

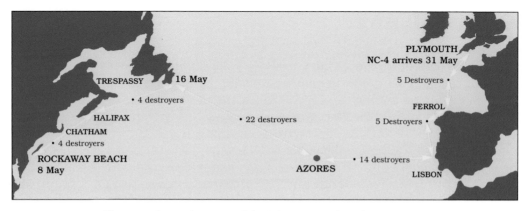

The map shows the route of the NC-4 across the Atlantic Ocean.

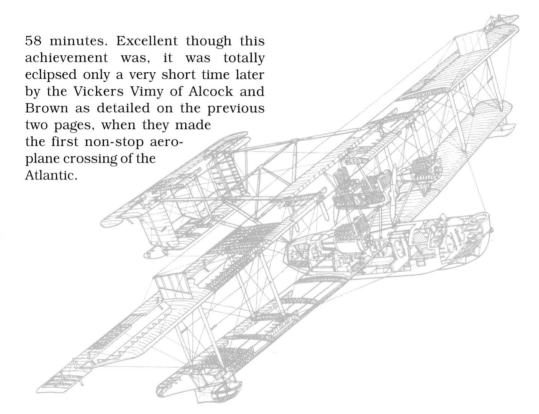

58 minutes. Excellent though this achievement was, it was totally eclipsed only a very short time later by the Vickers Vimy of Alcock and Brown as detailed on the previous two pages, when they made the first non-stop aeroplane crossing of the Atlantic.

Specifications – Curtiss NC-4

Wingspan	126 ft
Length	68 ft 5.5 in
Maximum speed	91 mph at sea level
Service Ceiling	4,500 ft
Range	1,470 miles plus
Engine	Four Liberty 12 inline piston engines, of 400 hp each
Crew	Six (for transatlantic flight)

125

Curtiss Jenny

Although particularly renowned for his pioneering work with seaplanes and flying-boats, American Glenn Curtiss created during the First World War period one of the classic land-planes of its era – although it did also have a seaplane spin-off. This classic aircraft was the Curtiss JN 'Jenny', which was to an extent an American equivalent of the similarly widely-used British Avro 504 series (see pages 82-83). Requirements for a tractor-type primary trainer originated with the U.S. military in 1914, and to meet these needs the Curtiss company employed B. Douglas Thomas, a British designer who had successfully worked with the British Sopwith company. The resulting Curtiss Model 'J' was a very practical tractor biplane. It also, however, retained a Curtiss peculiarity of an aileron control system in which the pilot was fitted with a yoke on his shoulders, the machine being banked by the pilot by leaning in the direction that he wanted to go. Luckily this archaic system was later dropped for what would eventually become the established means of controlling an aircraft with a control column and rudder pedals. Continuing Curtiss development resulted in the Model 'N', which also had the feature of interplane ailerons between the wings, fast becoming outmoded. Eventually these and other related Curtiss designs came together into the JN, which was developed into a famous family of trainers. The 'JN' designation led to the nickname 'Jenny', which persists to this day. Initially a series of basic trainers ensued, and production in the United States was supplemented by manufacture in Canada where an independent line of related models also

The smile on the face of the young boy in the front cockpit of this Jenny tells the story of the many thousands who got their first airplane ride as a passenger in the famous Curtiss trainer. As many as 6,700+ or even 7,500+ JN might have been built.

The Jenny was the vehicle for many crazy aerial stunts during the 'barnstorming' days of the 1920's, as shown here (Photo: John Batchelor Collection).

followed. Some of these were supplied to Britain for use as trainers, but the majority were used by U.S. forces. The most famous of the substantial Jenny line was the JN-4, which was produced from 1916 in the United States, the major production model being the JN-4D. The prototype U.S.-type JN-4D appeared in mid-1917. Up-engineing of the line resulted in the JN-4H powered by the Wright-built Hispano-Suiza (the so-called 'Hisso') engine, allowing the Jenny to be used for advanced training in gunnery, bombing, reconnaissance and even fighter training. Other developments ensued, including the related N-9 floatplane (see Pages 132-133). Post-war, the more powerful Jenny types remained in military service as train-ers, some being re-built as JNS (standardised) models. Many of the less-powerful Jenny aircraft were bought back by Curtiss for 'civilianization', but the U.S. government then sold off large numbers of the remaining lower-powered Jennies and scores of these were bought by private owners and ex-military flyers. The famous era of 'barnstorming' began, with these aircraft used for joy-riding across the width of the United States and for many crazy aerial stunts such as wing-walking. Others featured in movies. Government regulation in 1927/1928 eventually put many of these aircraft out of business, and the remaining military models were finally retired in 1927.

Specifications – Curtiss JN-4H Jenny

Wingspan	43 ft 7.25 in (43 ft 9 in sometimes also used)
Length	27 ft 0.5 in
Maximum speed	93 mph at sea level
Endurance	2 hr 30 min
Service Ceiling	18,000 ft
Engine	One Wright-built Hispano-Suiza 'A' inline piston engine, of 150 hp
Crew	Two

Ansaldo S.V.A.5

Apart from the Caproni bombers referred to on Pages 120-121, and 134-135, the most important indigenous Italian military aircraft of the First World War years were the S.V.A. (Ansaldo) series of light reconnaissance and bomber aircraft. S.V.A. stood for Savoia, Verduzio, (two of the type's designers) and Ansaldo (a major Italian industrial organisation, that came into aircraft production through the S.V.A. programme). Considerable Italian government money was put into the project and into the building or renovation of aircraft factories. The first S.V.A. flew in March 1917. It was a fast, fighter-like aircraft that was destined never to be used as a fighter in its own right. Instead, due to a perceived lack of manoeuvrability for air combat, it was relegated to long-range reconnaissance and light bombing roles. With its Warren truss-like wing struts and curious inverted triangle rear fuselage cross-section, the S.V.A. was

very distinctive. As a reconnaissance aircraft it was fast enough and long-legged enough to perform alone, being able to look after itself if enemy fighters challenged it. It also had an excellent climb rate. The S.V.A.3 and camera-carrying S.V.A.4 were important early production models, the former having short-span wings and was used amongst other duties as a local defence fighter. The main production model was the S.V.A.5. This entered service in early 1918, and the type performed useful reconnaissance missions until the end of the war. Some of these were of (for those days) very long length, including flights across the Alps from Italian-held territory over southern Germany. A famous leaflet-dropping 'raid' was flown over the Austro-Hungarian capital Vienna in August 1918, in which the celebrated Italian poet Gabriele D'Annunzio flew in a two-seater accompanied by several single-seaters. Two two-seat versions of the

S.V.A.5 reconnaissance/light bombers of the Italian air force's 87th Squadriglia carried some of the most beautiful fuselage artwork of any World War One aircraft.

S.V.A. were built, the S.V.A.9 and the S.V.A.10. A floatplane model was also manufactured. Post-war, the S.V.A. persisted in Italian air force service into the 1930's, latterly mainly as a trainer. S.V.A.s also operated with several other air arms. The type was employed in a celebrated flight from Italy to Tokyo in Japan during the first half of 1920. Some were used by private owners in the United States. Production ended in around 1928, by which time over 2,000 of all S.V.A. types are believed to have been built.

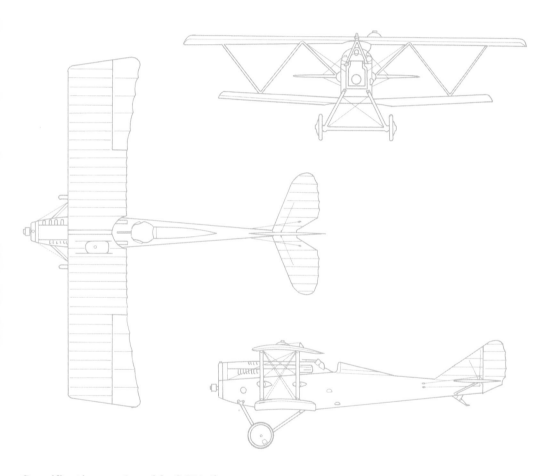

Specifications – Ansaldo S.V.A.5

Wingspan	29 ft 10.25 in
Length	26 ft 7 in
Maximum speed	143 mph at 6,500 ft
Endurance	typically 3 hr (up to six hours possible)
Armament	Two 0.303 in machine guns, various light bombs carried externally
Engine	One S.P.A. Type 6A inline piston engine, of 205-220 hp
Crew	One

Sopwith Snipe

The famous British aircraft company Sopwith had proven itself as one of the leading designers and manufacturers of fighter aircraft with the superlative Sopwith Camel (see Pages 98-99). When the official requirement arose for a potential replacement for the Camel, Sopwith competed with a number of other companies for the creation of a Camel successor. Although many Camels were powered by the Clerget rotary engine, some were powered by the Bentley B.R.1 rotary engine instead. In April 1917 early examples of a new, more powerful rotary, the Bentley B.R.2, were officially ordered. This new engine proved successful, and was sanctioned to be used to power the Camel successor. Sopwith's design proposal to replace the Camel was the 7F.1 Snipe, and this successfully beat off its competition to be officially selected in late 1917/early 1918. Some experimentation was subsequently involved, using several prototypes, before something approaching a production layout was decided upon, and the type entered production as the

Snipe Mk.I. Large orders were planned with several manufacturers, but in the event the end of the First World War resulted in cutbacks to the intended totals. Only three squadrons (one Australian, two British) used the Snipe operationally as their principal equipment over the Western front, the first deliveries being made in the summer of 1918. Nevertheless, the Snipe proved to be an excellent fighter. It was rather easier to fly than the somewhat unforgiving Camel, and it had fine manoeuvrability and rate of climb. It was also useful for ground attack duties. A long-range bomber escort model designated 7F.1a was developed but did not see widespread combat service. The Snipe became well-known due to an individual battle on 27 October 1918, when high-scoring ace Major William Barker flying a Snipe successfully fought solo against overwhelming numbers of German fighters. He was awarded the Victoria Cross for this action. 497 Snipes had been built by the end of 1918, and production continued after the war ended. The Snipe was developed into

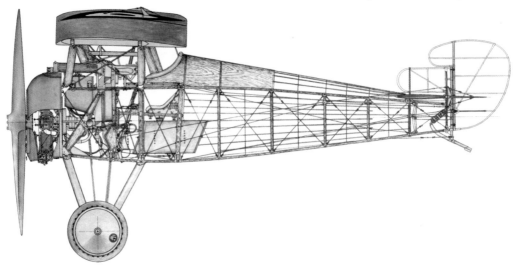

the Sopwith Dragon, which was built in small numbers and powered by the A.B.C. Dragonfly radial engine. Bentley-powered Snipes continued in service with the Royal Air Force well into the 1920's, for a time as night fighters.

Specifications – Sopwith 7F.1 Snipe

Wingspan	30 ft
Length	19 ft 10 in
Maximum speed	121 mph at 10,000 ft
Service Ceiling	19,500 ft
Endurance	3 hr
Armament	Two 0.303 in machine guns, up to 100 lb of bombs carried externally
Engine	One Bentley B.R.2 rotary piston engine, of 230 hp
Crew	One

Curtiss N-9

The Curtiss JN 'Jenny' was one of the most famous aircraft of its time (see Pages 126-127), but little is remembered of its floatplane close relative, the N-9. The likelihood of American entry into World War One (which actually happened in April 1917), encouraged the U.S. military during 1916 to considerably expand its training resources. The U.S. naval aviation needed a seaplane primary trainer in large numbers, and several manufacturers put forward proposals for a possible contender. Curtiss already had the Model 'N', which had been a part of the eventual JN Jenny conglomeration. With some amalgamation characteristic of the whole Jenny programme, the Curtiss naval trainer proposal eventually called the N-9 drew on features of the 'N' development programme together with the JN-4B landplane. It also included long-span wings as tried out on the N-8. A large wood veneer main float was rigged under the fuselage, plus small cylindrical metal wing-tip floats. There were other features peculiar to this model, including changes to the vertical tail and the adaptation of a different wing airfoil compared to the JN-4B. Production go-ahead was subsequently gained by Curtiss, and at least two different power plants were tried out on production N-9 models. These were the 100 hp Curtiss OX-6, but later examples designated N-9H were fitted with the 150 hp Wright-built Hispano-Suiza inline engine (the so-called

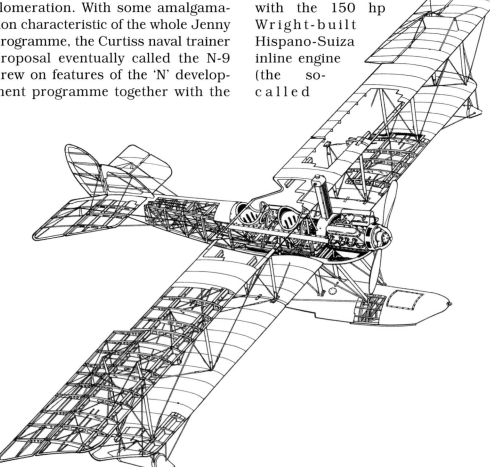

'Hisso', as used on some production Jenny models). These different power plants necessitated a variety of disparate radiator fittings. Delivery of the first N-9 examples was made prior to America's entry into World War One, these going to the major U.S. Navy training base at Pensacola in Florida. Historians disagree as to the number of N-9 that were built (as also is the case with the Jenny), but the best figure appears to be 560. Of these, 100 were built by Curtiss, the remainder by Burgess. The latter company has already appeared in our narrative on Pages 48-49, due to its association with the tail-less biplane designs of Englishman John Dunne. Most N-9 production was for the U.S.

Navy, but the U.S. Army managed to obtain several in trade for some JN-4 landplanes – and possibly 14 new-build N-9H for the Army were manufactured by Curtiss. In the early 1920's some 50 additional N-9 were constructed from stocks of spare and salvaged parts at Pensacola. The N-9 remained as the Navy's principal primary and gunnery trainer until replacement began (by Boeing types) in 1924, the final examples being retired in 1927. Mention must also be made of a completely separate seaplane model of the Jenny itself, which had early features of the JN series and was not directly associated with the N-9.

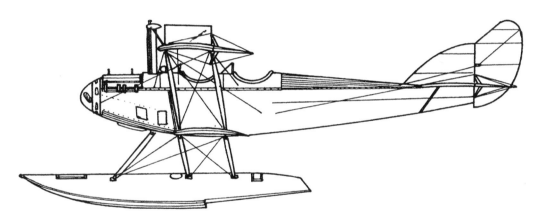

The cutaway drawing and line side-view show the Hispano-Suiza (Wright)-powered N-9H. This model was distinguishable from the Curtiss-powered N-9 by the tall 'stove-pipe' radiator ahead of the upper wing.

Specifications – Curtiss N-9H

Wingspan	53 ft 4 in
Length	30 ft 10 in
Maximum speed	77 mph at sea level
Range	approximately 200 miles
Service Ceiling	8,830 ft
Engine	One Wright-built Hispano-Suiza 'A' inline piston engine, of 150 hp
Crew	Two

Caproni Ca.5

The ungainly but successful Caproni Ca.1, Ca.2 and Ca.3 series of three-engined heavy bombers (see Pages 120-121) proved to be considerably useful in the long-range bombing role, and they were further developed into two quite different beasts. The first, in late 1917, was the Ca.40 series (Ca.4 military designation). This was an enormous triplane, with three engines and a distinctive bomb-carrier between the wheels of the huge main undercarriage. Although the configuration of these contraptions was basically similar to the Ca.3 models, the Ca.4 was probably one of the most ungainly contrivances that actually flew combat in World War One. With a wingspan of some 98 ft 1.25 in these were huge beasts. At least 20 production aircraft were built in several slightly different versions, some

seeing service with Italian forces, while six were taken on charge by Britain's Royal Naval Air Service in January 1918. It is believed that the British-operated examples did not fly in conflict. A civil version of the Ca.4 was flown post-war, and there was a seaplane model. However, more historically important was the Ca.5 series. This was a second-generation development of the Ca.3, and it retained the basic three-engined layout of the Ca.3, but was larger and more powerful, and featured a number of refinements. The first example flew in 1917, and considerable production was undertaken, believed to number almost 300 examples during and after the war. Several related models were developed including the Ca.45 and Ca.46, and the Ca.5 layout was built under licence in France.

Limited production also took place in the United States (where it was intended that Fisher Body, and Standard would produce large numbers; the end of the war curtailed this plan). Nevertheless, the type was put to good use by Italian and French units, as the ultimate combat expression of the curious three-engined layout of these Caproni aircraft. Interestingly, some combat units appear to have preferred the Ca.3 to the Ca.5, and post-war the Ca.3 persisted longer than some Ca.5 models. A Piaggio-built floatplane version was also manufactured.

The size of the Caproni bomber is well illustrated by the man in the cockpit. Note also the precarious gunner's 'cage' behind the wing.

Specifications – Caproni Ca.5

Wingspan	76 ft 9.25 in
Length	41 ft 4.25 in
Maximum speed	93 mph at sea level
Range	approximately 373 miles
Service Ceiling	15,092 ft
Armament	Two 0.303 in machine guns, up to some 1,984 lb of bombs or equivalent
Engine	Three Fiat A.12 inline piston engines, of 250 hp each
Crew	Four

Airco (de Havilland) D.H.9 and D.H.9A

The destructive German air raid on London of 13 June 1917 eventually led to a substantial increase in British military aviation elements, especially those intended for strategic bombing against German industrial targets. One of the aircraft to emerge in this period was the D.H.9, which though similar in appearance to the D.H.4 (see Pages 68-69) was a longer range aircraft that promised considerable improvements over the established D.H.4. Unfortunately the D.H.9 proved to be a disappointment in its intended bombing role in north-west Europe, although it did achieve more in other arenas of the war. The first D.H.9, converted from a D.H.4, flew in July 1917. A major problem with this new aircraft was its engine, the 230 hp B.H.P. sometimes called the Galloway Adriatic, and produced as the Siddeley Puma. This engine type proved troublesome in development and production. The D.H.9 therefore was found to be inferior to the D.H.4 in almost all respects, except that the two-man crew were placed further

together than in the D.H.4, where they were separated dangerously by a fuel tank. Large batches of D.H.9 were rashly ordered before the aircraft had been proven, and found to have generally inferior performance compared to the D.H.4. Squadron deliveries started in earnest early 1918, and the type entered operations in April 1918. 3,204 had been built by the end of 1918. Although the type was still in service at the end of World War One, and a batch were operated by Belgium, by then they had been superseded by an excellent re-design of the D.H.9 known as the D.H.9A. Development of this new model was performed by Westland in Yeovil, southern England, and included a new engine, and many alterations including re-designed wings. Powered by the American Liberty engine, production of the D.H.9A was underway in the summer of 1918, and the first major Royal Air Force mission of the D.H.9A took place in September 1918. The type did not have a real opportunity to show its potential

Installation of the American Liberty engine gave the D.H.9A a completely different nose shape compared to the D.H.9.

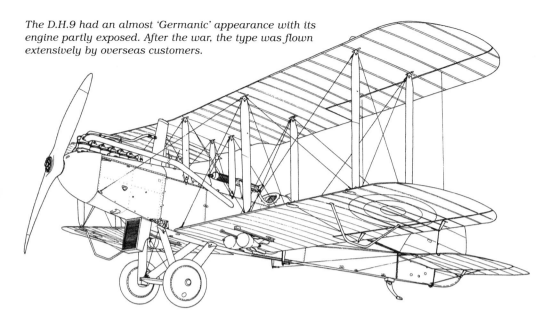

The D.H.9 had an almost 'Germanic' appearance with its engine partly exposed. After the war, the type was flown extensively by overseas customers.

before the end of the war, but it was a highly capable aircraft that gave valuable service after the war in Britain and in other parts of the British Empire. Production of the 'Nine-Ack' as it became affectionately known, reached some 885 by the end of 1918. Total production was probably over 2,000, and the type served with the R.A.F. until the early 1930's, latterly in training and second-line duties. A small number were built in the United States, and an unlicensed copy was made in Russia as the R-1, powered by the M-5 copy of the Liberty engine.

A classic painting of a D.H.9A on 'policing' duties over Iraq in the mid-1920's.

Specifications – Airco (de Havilland) D.H.9A

Wingspan	45 ft 11.5 in
Length	30 ft 3 in
Maximum speed	123 mph at sea level
Service Ceiling	16,750 ft
Endurance	5 hr 15 min
Armament	One 0.303 in machine gun fixed forward-firing, one or two 0.303 in flexible ring-mounted machine guns in rear cockpit, up to 460 lb of bombs
Engine	One Liberty 12 inline piston engine, of 400 hp (other options available)
Crew	Two

Blackburn Kangaroo

The ugly and ungainly Blackburn Kangaroo was a British late World War One anti-submarine patrol aircraft that managed to pursue a new career in civil guise after the war ended. Originating in the Blackburn G.P. and S.P. patrol bomber/torpedo-carrying floatplane designs of 1916 that did not enter production, the landplane Kangaroo was developed as a bomber for Royal Flying Corps service. The prototype flew in or just before January 1918, and up to 24 were ordered although only 16 were completed. The majority of these served with only one squadron, No.246, which received its first aircraft in April 1918. This unit carried out anti-submarine patrols with the Kangaroo until the end of the war, supplementing aircraft such as the Felixstowe and Curtiss Large America flying-boats (see Pages 70-71) in this role. A Kangaroo successfully participated in the sinking of a German U-boat in August 1918. With reasonably good performance for such a large aircraft, the Kangaroo nevertheless had a peculiarly thin fuselage that was subject to twisting during manoeuvres in flight. Post-war some Kangaroos were converted into airliners or used as joy-riders with an enclosed 'humped' fuselage cabin to allow up to eight passengers in the fuselage to fly in some degree of comfort. Some were flown on an international airline route in 1919/1920 from Leeds to Hounslow in England, and thence to Amsterdam in the Netherlands by the North Sea Aerial Navigation Co. Ltd. Several civilian-owned Kangaroos were also used as dual-control trainers until 1929 for Royal Air Force aircrew training.

Specifications – Blackburn Kangaroo

Wingspan	74 ft 10.25 in
Length	46 ft
Maximum speed	100 mph at sea level
Endurance	8 hr
Service Ceiling	10,500 ft
Armament	Two 0.303 in machine guns, four 230 lb bombs or equivalent
Engine	Two Rolls-Royce Falcon III inline piston engines, of 275 hp each
Crew	Four

Aero A-10

At the end of World War One several new nation states were created in Central and Eastern Europe out of the remains of the old empires. Some of these new countries soon established their own major aviation industries, underlining the importance that was by then attached to the aviation industry. In the newly-formed state of Czechoslovakia, several new aviation companies were set up, there already being some pioneering aviation heritage in the Czech lands prior to this. The need for new transport aircraft following the end of the First World War, fuelled by the establishment of completely new air routes for civil transport, led to the creation of a variety of entirely fresh passenger-carrying aircraft designs in a number of countries. In Czechoslovakia, the recently formed Aero company created the Aero A-10. This was one of the first civil passenger aircraft specially developed for the civil air transport market after World War One, and was in stark contrast to the converted bombers that were used by a number of airlines across Europe after the war as makeshift civil transports. In common with some of its contemporary civil aircraft, the Aero A-10 had an open cockpit for its pilot (plus second crew member if required), and enclosed accommodation within the fuselage for its passengers and baggage. The prototype first flew in 1922 and the type served until 1924/1925. It was built only in small numbers, reflecting the fact that few of the newly formed airlines that existed at that time had much money to spare on brand-new aircraft.

Specifications – Aero A-10

Wingspan	46 ft 7 in
Length	33 ft 3.25 in
Maximum speed	99.5 mph
Ceiling	19,029 ft
Range	323 miles
Engine	One Maybach Mb IVa inline piston engine, of 240 hp
Accommodation	One pilot (plus mechanic if required), up to four/five passengers

Dornier Komet

Following Germany's defeat in World War One, the German aircraft industry of the war years was scaled down as new orders diminished and restrictions were imposed by the victorious Allies. One of the German designers who was nevertheless able to persist despite the peacetime austerity was Claude Dornier. He had worked during the war with the Zeppelin company, albeit on the aircraft side of that organisation's business at Lindau. He was also one of a number of pioneers of all-metal aircraft design and construction, and in the early 1920's he was responsible for a series of all-metal aircraft that were advanced for their time. They in fact pre-dated by many years the even more technologically advanced commercial aircraft that were conceived by the American John K. Northrop (see Pages 162-163). An early product of Dornier's new, post-war company was the Libelle (Dragonfly) shoulder-wing monoplane amphibian or flying-boat, which was of all-metal construction but with some fabric covering. It led on to the unusually-configured monoplane Delphin (Dolphin) commercial flying-boat series, while at the same time a series of monoplane passenger-carrying landplanes was also being developed. With its first flight in 1921, the Dornier Komet (Comet) I was a revolutionary aircraft for its day. It was of all-metal construction, with an unusual tailwheel-type undercarriage in which the main wheels were set

An all-metal Pullman of the air, this Dornier Komet was pictured prior to leaving on a scheduled air service from Berlin to London (Photo: Philippe Jalabert Collection).

140

The pilot in early models of the Dornier Komet had an exposed open location in the top of the fuselage.

beside rather than lower than the bottom of the deep fuselage. The pilot sat in an exposed cockpit in the upper fuselage, but the type's four passengers were seated a little more comfortably within the fuselage. It appears that production models were flown by early airlines such as Deutscher Aero Lloyd. The improved Komet II first flew in October 1922, with a relocated cockpit further forward relative to the Komet I, to give the pilot a better view. It also carried four passengers, and gained some export success as well as service in Germany itself. The Komet III, which first flew in December 1924, was a larger development with two crew and accommodation for six passengers. The improved and more powerful Merkur (Mercury) series of commercial transports followed, before Dornier became involved in other programmes such as the fantastic Dornier Do X flying-boat (see Pages 158-159).

Specifications – Dornier Komet I

Wingspan	55 ft 9.5 in
Length	31 ft 2in
Maximum speed	99.5 mph at sea level
Maximum take-off weight	4,674 lb
Service Ceiling	13,125 ft
Engine	One BMW III/IIIa inline piston engine, of 180/185 hp
Accommodation	One pilot, four passengers

De Havilland D.H.50

The wartime military aircraft that were pressed into civil passenger-carrying work following the end of World War One did valuable service as interim commercial aircraft. However, many of these types were not particularly suitable for conversion into civil aircraft, and in any case after several years of service some were completely worn out. The de Havilland company in Britain realised that at least some of these former military aircraft would eventually need replacing by purpose-designed and newly-built types. The result was a number of comparatively successful commercial designs, an early major representation of which was the D.H.50. With a seating capacity for four passengers enclosed in a cabin within the fuselage between the biplane wings, and an open cockpit for the pilot, the D.H.50 looked like a refined civil model of the D.H.9A. The first aircraft flew in August 1923, and production by

a number of companies in several countries amounted to some 38 examples. Of these, just under half were built by de Havilland, although few served in Britain, with the D.H.50 instead being operated by a diversity of operators as far away as Australia (where licence production also took place). In Czechoslovakia, seven were built by Aero (in addition to one supplied from Britain), and these aircraft were powered by a 240 hp Walter engine of Czechoslovakian manufacture – one of several options available to the D.H.50 line. The type is best remembered for the long-distance exploits of British pioneer and entrepreneur Alan (later Sir Alan) Cobham. Forever associated with the development of in-flight refuelling, Cobham also achieved many other aviation firsts. Between 16 November 1925 and 17 February 1926, Cobham used a special D.H.50J, powered by a 380-385 hp Armstrong Siddeley Jaguar radial

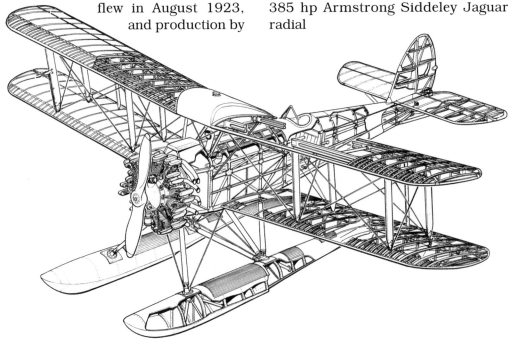

engine, for an epic flight from Croydon in London, England to Cape Town in present-day South Africa. Flights such as this helped to open up the African continent for commercial aviation. Cobham subsequently flew home by the same route, arriving in London on 13 March 1926. Leaving England on 30 June 1926 in the same aircraft, G-EBFO, Cobham then had an equally adventurous survey and route-proving expedition to Australia and back. Cobham eventually reached Darwin, Australia on 8 August 1926, and then moved on across Australia. The D.H.50J operated on floats for a part of this work.

D.H.50J G-EBFO flies in triumph past the Houses of Parliament and Big Ben in London, on its way to landing on the River Thames. This aircraft was used by Alan Cobham in 1925/1926 for his famous flights to Cape Town and out to Australia (Photo: Flight Refuelling Ltd.).

Route-proving for commercial aviation over the Pyramids in Egypt, in an evocative painting that captures the splendour of this age of pioneering aviation after the First World War.

Specifications – de Havilland D.H.50

Wingspan	42 ft 9 in
Length	29 ft 9 in
Maximum speed	112 mph at sea level
Service Ceiling	14,600 ft
Range	380 miles
Engine	One (Armstrong) Siddeley Puma inline piston engine, of 230 hp (other options available)
Crew	One pilot, plus up to four passengers

Lockheed Vega

A famous line of American civil transports that was made in a number of versions, the Lockheed Vega first flew on 4 July 1927. Several American aviation pioneers were involved in its creation, including the Loughead brothers who (with a change of spelling) gave the famous Lockheed company its name, and John K. Northrop (later of flying wing development fame). In the following years the Vega became a famous line that included seven-seat commercial models, and specific one-offs that were used for a number of pioneering flights or explorations. The Vega was for its time a very 'clean' design, with a cantilever wing and a 'cigar-shaped' monocoque fuselage construction, employing mainly wood in its construction (although the final Vegas featured a metal fuselage). Several engine types were used during the Vega production run, which was mainly carried out by Lockheed, but also by Detroit (of which Lockheed temporarily became a division). Some 128 Vegas of all types were built, and a related model was the parasol-wing Lockheed Model 3 Air Express four-passenger airliner that was created for the airline Western Air Express. A famous Vega Model 5-B was the 'Winnie Mae' (see Pages 168-169). Also well-known was the Vega Model 1 derivative used for the first-ever trans-Arctic flight, by the explorers Hubert Wilkins and Carl Eielson in April 1928.

The Wilkins Arctic Expedition of April 1928 used this specially- configured and very distinctive Vega Model 1 registered as X3903.

Specifications – Lockheed Model 1 Vega

Wingspan	41 ft
Length	27 ft 8 in
Maximum speed	138 mph at sea level
Service Ceiling	15,000 ft
Range	900 miles
Engine	One Wright J-5 series Whirlwind radial piston engine, of 220-225 hp
Accommodation	One pilot, plus up to four passengers (later models were up to seven-seat capacity)

Lockheed Sirius

Lockheed developed the Sirius principally due to a request from Charles Lindbergh of transatlantic flight fame. Lindbergh needed a long-range monoplane with good all-round performance for various long-distance and route-proving flights that he intended to make. As with the Lockheed Vega (see previous Page), the Sirius had design input from John K. Northrop and Gerard Vultee, and the result was an advanced-looking, low-wing cantilever monoplane with a wooden monocoque fuselage construction similar to the Vega. The original Sirius was a two-seater with open cockpits, but thanks to the suggestion of Lindbergh's wife the open cockpits were covered with neat sliding enclosures. The first flight is believed to

have been made in late 1929 and the type certificate for the Model 8 Sirius was issued in March 1930. The basic Model 8 was joined by the 8-A with altered tail surfaces and different operating weights, and the 8-C provided a cabin for two passengers within the fuselage. Approximately 14 of all types were built, and several of them made exceptional flights. Lindbergh's special Sirius was up-engined with a 575 hp Wright Cyclone radial, and at times it operated with a twin-float undercarriage as a seaplane. It was later fitted with a more powerful version of the Cyclone engine. A retractable undercarriage derivative of the Sirius was known as the Model 8-D Altair.

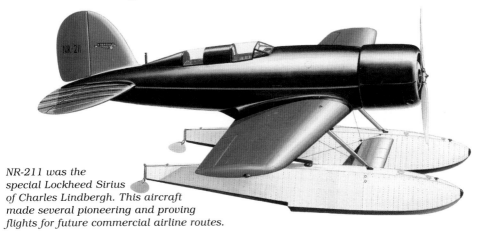

NR-211 was the special Lockheed Sirius of Charles Lindbergh. This aircraft made several pioneering and proving flights for future commercial airline routes.

Specifications – Lockheed Model 8 Sirius

Wingspan	42 ft 10 in
Length	27 ft 6 in
Maximum speed	175 mph at sea level
Service Ceiling	20,000 ft
Range	975 miles
Engine	One Pratt & Whitney Wasp radial piston engine, of 420-450 hp
Accommodation	Two crew, plus two passengers in Model 8-C Sport Cabin Sirius

Douglas World Cruiser

The years after World War One witnessed many aviation achievements and long-distance endeavours. The accolade for the first round-the-world flight – in many stages – goes to the U.S. Army Air Service and its small fleet of Douglas World Cruisers. The idea of a round-the-world flight seems to have taken hold during 1923, and official approval led to a prodigious feat of planning and organisation – similar in scope, but much larger in scale, to that which accompanied the Atlantic crossing of the U.S. Navy-operated Curtiss NC-4 in 1919 (see pages 124-125). The Army needed a rugged, reliable aircraft with good range potential to make the trip, plus the ability to operate on floats and when necessary on wheels. The almost natural choice was a version of the Douglas DT-2, which the fledgling Douglas company had been developing for the U.S. Navy (see pages 152-153). During 1923 a prototype for what came to be called the Douglas World Cruiser was ordered, and it was followed by four production aircraft – No.1 'Seattle', No.2 'Chicago', No.3 'Boston', and No.4 'New Orleans'. They differed from the U.S. Navy's DT series in several respects, including having around six times the fuel capacity, special survival gear, and other equipment relevant to the flight although keeping very basic flight instrumentation. The adventure began in Seattle, in the north-western United States, on 6 April 1924. It went westwards into western Canada, Alaska, the Aleutians, Japan, across Asia to India, and thence to the Middle east, Central Europe, Western Europe and Britain, then across the northern Atlantic via Iceland and Greenland to Newfoundland, eastern Canada, and across the United States. The arrival point was Seattle, which was reached on 28 September 1924. En route, No.1 'Seattle' crashed into a mountainside early in the flight, and crossing the Atlantic No.3 'Boston' had to alight on the sea and was lost. It was replaced by the original prototype, christened 'Boston II', for the final

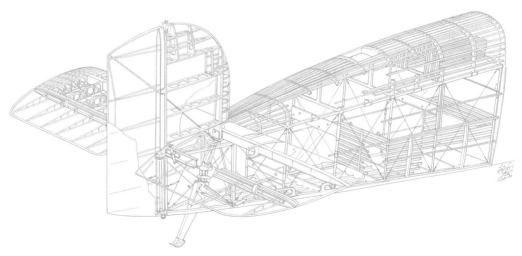

Partial cutaway illustration of Douglas World Cruiser showing complex structure of the rear fuselage.

Douglas Would Cruiser No.4 was called 'New Orleans', and was one of two from the original four starters to complete the 1924 round the world flight (Copyright: Boeing Corporation).

legs across the United States. Fortunately no crew members were lost, and the flyers received a warm welcome along their route. The whole flight was a remarkable achievement, and was accomplished in over 70 individual legs, for a total distance covered of some 28,000 miles, although many conflicting figures have arisen over the years for the flight's statistics –

and indeed for the specifications of the aircraft involved.

Cockpit instrumentation was basic in the Douglas World Cruisers. Each aircraft carried a crew of two in open cockpits (Photo: John Batchelor Collection).

Specifications – Douglas World Cruiser (landplane configuration)

Wingspan	50 ft
Length	35 ft 2.5 in
Maximum speed	104 mph at sea level
Service Ceiling	10,000 ft
Range	2,200 miles plus
Engine	One Liberty inline piston engine, of 400-420 hp
Crew	Two

Cierva Autogyros

The development of the helicopter as a viable means of aerial transport proved to be a very difficult concept to master, and as described on pages 50-51, many early pioneers toyed with the problems of vertical flight without really perfecting the means to achieve it. It was not until the 1930's that any degree of real success was gained in helicopter operation (see pages 272-273). A different train of thought was tried out by the Spanish pioneer Juan de la Cierva. He was the main instigator of a completely different form of short take-off machine, the autogyro. In an autogyro there is usually a conventional engine at the front or back end of a normal fuselage, but with no wings so to speak of, and a main rotor above the fuselage at the centre of gravity position. Unlike modern helicopters, there is

no constant main drive to the main rotor to give lift to the machine. The idea of an autogyro in a nutshell is that the lift required for flight is derived from the main rotor, which freely windmills for flight and is independent of the engine at the front or back which serves to give the machine power to move forward and to move through the air. This concept also took some time to perfect, Cierva beginning his experiments in 1920. However, success eventually followed, so that during January 1923 in Spain the first real autogyro flight was achieved after a number of false starts. Cierva, with input from interested parties in several other countries, was able to develop the autogyro into a completely practical machine, its docile handling (once the pilot has got used to its unusual oper-

G-ACUU was officially registered in Britain as a Cierva C.30A (Avro 671). It was impressed (requisitioned) for Royal Air Force service in 1942 as HM580, and it exists today on display at Duxford north of London belonging to the Imperial War Museum.

ation) and slow operating speeds in addition to very short landings and take-offs making the autogyro a very safe type of machine. An early model was the C.6 series of 1924 onwards, which used the fuselage of the Avro 504. A British Cierva autogyro company was later established. A large number of individual models and one-offs followed, the first really mass-produced autogyro being the C.19. Eventually Cierva perfected a means of spinning the main rotor prior to take-off so that the autogyro could make a 'jump start',

the closest that an autogyro can come to making a vertical lift-off. The best-known model was the C.30, built by Avro in Britain as the Rota, and by Lioré et Olivier in France as the LeO C.30. These machines saw military service, the British examples being used for radar calibration during World War Two while the French machines were employed by the French navy mainly for observation. The autogyro gained prominence again in the 1960's, but has never really 'taken off' as a mass-produced flying machine. In the United States, a major autogyro collaborator was Pitcairn (see the next two pages for Pitcairn's aircraft activities).

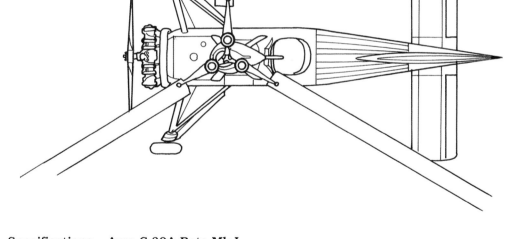

Specifications – Avro C.30A Rota Mk.I

Rotor diameter	37 ft
Length	19 ft 8.5 in
Maximum speed	110 mph at sea level
Range	285 miles
Maximum take-off weight	1,800 lb
Engine	One Armstrong Siddeley Genet Major IA radial piston engine, of 140 hp
Crew	Two

Pitcairn PA-5 Mailwing

The first official occasion when mail was carried by air in Europe took place on 9 September 1911 in England. In the same month, an air-carried mail service started in New York State in the United States. During the following years, and especially from the 1920's onwards, the carriage of mail by air grew massively. Specific types of aircraft were developed for carrying mail and cargo by air, in addition to aircraft such as the D.H.4 (see pages 68-69) that were converted to mail-carrying from other uses. In the United States, an early exponent of air-carried mail was Harold Pitcairn. His series of Mailwing biplanes from 1927 onwards represented the state of the art of this type of aircraft during that era, and commenced with the PA-5 Mailwing of mid-1927. At that time new air-carried mail routes were starting to be developed by the U.S.

postal authorities. The Mailwing series proved to be well-suited to these routes, combining strength and reliability with range and useful load-carrying capacity. The price of a new PA-5 was $9,850, and some 18 PA-5s were built. Later the PA-5 was followed by the PA-6 and more-powerful PA-7 and PA-8 series, the PA-7M Super Mailwing having a mail/cargo payload capacity in a special fire-proof fuselage compartment of up to 559 lb – the PA-5 could carry 500 lb. A number of cargo-carrying organisations and airlines successfully operated Mailwing aircraft; they have been likened to a late 1920's version of the old land-based 'Pony Express', and they helped to bring the far-flung corners of the United States closer together by carrying the mail (at least for a time) speedily and efficiently. Three-seat 'sport' versions of the Mailwing series were also developed by Pitcairn.

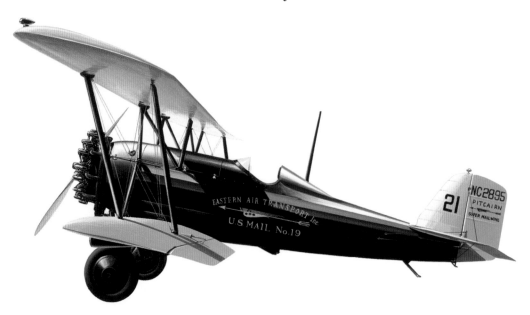

The Pitcairn Mailwing and Super Mailwing were classic biplanes of their day.

A preserved Pitcairn biplane in the United States. Thanks to unsung individuals in the world of aircraft preservation such as the American Cole Palen, it is still possible to see fantastic old aircraft such as this (Photo: John Batchelor).

Specifications – Pitcairn PA-5 Mailwing

Wingspan	33 ft
Length	21 ft 11 in
Maximum speed	130 mph
Ceiling	18,000 ft
Range	600 miles
Engine	One Wright J-5 Whirlwind radial piston engine, of 220 hp
Crew	One

Douglas DT

The fledgling aircraft company of Donald Douglas had two lucky breaks at the time of its creation. As related on pages 146-147, it will forever be associated with the first-ever circumnavigation of the globe by the Douglas World Cruisers of the U.S. Army Air Service. Douglas had started well in any case with his first military aircraft design, which was to become a standard torpedo-bomber for the U.S. Navy. This was the DT series, and this model also formed the basis for the World Cruiser aircraft. Douglas set up his aircraft company in July 1921, and in later years it was to become one of the world's principal aircraft designers and manufacturers until absorbed by Boeing in the 1990's. The DT series was already on the drawing boards at the time of the creation of the company in 1921, Douglas having by then gained a contract for three aircraft earlier in 1921. These were designated DT-1 (Douglas, Torpedo-bomber), and they drew on experience with the Davis-Douglas Cloudster with which Douglas had previously been associated. The DT-1 began life as a big, solid

single-seat biplane powered by a 400 hp Liberty engine. The first aircraft flew in November 1921, but the U.S. Navy duly decided on a two-seat layout and so the other two intended DT-1 were finished as DT-2 two-seaters. Evaluation in the first half of 1922 proved the DT-2 to be superior to other possible contenders for the Navy's new torpedo-bomber, and 38 more production DT-2 were ordered from Douglas. The Naval Aircraft Factory additionally built six, and L.W.F. Engineering 20 others. These entered service in 1922/1923, being the U.S. Navy's standard floatplane torpedo-bomber until 1926. They could actually be operated as seaplanes, or as landplanes with a conventional wheeled undercarriage. A number of later DT models were created through conversions, mostly with different engines installed. A related model, the SDW-1 also existed. This was a conversion by Dayton-Wright of three L.W.F.-built DT-2 as long-range scout/reconnaissance floatplanes, with a revised fuselage, changed crew stations and provision for more fuel.

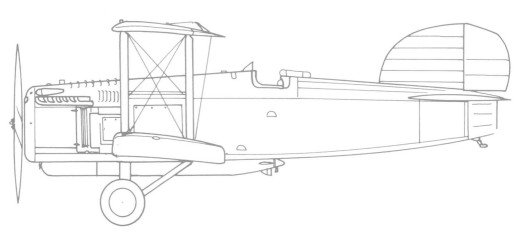

The Douglas DT-1 of 1921 was a single-seater. Only one was built in this configuration.

The two-seat production Douglas DT-2 served with the U.S. Navy as a torpedo-bomber until 1926.
Illustration by John Batchelor. Picture courtesy Boeing Corp.

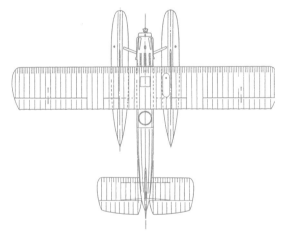

*The line drawings show
the production layout
of the Douglas DT-2.*

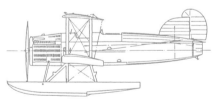

Specifications – Douglas DT-2 (landplane)

Wingspan	50 ft
Length	34 ft 2 in
Maximum speed	101 mph at sea level
Range	293 miles
Service Ceiling	7,800 ft
Armament	One 1,835 lb torpedo
Engine	One Liberty 12A inline piston engine, of 420 hp
Crew	Two

Junkers F 13

The German aircraft designer and pioneer Hugo Junkers was one of the great early exponents of metal construction in aviation. As described on pages 78-79, his early Junkers J 1 and J 4 were important early all-metal production aircraft. In 1910 Junkers had patented a thick cantilever wing design, and in the post-World War One years the Junkers company became a world-leader in all-metal landplane commercial aircraft based on his early concepts. Late in World War One the J 10 two-seat single-engine ground attack aircraft had been introduced (and was operated as the CL I), and this type had a design impact on the commercial aircraft that followed it. In fact a demilitarised J 10 flew, in March 1919 between Dessau and Weimar, probably the world's first commercial flight using an all-metal aircraft. Design work by Junkers led to the J 13 (later called the F 13), which first flew on 25 June 1919. This was a ground-breaking aircraft, one of the world's first all-metal commercial aircraft (some claim it to be truly the first). A

very clean cantilever monoplane of all-metal construction, covered with corrugated duralumin, this little passenger aircraft played a major role in developing post-war air transport. It was eventually built in a wide variety of versions (possibly up to 70), with several different engine options. The total production was possibly 328, but many key records from that period have not survived which also makes accurate specifications of many of the production models difficult to assess (a situation that also covers various other aircraft types) – the specifications given here are representative rather than specific. Some F 13 operated on floats or skis, some had enclosed cockpits for their two-man crew, and the F 13 effectively acted as the basis for many more of Junkers' successful all-metal commercial aircraft. Continuing development led to the single-engine all-metal W 33 and W 34 series from 1926, which were used for commercial operation (on floats or land undercarriage), and the W 34 also saw important service as a transport and trainer with Nazi Germany's Luftwaffe. Almost 1,800 W 34 were built in Germany and Sweden. These single-

The Junkers W 34 was an important all-metal aircraft for both commercial and military use, and could be operated on floats. 1,791 of all sub-types are believed to have been built.

1926. The G 31 was only built in comparatively small numbers, and is best known for the exploits of four aircraft in New Guinea, some of which were specially converted to haul oversize loads.

engine all-metal aircraft were joined by a line of three-engined all-metal monoplane transports, including the G 31 which first flew in September

The Junkers F 13 was a very advanced aircraft for its day, and was the forerunner of the sleek all-metal transports of the later inter-war period. In the photograph, claimed to be a night scene at Tempelhof airport in Berlin, several F 13 transports are in the foreground. F 13s were used world-wide by many operators, including Germany's Deutsche Luft Hansa (Photo: Hans Meier Collection).

The best-known service of the three-engined Junkers G 31 was in New Guinea, where four were operated pre-World War Two in the New Guinea gold-fields. They hauled cargo, heavy plant and even the odd car as shown here, into inaccessible airstrips. The aircraft shown is almost certainly VH-UOW of Guinea Airways (Photo: Deutsches Museum, Munich).

Specifications – Junkers F 13a (early production)

Wingspan	48 ft 7.5 in
Length	31 ft 5.5 in
Maximum speed	106 mphat sea level
Service Ceiling	15,092 ft
Range	746 miles plus
Engine	One BMW III/IIIa inline piston engine, of 180/185 hp
Accommodation	Two crew, up to four passengers

Douglas M-2

The carriage of mail by air had been successfully pioneered before World War One, as explained on pages 150-151. In the United States, the development of aircraft capable of flying long distances with a useful payload promised the possibility of carrying the mail to the far-flung corners of the vast North American continent much more speedily that ever before possible. In 1918 the fledgling mail routes in various parts of the United States became the responsibility of the U.S. government's Post Office Department. One of the first aircraft to be used successfully on the subsequently growing air-carried mail routes within the United States were civilianised and specially-converted American-built D.H.4 aircraft (see pages 68-69). The need to replace these aircraft from the mid-1920's led to the creation of the M-series of mailplanes. Manufactured by Douglas, the M-series were based on the legendary Douglas O-2 series of military observation biplanes built by Douglas for the U.S. Army. The first production model was the M-2, which used a similar power plant and layout as the O-2 series but featured a mail compartment within the fuselage where the pilot of the O-2

sat, the M-2's pilot and controls being moved to the observer's position of the O-2 layout. With the introduction of Contract Air Mail (CAM) routes, the civilian operator Western Air Express (a forerunner of the famous airline Western Air Lines) put the M-2 into service, the Douglas design having won a competition in 1925 to replace the D.H.4 mail-carriers. A quick-change interior layout was used in which the forward mail areas in the fuselage could be converted into a passenger compartment for up to two intrepid passengers. The total mail capacity was approximately 1,000 lb (453.6 kg). Following the M-2 was the M-3 with detail differences, and subsequently the M-4 sub-type again with minor differences and the provision for increased span upper wing surfaces. The Post Office relinquished its hold on air-carried mail routes in 1926, allowing operators such as National Air Transport to take on these growing route networks. The M-series Douglas continued in service in this way until 1929/1930, approxi-

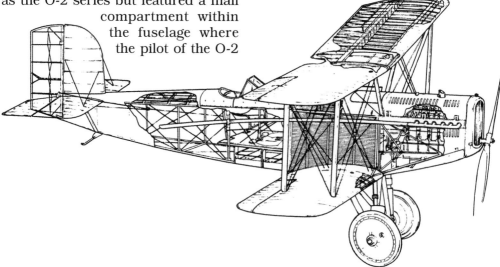

A Western Air Express Douglas M-series mail-carrier in a late 1920's period setting.

mately 57 production models having been built of all types.

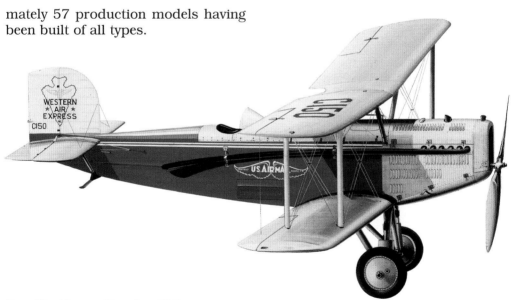

Specifications – Douglas M-2

Wingspan	39 ft 8 in
Length	29 ft 3 in
Maximum speed	140 mph
Ceiling	16,500 ft
Range	700 miles
Engine	One Liberty 12 inline piston engine, of 400 hp
Crew	One

Dornier Do X

The Dornier Do X was one of the world's most remarkable aircraft, a massive flying-boat that sadly was to prove as generally unsuccessful as many other larger-than-life aviation projects. The German Dornier company had created a series of all-metal aircraft in the post-World War One period. These included the highly-successful Wal flying-boat (see pages 238-239), which achieved good sales successes and was also used for a variety of long-range and route-testing flights. The ultimate development of the design layout used on the Wal was the Do X. This enormous transoceanic flying-boat was intended to carry up to 100 passengers on Atlantic crossings in the luxury often found in contemporary ocean liners. Design work began in earnest during 1927. The Do X was basically of metal structure, but large areas of the wings and control surfaces were fabric-covered. The intention was to power the aircraft with 12 Siemens-built Bristol Jupiter radial engines, the original layout being of six pairs of back-to-back engines on an over-wing structure.

This proved problematical, particularly with the cooling for the rear six pusher engines, and eventually a simpler installation using 12 American Curtiss Conqueror inline engines was adopted (once more with six of the engines as pushers). Aboard the flying-boat's fuselage/hull were three decks including sleeping quarters, a lounge, a smoking room, bathrooms, a galley, and a dining room. The first flight of this giant was made on 25 July 1929. At that time the Do X, registered D-1929, was the world's largest aircraft. Its load-carrying capability was demonstrated on 21 October 1929 when it carried aloft a ten-person crew, 150 passengers and nine stowaways. The normal capacity was actually some 72 passengers. On 2 November 1930 the aircraft departed from Friedrichshafen on Lake Constance for what turned out to be a leisurely 'world tour' that actually took in north-west Europe, the Canary Islands, and various other Atlantic stops including Brazil, Miami and New York, which was reached on 27 August 1931. Some of this time was

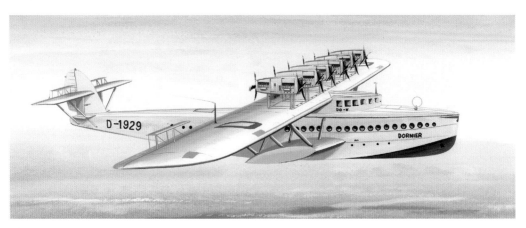

Do X D-1929 was eventually powered with inline Curtiss Conqueror engines. The construction of this huge aircraft was a major undertaking in its own right.

The Do X D-1929 in flight, showing
the original installation of 12
Siemens-built Jupiter radial engines
(Photo: Hans Meier Collection).

taken up with repairs, but on its return to Germany the aircraft was on the books of Deutsche Luft Hansa for a time, before being relegated to various development and testing work. It was destroyed in an aviation museum in Berlin by Allied bombing during World War Two. Two further Do X were built, these going onto the Italian civil register as I-REDI and I-ABBN and powered by Fiat engines, but they were not put into passenger service and operated for a time on trials with the Italian military before being scrapped.

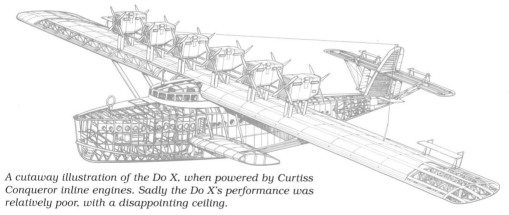

A cutaway illustration of the Do X, when powered by Curtiss Conqueror inline engines. Sadly the Do X's performance was relatively poor, with a disappointing ceiling.

Specifications – Dornier Do X

Wingspan	157 ft 5.75 in
Length	131 ft 4.75 in
Maximum speed	134 mph at sea level
Maximum take-off weight	123,458
Service Ceiling	1,640.4 ft
Range	1,367 miles plus
Engine	Twelve Curtiss Conqueror inline piston engines, of 600 hp each
Accommodation	Up to 10 crew, accommodation for approximately 72 passengers

Potez 25

The rugged and purposeful Potez 25 was one of the most – if not the most - widely-produced aircraft of the inter-war period, and it found its way to most parts of the world with a large variety of different military operators. The French Potez company in its post-World War One form dated back to 1919, and the two-seat Potez 25 was immediately derived from the Potez 24 of the early 1920's. It made its debut at the 1924 Paris aeronautical exhibition (the predecessor of today's Paris Salon de l'Aéronautique et de l'Espace). It is possible that the aircraft exhibited had not at that time flown, but sufficient progress had been made with flight testing by 10 August 1925 to allow a prototype to perform a gruelling but successful tour of Northern and Central European capitals. The following year a similar flight in stages was accomplished of Southern European and North African cities. This established the reputation of the Potez 25, and in the following years orders flowed in from overseas operators in addition to widespread French military use. A very large number of sub-types and different engine options were developed, with as many as 87 sep-

arate versions being claimed. In addition to the inline-engines models, several radial engine options were tried, some using French-built derivatives of the ubiquitous British Bristol Jupiter radial. Particularly prolific were the Potez 25A.2 reconnaissance and 25B.2 bomber versions, but the most widely-produced was the 25TOE and related models for use primarily in French overseas colonies. In addition to these and other military options, a number of civil models of the Potez 25 existed, although two planned transatlantic flight attempts were (perhaps wisely) abandoned. Including licence-production and French manufacture by several companies, over 4,000 Potez 25 planes were built – an enormous total for the late 1920's/1930's. Possibly the best-known of all the Potez 25 models were the aircraft flown by Aéropostale, the French mail carrier and route-proving pioneer. This company also operated the Latécoère 28, described on Pages 170-171. Five Potez 25A.2 were received

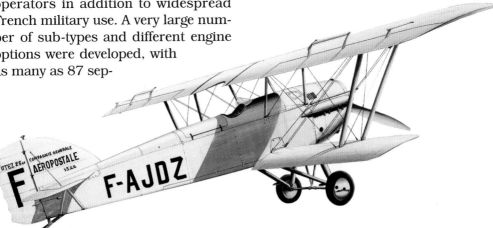

This single-seat mail-carrying Aéropostale Potez 25A.2 (22/55) was crash-landed by French pioneer pilot Henri Guillaumet in the Andes during June 1930. Both pilot and aircraft survived to fly again, a testament to the ruggedness of both.

Captioned as a Potez 25TOE, this picture shows the military layout of many of the Potez 25 line, with a mounting in the rear cockpit for the observer/gunner's machine gun(s) and what appear to be bomb rack fittings beneath the aircraft (Photo: E.C.P.-Armées).

by Aéropostale in 1929 and 1930. They eventually passed to Air France after the demise of Aéropostale in 1931/1932, but by then had established a reputation for incrediable ruggedness. They flew the mail in South America, across the Andes Mountains in some of the most difficult flying conditions over some of the most rugged terrain, and were piloted by several famous French pioneering pilots.

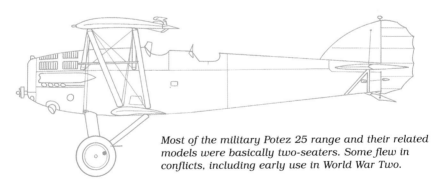

Most of the military Potez 25 range and their related models were basically two-seaters. Some flew in conflicts, including early use in World War Two.

Specifications – Potez 25TOE

Wingspan	46 ft 4.75 in
Length	29 ft 10.25 in
Maximum speed	130.5 mph at sea level
Service Ceiling	19,029 ft
Range	783 miles plus
Armament	One fixed forward-firing, and two flexible ring-mounted 0.303 in machine guns, up to 441 lb of bombs
Engine	One Lorraine 12Eb piston engine, of 450 hp
Crew	Two

Northrop Alpha

By the late 1920's and early 1930's, advances in design, materials and construction were allowing for ever more streamlined and advanced aircraft to be conceived. One of the flagship aircraft in the advance towards the modern aircraft configuration that we recognise today was the ground-breaking Northrop Alpha. A gleaming, all-metal commercial monoplane for passenger and cargo operation, the Alpha owed its existence to the design inspiration of John K. Northrop. Northrop had worked in the American aircraft industry for some years, and in 1929/1930 his Northrop Aircraft Corp. was created. This was a division of the United Aircraft and Transport Corp., which was interested in Northrop's work with metal airframes and counted amongst its members the famed William E. Boeing. Northrop was associated with advanced work on flying wing aircraft, and his Alpha design was also revolutionary but in very different ways. The Alpha has sometimes been regarded as one of the first true modern airliners. Its stressed-skin all-metal construction, comprising a monocoque fuselage and cantilever

wing with a long fatigue life were all exceptional features for their day. Nevertheless, in a throw back to the past, the Alpha's pilot sat in an open cockpit. Additionally, the type never had a retractable undercarriage, although later configurations featured neatly 'trousered' main undercarriage fairings. In its Alpha 2 passenger version, six passengers were carried in the aircraft's fuselage, but the carriage of mail and freight were rather more lucrative and so the Alpha 3 included mixed passenger (three) and cargo configuration. The Alpha 4-A established a cargo-only layout with a single window in each side of the fuselage, and a cargo capacity of 1,250 lb. This model also introduced Goodrich de-icing installations for its wings, and the most modern radio and navigation equipment to allow flights even in (comparatively) bad weather. During 1931 the Alpha was integrated into the transcontinental air route across the United States of the airline Transcontinental and Western Air, and the famous exploits of this aircraft commenced. It appears that 14 commercial and three military Alphas were built, and the civil-operated Alphas were retrospectively upgraded

as each new model configuration was introduced. These advanced all-metal aircraft heralded the decline of the biplane as a commercial aircraft.

A Transcontinental and Western Air Northrop Alpha has some very lucrative mail loaded into its fuselage cargo hold (Photo: Boeing Corporation).

The colour drawing shows the Northrop Alpha 4-A all-cargo configuration, with a single window in the fuselage side.

Specifications – Northrop Alpha Model 4-A

Wingspan	43 ft 10 in
Length	28 ft 5in
Maximum speed	177 mph at sea level
Ceiling	17,500 ft
Range	900 miles
Engine	One Pratt & Whitney Wasp SC1 radial piston engine, of 450 hp
Crew	One

163

Sikorsky S-38 and S-39

Sometimes described as a collection of spare parts flying in formation, the Sikorsky S-38 was a gloriously unconventional contraption that nonetheless gained important orders and helped to spread commercial air services into such areas as the Caribbean. Russian Igor Sikorsky had set up his aircraft company in the United States in 1923 (after several years of successful design and manufacture in Russia), and he was subsequently able to pursue two forms of air transport – the amphibian/flying boat, and the helicopter. The sesquiplane twin-engine amphib-

ian S-38 was the first commercially successful aircraft built by Sikorsky in the United States, after a series of limited and mainly experimental types. The initial S-38 flew in 1928, with the type certificate for the S-38A initial production model being issued in August 1928. The S-38 was built in three main production versions, the S-38B being the most widely produced. The type was basically an airliner, with a wood and metal fuselage/hull, able to carry up to ten passengers – the S-38C could seat more, with reduced fuel. The main claim to fame of the passenger-carry-

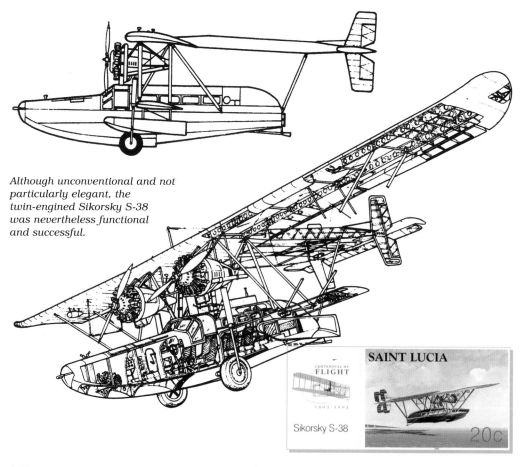

Although unconventional and not particularly elegant, the twin-engined Sikorsky S-38 was nevertheless functional and successful.

SAINT LUCIA

CENTENNIAL OF
FLIGHT

1903-2003

Sikorsky S-38

20c

164

ing S-38 models was their pioneering work in establishing commercial air routes for American and overseas airlines, one of the chief early operators being Pan American Airways. However, some executive models were also created with luxury interiors, and a comparatively small number were operated by the U.S. Army Air Corps (as the C-6), and the U.S. Navy and Marine Corps. The S-38 also achieved a number of world records for its class of aircraft. Most historians agree that 111 S-38 of all models were built, although the real number could be a little higher. Production ended in the early 1930's. Further development resulted in the smaller, single-engine S-39 sports amphibian. This model first flew in December 1929, and generally resembled the S-38's unconventional twin boom fuselage pod layout but did away with the sesquiplane small lower wing, and was instead simply a parasol wing amphibian with an all-metal hull that could seat four or five. The S-39A's type certificate was issued in July 1930. This model was powered by a 300 hp Pratt & Whitney Wasp Junior radial engine. Approximately 20 to 23 S-39 were built. The best-known examples of both the S-38 and S-39 were the two aircraft, one of each, used by the aerial explorers Martin and Osa Johnson in Africa.

Martin and Osa Johnson used an S-38 named 'Osa's Ark', and an S-39 called 'Spirit of Africa', for their 1930's aerial explorations in Africa.

Specifications – Sikorsky S-38B

Wingspan	71 ft 8 in
Length	40 ft 3 in
Maximum speed	125 mph at 5,000 ft
Service Ceiling	18,000 ft
Range	approximately 750 miles
Engine	Two Pratt & Whitney Wasp radial piston engines, of 425 hp each
Accommodation	One or two crew, up to 10 passengers

Ryan NYP 'Spirit of St. Louis'

One of the most famous feats in aviation history was the May 1927 nonstop first-ever solo crossing by air of the Atlantic Ocean by Charles A. Lindbergh in his Ryan NYP 'Spirit of St. Louis'. Lindbergh's triumph made headlines around the world, and the Ryan monoplane that accomplished the flight has a revered place in aviation's hall of fame. In 1919 wealthy hotelier Raymond Orteig had offered a $25,000 prize to the first person to fly non-stop from New York to Paris. That same year, Alcock and Brown had flown across the North Atlantic to Ireland in a specially-prepared Vickers Vimy (see pages 122-123), but the Orteig prize was for a genuine capital city to capital city flight. In 1927 there were three contenders for

the prize. Of them, Charles Lindbergh was a little-known air mail pilot. The other two challengers were Richard Byrd (the explorer and first man to fly over both Poles) with a Fokker, and Clarence Chamberlin with a Bellanca. In the event all three attempts managed the Atlantic crossing (although Byrd's aircraft came down in the English Channel, and Chamberlain flew as far as Germany), but Lindbergh was the first, the only solo pilot, and the only one of the three to genuinely reach Paris. Named 'Spirit of St. Louis' and known as the NYP (for New York to Paris), Lindbergh's aircraft was a 'one-off' which was based on one of Ryan's contemporary products, the M-2 five-seat light transport, while drawing also on the

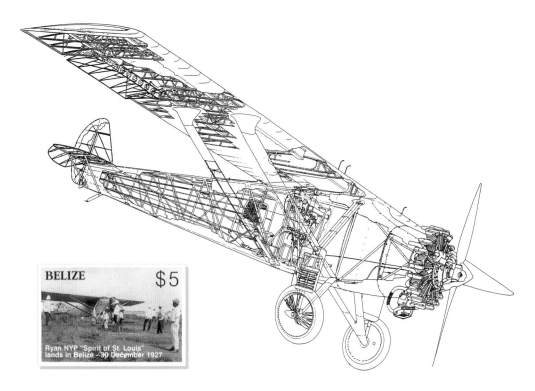

BELIZE $5

Ryan NYP "Spirit of St. Louis" lands in Belize - 30 December 1927

The 'Spirit of St. Louis' had no real forward vision, because a large fuel tank sat in front of the pilot.

B-1 Brougham which was then being developed. Known as **Mahoney-Ryan** at the time of its build, Ryan constructed the NYP to Lindbergh's exacting specifications. It first flew in late April 1927, and was capable of flying some 4,210 miles. On 20 May 1927 Lindbergh departed from Roosevelt Field, Long Island, New York, and headed east. He flew in effect on a Great Circle route, almost making this the first of his subsequent route-testing flights made in later years for commercial airline travel. He arrived at Le Bourget airfield north of Paris on 21 May, to a huge reception, having successfully flown some 3,610 miles, in just over thirty-three and a half hours.

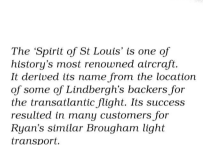

The 'Spirit of St Louis' is one of history's most renowned aircraft. It derived its name from the location of some of Lindbergh's backers for the transatlantic flight. Its success resulted in many customers for Ryan's similar Brougham light transport.

Specifications – Mahoney-Ryan NYP 'Spirit of St. Louis'

Wingspan	46 ft
Length	27 ft 8 in
Maximum speed	119.5 mph at sea level
Range	4,210 miles plus
Take-off weight	5,250 lb
Engine	One Wright J-5C Whirlwind radial piston engine, of 237 hp
Crew	One

'Winnie Mae'

The Lockheed Vega series, as described on page 144, was a famous and successful line of light civil transports that was also suitable with relevant modifications for various special individual flights and exploration missions. By far the most famous of the line was a Lockheed Model 5-B Vega used by American pilot Wiley Post, which achieved two spectacular, headline-making long-distance flights. Post, who was blind in one eye, was one of America's most famous pilots of the early 1930's, in an age when many solo aviators and pioneers were household names. How different those days are compared to our own time! Post was the personal pilot of Oklahoma oil tycoon F.C. Hall, and he is well remembered for his praise of the Lockheed Vega. In 1930 he won a non-stop air race from Los Angeles to Chicago, defeating several other Vega pilots in the attempt. His subsequent

comment "It takes a Lockheed to beat a Lockheed" was tremendous publicity for the company. Post's famous 'Winnie Mae' was a Vega Model 5-B registered NR-105W. It was specially converted for long-distance flights, and it achieved two remarkable pioneering achievements. On 23 June 1931, Post and his co-pilot Harold Gatty began a headline-creating round-the-world flight, in which a northern hemisphere route was flown with calls in several countries including the Soviet Union. The Vega successfully returned to New York, its starting point, on 1 July. Two years later, Post achieved immortality in the aviation world with the first-ever solo round-the-world flight. Taking off from New York, on 15 July 1933, Post flew a number of legs in a flight that ended back in New York on 22 July. The first round the world flight had been made during almost six months

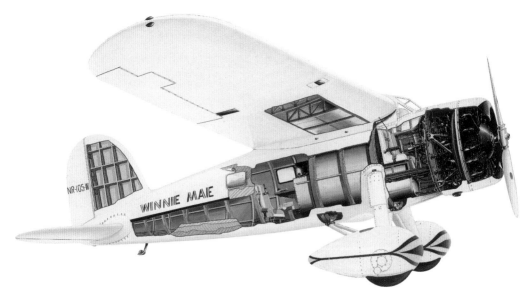

The 'Winnie Mae' was specially configured for its long-distance flights. Note in particular the large additional fuel tank inside the fuselage.

in 1924 by military Douglas World Cruisers (see pages 146-147) – Post had made his solo circumnavigation in only seven days, 18 hours, and 49 minutes! Sadly, Post was killed in 1935 during another round-the-world flight in a different aircraft. 'Winnie Mae' NR-105W was later preserved at America's National Air and Space Museum – it was named after the daughter of F.C. Hall.

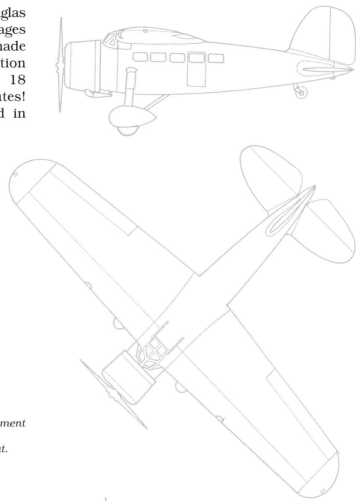

A three-view general arrangement drawing showing a standard Lockheed Vega Model 5 layout.

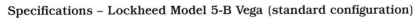

Specifications – Lockheed Model 5-B Vega (standard configuration)

Wingspan	41 ft
Length	27 ft 6 in
Maximum speed	180 mph at sea level
Service Ceiling	20,000 ft
Range	690 miles
Engine	One Pratt & Whitney Wasp radial piston engine, of 450 hp
Accommodation	One or two crew, plus up to five passengers

Latécoère 28

The carriage of mail became big business in the 1920's, as the clouds of the First World War dispersed and new air routes opened up all over the world. Yet it was far easier to establish these commercial air routes in some parts of the world than in others. In some areas, inhospitable climate, unwelcoming locals and lack of basic infrastructure made the building of airfields and staging posts very difficult and sometimes hazardous. There were always pioneers who were willing to take on these odds, however, and some of the best-known early air mail carriers, who blazed a trail not just in Europe but into Africa and on into South America, were French. In the 1920's the French overseas territories included key areas of North Africa, and carrying mail to these French colonies became big business for aircraft manufacturer and air mail carrier Pierre Latécoère. He had a vision of carrying mail not just to the French colonies, but on from there across the South Atlantic to South America. This he started to achieve during the 1920's, with the help of celebrated French pilots such as Jean Mermoz. For the developing French air mail routes, the large, tough Latécoère 28 was devised as a mail and passenger carrier. The first production example was built in 1929, and roughly 50 are believed to have been manufactured in a number of different models including landplane and floatplane versions. Principal initial production models were the Latécoère 28-0 and 28-1. These served with Aéropostale, the successor to Latécoère's own airline, while others flew with some South American carriers. Routes in Europe and North Africa were graced by these strong metal and fabric high-wing monoplanes. On 12/13 May 1930 a Latécoère 28 floatplane flown by Mermoz successfully traversed nonstop the South Atlantic in 21 hours from Saint-Louis, French West Africa

The classic lines of an Aéropostale Latécoère 28.

An Aéropostale Latécoère 28 in its element – flying the air mail and a group of intrepid passengers over rugged terrain.

(now Sénégal) to Natal, Brazil. This was another of the world's great pioneering flights. A French naval pilot, Lieutenant de Vaisseau Paris, established several world records for speed, endurance and distance carrying various weights in a Latécoère 28. The French navy later operated a developed, navalised torpedo-carrying model, the Latécoère 290 series from the early 1930's.

Specifications – Latécoère 28-1

Wingspan	63 ft 1.75 in
Length	44 ft 9 in
Maximum speed	138.5 mph at 6,562 ft
Service Ceiling	18,045 ft
Range	621 miles plus
Engine	One Hispano-Suiza 12Hbr inline piston engine, of 500 hp
Accommodation	Two crew, up to eight passengers

Supermarine S.6B

Progress in the science of aeronautics has been stimulated by many factors over the years, including single events or specific objectives. Arguably one of the greatest incentives to the advancement of high-speed flight, which created so many important spin-offs in engine design, aerodynamics, and in encouraging progress towards high-performance front-line military aircraft, was the Schneider Trophy competition. Created by Frenchman Jacques Schneider primarily as a fillip to advancement in water-borne aircraft design and development, it grew eventually into a contest for high-performance machines that became so costly to create that only well-financed or officially-backed competitors could produce the necessary participants. At first annually contested but later biennially, this event was on a completely higher level than the type of air racing of, for example, the Gee Bee racing aircraft described on pages 194-195. The first Schneider Trophy contest was staged at Monaco in 1913, and after World War One it developed into a flag-waving competition mainly between the Italians, Americans and British. Out of it grew a winning combination on the British side, comprising the Supermarine company and its brilliant and far-sighted designer Reginald J. Mitchell, in concert with the Rolls-Royce aero engine company. Mitchell has become over the years one of the world's most celebrated aircraft designers, and he was responsible for the superlative Supermarine Spitfire (see pages 274-275). For the 1925 Schneider Trophy contest, Mitchell designed the S.4, a sleek cantilever wing monoplane on floats. This was subsequently developed into the S.5, which first flew in June 1927 and was operated by the Royal Air Force's High Speed Flight, which was formed in October 1926. This unit flew the S.5 and all subsequent Supermarine

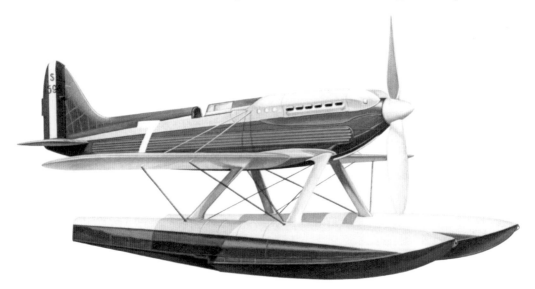

The Supermarine S.6B won the 1931 Schneider Trophy contest (S1595) on 13 September 1931, and also took the world speed record on 29 September. Two S.6B were built.

S1595, the Supermarine S.6B that won the Schneider Trophy in 1931.

entries. The S.5 won the 1927 contest, and the developed S.6 was victorious in the 1929 event. The 1931 competition was the final Schneider Trophy, which was won outright by Britain for the third time running when S.6B S1595 won the contest unopposed. The S.6B had first flown in July 1931, and on the day of the event, 13 September 1931, the second S.6B (S1596) beat the world speed record at just over 379 mph. This was bettered on 29 September by S1595 at just over 407 mph (655 km/h) – a graphic representative of how the Schneider Trophy had helped to stimulate high-speed flight and the aerodynamics and engine performance that went with it.

Specifications – Supermarine S.6B

Wingspan	30 ft
Length	28 ft 10 in
Maximum speed	over 407 mph at sea level
Maximum take-off weight	6,086 lb
Engine	One Rolls-Royce R inline piston engine, of 2,330-2,350 hp (uprated to 2,600 hp for 407 mph speed)
Crew	One

Fokker F VII

Dutchman Anthony Fokker successfully re-established his aviation interests after World War One, as described on pages 116-117. His Dutch-based Fokker company subsequently made a considerable name for itself as a creator and manufacturer of both civil and military aircraft. Several of the civil aircraft designs were highly successful, and there also developed an important Fokker presence in the United States (see pages 198-199). One of Fokker's most enduring commercial designs was the F VII, which gained great fame as the mount of pioneer aviators even though it was conceived as an airliner. The F VII family comprised the original single-engined F VII, the aerodynamically improved single-engine F VIIA, and then the big advance to the three-engined F VIIA-3m, and the long-range F VIIB-3m. This family became one of the most successful and important airliner series of its time, helping to bring long-distance commercial aviation to a wider audience and more general acceptance. The original single-engine F VII flew in 1924, and the groundbreaking F VIIA-3m was conceived as a logical development of the successful F VII single-engined format, using much the same fuselage and wing lay-

out of the single-engine model – but with two additional engines added, one below each wing. The first three-engined F VIIA-3m won the highly-publicised Ford Reliability Tour in the United States in 1925, and the type went on to considerable commercial success. It had a direct bearing on the development of the all-metal Ford Tri-Motor series (see pages 182-183). Production was carried out in Holland and under licence elsewhere. Some disagreement exists over the number manufactured, although well over one hundred is likely. The long-range F VIIB-3m featured several alterations including the wing, and was manufactured under licence elsewhere in addition to the 63 or so constructed by Fokker in Holland. The Avro Ten was the equivalent model that was built in England. Military orders included the C-2 for the U.S. Army Air Corps. The F VII was immortalised, however, by its use in long-distance and pioneering flights, including the Byrd Arctic Expedition of May 1926, and the first-ever pioneering flight across the Pacific Ocean in stages by Charles Kingsford Smith and his crew in the famous 'Southern Cross' during May and June 1928.

In May 1926, Richard E. Byrd made the first flight over the North Pole in this Fokker F VII-3m, the 'Josephine Ford'.

The coveted accolade of being the first person to fly over the North Pole went to Richard Byrd in this Fokker F VII tri-motor named 'Josephine Ford'. She was the daughter of the Byrd Arctic Expedition's sponsor, Edsel Ford of Ford car fame.

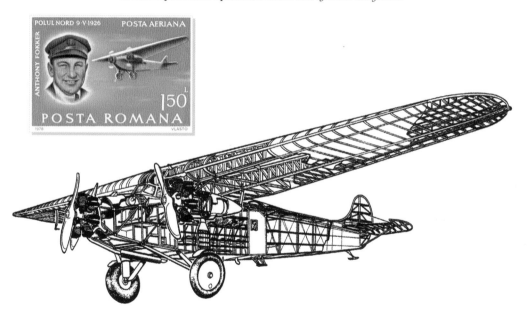

Specifications – Fokker F VIIB-3m

Wingspan	71 ft 2.75 in
Length	47 ft 7 in
Maximum speed	129 mph at 6,000 ft
Maximum take-off weight	11,684 lb
Range	746 miles
Engine	Three Wright J-5C or J-6 Whirlwind radial piston engines, of 300 hp each
Accommodation	Two crew, up to 10 passengers

De Havilland D.H.60 Moth

Real efforts were made during the 1920's to make aviation more available to the masses, and a golden era of aviation for private flyers was fostered by a number of companies that produced aircraft which gained widespread appeal and acceptance. This was in the great tradition of pre-First World War pioneers like Alberto Santos-Dumont (see pages 44-45). In Britain there were a number of light aircraft producers during this period, but none were more prevalent than de Havilland. Although this company eventually broadened out to larger types such as the D.H.91 Albatross airliner (see pages 228-229), and made many successful military aircraft, in the 1920's and early 1930's a series of light aircraft from this company helped to revolutionise the aviation scene in Britain and elsewhere in the world. The first really successful aircraft in this tradition was the

D.H.60 Moth series. Built in a series of evolving models, the D.H.60 had its ancestry in the original private-owner aircraft that were introduced by de Havilland in the early to mid-1920's such as the D.H.37. De Havilland hit the right formula with the smaller and lighter D.H.60, the first of the famous Moth series. The original D.H.60 flew in February 1925, powered by a 60 hp Cirrus I inline engine. The type was an instant success, and orders for several aero clubs meant that deliveries began in the summer of that year. Continuing success led to orders from overseas as well, encouraging development to continue into a line of Cirrus-powered models. However, de Havilland also ventured into engine design and development, leading to an equally successful series of light aircraft engines. The de Havilland Gipsy I was fitted to the established D.H.60 airframe in 1928, resulting in the highly successful D.H.60G models known as the Gipsy Moth. This type

Possibly the most famous D.H.60G Gipsy Moth was 'Jason', the aircraft in which intrepid British aviator Amy Johnson flew solo to Australia from England in May 1930 in nineteen and a half days, the first woman to achieve this feat.

The ultimate development of the basic D.H.60 line was the D.H.60T Moth Trainer, exemplified here by G-ABKM which was sold to Sweden (Photo: Philippe Jalabert Collection).

was subsequently used for many long-distance or record-breaking flights by famous aviators including Amy Johnson, in addition to being bought by private buyers all over the world. Licence production also took place in several countries, including the United States which underlined the success of the type. The all-wood construction D.H.60G was joined by the D.H.60M with a metal frame fuselage, and continuing development of the airframe and Gipsy engine led to several further developed models – and ultimately continued to the world-famous D.H.82 Tiger Moth which had its finest hours as a trainer during World War Two. Many hundreds of the D.H.60 Moth series were built, de Havilland's own production of the D.H.60G alone amounting to over five hundred.

Specifications – De Havilland D.H.60G Gipsy Moth

Wingspan	30 ft
Length	23 ft 11 in
Maximum speed	98 mph at sea level
Service Ceiling	14,500 ft
Range	290 miles
Engine	One de Havilland Gipsy I inline piston engine, of 100 hp
Crew/accommodation	One pilot, plus one passenger or further crew member

Boeing Model 40

Originally designed in 1925 as a mail carrier, and intended to meet the same requirement for a D.H.4 replacement that had led to the Douglas M-2 (see Pages 156-157), the Boeing Model 40 biplane was developed into a successful series of rugged mail and passenger carrying aircraft. The first, single-seat Liberty-engined example flew in July 1925. Initially unsuccessful against the Douglas M-2, Boeing nevertheless persisted with the Model 40 design, the type receiving a large shot in the arm with the purchasing power of Boeing's related commercial mail/passenger carrier, Boeing Air Transport. The first production model was the Model 40A.

This differed from the original 1925 'Mailplane' principally in having a Pratt & Whitney Wasp radial engine of 400-420 hp, and accommodation in the fuselage not just for mail/cargo, but also a cabin for two passengers – plus an open cockpit for the pilot. The initial Model 40A flew in May 1927, and was one of the first aircraft to receive a type certificate under new regulations specific to civil aviation that were introduced in the United States at that time. Gaining Approved Type Certificate No.2 from the aeronautical branch of the U.S. Department of Commerce, in July 1927, the production Model 40A was sold in moderately successful num-

Unloading cargo from the front fuselage compartment of a Boeing Model 40-series aircraft, with seating for two passengers in the fuselage (Photo: Boeing Corporation).

bers, 24 being bought by Boeing Air Transport. A payload of cargo and mail could be carried in two fuselage compartments. The Boeing 40A entered service on Boeing's new contract air-carried mail route from San Francisco to Chicago in July 1927. Further development led to the Model 40B. This introduced the more powerful Pratt & Whitney Hornet radial engine of 500-525 hp, and was basically a conversion of the earlier Model 40A, 19 being so up-engined. Additional work led to the Model 40C, which was a four-seat transport and cargo/mail carrier, based on the earlier models but reverting to the Pratt & Whitney Wasp radial engine. Some of these were used on the Pacific Air

Transport (also eventually a part of Boeing's then-growing airline business) Pacific coast services. The type certificate for this model was issued in July 1928, and ten were built. Their success led to the Model 40B-4, a four-seat development of the basic Model 40B series. In addition to the four passengers, 500 lb of mail or cargo could also be carried. Approximately 38 were built, the last 20 or so examples having a Townend ring cowling around their 525 hp Hornet radial. Some Model 40C reverted to this standard. However, during the early 1930's the days of the open-cockpit, lumbering biplanes were quickly drawing to a close.

Initially defeated by the Douglas M-2 as an official mail carrier in 1925, the Boeing Model 40 benefited from deregulation of postal services in 1926/1927 and then operated successfully on commercial contract mail routes. The drawing shows a Model 40B.

Specifications – Boeing Model 40B

Wingspan	44 ft 2 in
Length	33 ft 4in
Maximum speed	132 mph at sea level
Service Ceiling	15,000 ft
Range	approximately 550 miles
Engine	One Pratt & Whitney Hornet radial piston engine, of 525 hp
Accommodation	One pilot, two passengers

Curtiss Condor

Although the Curtiss aircraft company of Glenn Curtiss can rightly be seen as one of the pioneers and innovators of the early years of successful manned flight, some of the company's later designs were not exactly groundbreaking. In 1929 a new biplane commercial transport emerged from the company under the name Condor. This huge biplane airliner was developed from the Curtiss B-2 military bomber design, and first flew in the summer of 1929. It featured a biplane tailplane and even at that time it looked rather out of place amongst the newer design concepts that were then emerging. It entered service during 1930. It could carry 18 passengers in a luxurious cabin and gained sufficient success (at least six were built for airlines in the United States) to promote Curtiss to look towards refining and further developing the design. However, as pointed out on pages 250-251, Curtiss preferred to hang on as long as possible to the biplane concept. When the new Condor came out in 1933, it was once

more a biplane, smaller but by that time out of place amongst the monoplane airliners that were then being developed. Known as the T-32 Condor II, the first flight was made in January 1933. The Condor II was a considerably cleaner design that the original Condor airliner, with radial rather than inline engines and a conventional monoplane tailplane (albeit strut-braced), but its layout represented the end of an era rather than the start of a new one. It was the ultimate in biplane airliner design in the United States. Accommodation varied between customers, but some T-32 were fitted out with a 12-passenger night-sleeper layout. The first of 21 T-32 entered service in 1933 with such airlines as American Airways, and a developed model – the AT-32 – also saw airline use. Several T-32 were later updated to T-32-C standard. Military orders included two T-32 transports as the YC-30 for the U.S. Army, and a small number of AT-32-type models were purchased not only by the American military but by

Perhaps the best-known of the Curtiss Condor line was the floatplane (it could also be equipped with skis) used by the Byrd Antarctic Expedition.

several export customers. A bomber development, the BT-32, was purchased in small numbers by Colombia (as seaplanes), Peru and China. Argentina bought a military cargo model, and two R4C-1 were used by the U.S. in Antarctica. The Byrd Antarctic Expedition also used a T-32 Condor, with a fixed undercarriage.

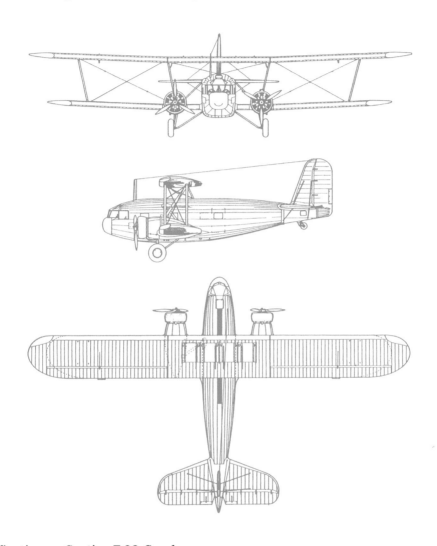

Specifications – Curtiss T-32 Condor

Wingspan	82 ft
Length	48 ft 10 in
Maximum speed	170 mph at sea level
Service Ceiling	15,500 ft
Range	580 miles
Engine	Two Wright GR-1820-F11 Cyclone radial piston engines, of 650-670 hp each
Accommodation	Two crew, up to 15 passengers, or less on night-sleeper models

Ford Tri-Motor

Known and much-loved as the 'Tin Goose', the Ford Tri-Motor was a highly significant aircraft for several reasons, not least in aiding the development of the airline system in the United States, and for bringing the concept of the all-metal airliner to America's aircraft industry. Tough and versatile, the Tri-Motor was a contemporary of the all-metal airliners of the German Junkers company (see pages 154-155), and like the Junkers it was of all-metal construction and even had control surfaces clad in corrugated metal. It featured a configuration similar to that established by Anthony Fokker in the Fokker F.VII airliner described on pages 174-175, but it partly owed its existence to the Stout company that motor car producer Henry Ford's organisation absorbed in 1925. Some of the ground work that Stout had achieved with its own metal aircraft found its way into the Ford aircraft when design work on what would be Ford's first airliner began during 1925. The original three-engined Model 3-AT was unsuccessful, but further design work led to the Model 4-AT which was the first of the line of successful Tri-Motors that eventually evolved into the Model 5-AT and a number of military models. The initial 4-AT featured an open cockpit

for its two crew members (replaced with an enclosed flight deck on later models), and accommodation for eight passengers. The control cables for the tail control surfaces ran on the outside of the fuselage, and the strut-braced and mounted separate engine nacelles for the two below wing engines also doubled as part of the attachment for the fixed main undercarriage – which was neatly spatted on some examples. The first Model 4-AT flew on 11 June 1926, and the initial main production model was the 12-passenger 4-AT-B which gained its type approval later, in November 1928. One of the first customers was Maddux Air Lines of California, but many other airlines – large and small – eventually operated the 'Tin Goose'. Continuing development led to the larger and more powerful 5-AT series, and a list of 'one-off' and short-run models also existed. Production ceased in the early 1930's at over 200, the model being dealt a blow by the Great Depression, but at that time more streamlined and capable airliners were in any case starting to be created. Nevertheless, Tri-Motors were very successful for both their civil or military operators, and they literally flew in just about every corner of the world.

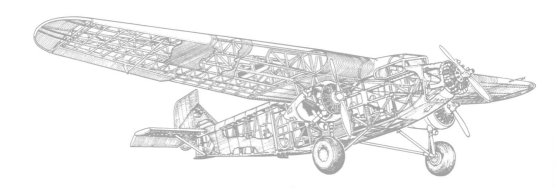

*Perhaps the best-known Tri-Motor was the Byrd Antarctic Expedition's 'Floyd Bennett',
in which the U.S. Navy's Richard Byrd overflew the South Pole in November 1929.
This made him the first person to overfly both Poles.*

*Dating from the late 1920's, this beautiful period picture captures a Model 4-AT Tri-Motor
with Wright Whirlwind radial engines (Photo: Ford).*

Specifications – Ford Model 5-AT-C Tri-Motor

Wingspan	77 ft 10 in
Length	50 ft 3 in
Maximum speed	152-164 mph depending on load
Service Ceiling	18,500 ft
Range	approximately 630 miles
Engine	Three Pratt & Whitney Wasp C-series radial piston engines, of 420-450 hp each
Accommodation	Two crew, up to 15 passengers, or less on night-sleeper models or with steward

De Havilland D.H.80 Puss Moth

The famous British company de Havilland produced many fine light aircraft in the inter-war years. As described on pages 176-177, some of these aircraft were used for headline-making long-distance flights. The de Havilland design offices were always busy, and in 1929 a new light aircraft for private owners first appeared. Given the de Havilland number D.H.80, it was also named Puss Moth in line with de Havilland's tendency to name its products after moths and other small (and some not so small) flying creatures. In the late 1920's prior to the Wall Street Crash and the Great Depression, there were sufficient affluent pilots to encourage the creation of well-appointed civil touring aircraft with an enclosed, comfortable cabin. The prototype Puss Moth flew in September 1929, and was a neat strut-braced cabin mono-

plane with seating for a pilot and up to two passengers. Production aircraft to D.H.80A standard introduced a welded tubular metal fuselage frame with fabric covering, and a Gipsy III inline engine. This power plant was mounted inverted, rather than the upright installation on the D.H.60 Moth series, thus setting a trend that was followed on many subsequent de Havilland light aircraft. Production examples were delivered from 1930 onwards, with manufacture continuing into 1933, 259 or 261 being built in Britain plus 25 manufactured in Canada by de Havilland Aircraft of Canada. Although most Puss Moths quietly flew with their private owners, several were used for some pioneering long-distance flights. In November 1931, for example, the famous Australian pilot Bert Hinkler flew a Puss Moth from Natal,

There were a number of famous Puss Moths. This one, named 'The Heart's Content',
was flown by James Mollison solo across the North Atlantic from east to west in August 1932,
the first time that this feat had been achieved.

Brazil, to Senegal to complete the first solo west to east crossing of the South Atlantic. In an equally spectacular testimony to this reliable little light aircraft, famous pilot 'Jim' Mollison flew his Puss Moth named 'The Heart's Content' across the North Atlantic from Ireland to New Brunswick, Canada, in August 1932 to mark the first non-stop east to west solo North Atlantic crossing. In November 1932 Mollison's wife, Amy Johnson, gained the record for an England to Cape Town (South Africa) flight in stages using the Puss Moth 'Desert Cloud' in just over four days and six hours.

The Puss Moth was for a rather more affluent clientele than the D.H.60 Moth series described earlier in this book. The Puss Moth illustrated here was used by the Duchess of Bedford, flown for her by former R.F.C. and R.A.F. pilot Flt.-Lieutenant Bernard Allen.

Specifications – De Havilland D.H.80A Puss Moth

Wingspan	36 ft 9 in
Length	25 ft
Maximum speed	128 mph at sea level
Service Ceiling	17,500 ft
Range	300 miles
Engine	One de Havilland Gipsy III inline piston engine, of 120 hp
Accommodation	One pilot, up to two passengers

Tupolev ANT-20 'Maxim Gorky'

The majority of aircraft in the first few decades of successful manned flight included wood and fabric covering as a significant part of their overall construction and finishing (together with later innovations such as welded steel tube for fuselage structures). However, from early on there were designers in several countries who recognised the potential of metal for aircraft structures and even covering. They included Hugo Junkers in Germany (see page 78), and also Andrei N. Tupolev in the Soviet Union. Tupolev created a series of aircraft from the mid-1920's onwards which were remarkable for their metal structures, often with corrugated metal skinning. These includ-

ed a number of military and 'civil' aircraft (although there was no civil aviation as such in the Soviet Union), including some impressive large and super large aircraft. The ANT-6 four-engined bomber of 1930 was the first of these grand aircraft, some examples being used in support of Soviet bases in the Arctic. The greatest of them all, however, was the ANT-20 series, which in their day were amongst the most impressive aircraft on earth. Developed from the six-engined TB-4 bomber, the eight-engined ANT-20 was named 'Maxim Gorky', a name derived from the pen-name of the famed Russian writer Alexei Maximovich Peshkov (1868-1936). It was a spectacular aircraft, two of its engines being pod-mounted back-to-back above the fuselage, with the other six in the wing leading edges. It spanned 206 ft

The ANT-20 was an amazing aircraft in all respects, and included many features within its fuse-lage and inner wing areas. The name 'Gorky' is often spelt differently in English, such as 'Gorki' or 'Gorkii'.

8.25 in, making it the largest land-plane in the world when it appeared in 1934. Construction work began in 1933, following inspiration from an association of Soviet writers and editors/publishers to celebrate an anniversary in Gorky's literary career. Six million roubles are said to have been raised by public subscription to build the 'Maxim Gorky'. It was a remarkable aircraft, containing within its fuselage and inner wing areas a printing plant, photographic studio, small cinema, and radio station. Illuminated signs could be mounted on the aircraft's undersides, and it could broadcast from loudspeakers.

It first flew in mid-1934. A crew of up to 20 could be carried, and between 43 and 76 passengers, although more could be taken aboard if crew numbers were reduced. Sadly, this fantastic propaganda showpiece had a tragic end. On 18 May 1935, a small fighter that was 'escorting' the 'Maxim Gorky' crashed into it, bringing down both aircraft with the loss of all onboard. Public subscriptions later resulted in the building of the altered but similarly impressive all-metal ANT-20bis, which had only six engines and did away with the engine pod above the fuselage.

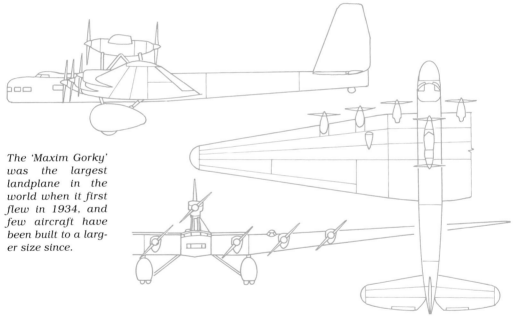

The 'Maxim Gorky' was the largest landplane in the world when it first flew in 1934, and few aircraft have been built to a larger size since.

Specifications – Tupolev ANT-20 'Maxim Gorky'

Wingspan	206 ft 8.25 in
Length	106 ft 6 in
Maximum speed	152.2 mph at sea level
Service Ceiling	19,685 ft
Range	1,242.8 miles
Maximum take-off weight	92,593 lb
Engine	Eight Mikulin AM-34FRN inline piston engines, of 900 hp each
Accommodation	Up to 20 crew, between 43 and 76 passengers

Tupolev ANT-25

In a period of record-breaking pioneering and headline-making long-distance flights, a particular aircraft type stands out for its remarkable achievements in long-distance flying – the Soviet Tupolev ANT-25. It is possible that the design of this ultra long-range aircraft was inspired by political needs in addition to those of pure aviation and aerodynamic interest, for the achievements of the ANT-25 were certainly useful to the dictatorship of Stalin in the Soviet Union. The ANT-25 was designed by a team under the direction of Andrei N. Tupolev, hence the 'ANT' in the aircraft's designation. Tupolev was interested in all-metal structures (see the previous two pages), and so the ANT-25 was also of this construction. The first aircraft flew on 22 June 1933, and for its day it was a remarkable machine. With a wingspan of 111 ft 6.5 in, its advanced all-metal construction, complete with long high aspect ratio cantilever wings, certainly pointed to the future. The ANT-25 type eventually achieved several

remarkable flights which gained global attention. The most important of these were in 1937, when two famous long-distance flights were made. On 18-20 June 1937, an ANT-25 with a crew led by Valery Chkalov flew from Moscow, over the North Pole, and on to the western United States, finally stopping near the American township of Vancouver near Seattle. A total flying time of over 63 hours was achieved on this flight. On 12-14 July 1937, an ANT-25 whose three-man crew was headed by Mikhail Gromov, flew from Moscow direct to California over the North Pole, landing through a break in the fog in a field near San Jacinto. This incredible non-stop flight was of 6,306 miles in 62 hours 17 minutes (historians disagree about the exact distance covered). This was a world record for a route of this type, and a fantastic advertisement for Soviet aviation – and for all-metal aircraft in general. There continues to be disagreement as to how many ANT-25 were actually built, the number possibly being just two.

A view of the ANT-25 after arrival in California at the end of its July 1937 flight. Some controversy continues to exist about the ANT-25 type, not only its true specifications, but the authenticity of the record-breaking flights themselves (Photo: Philippe Jalabert Collection).

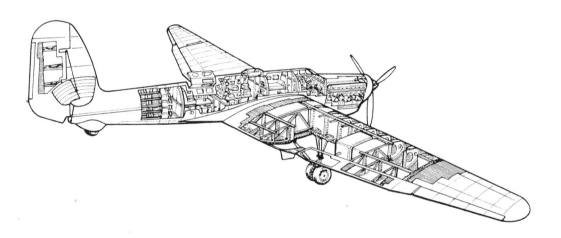

Specifications – Tupolev ANT-25

Wingspan	111 ft 6.5 in
Length	43 ft 11 in
Maximum speed	153 mph at sea level
Service Ceiling	22,966 ft
Range	nominally 6,214 miles
Engine	One Mikulin M-34R or RF inline piston engine, of up to 950 hp
Crew	Three

Loening OL Series

Grover C. Loening was one of America's chief exponents of the amphibian, and his company created a series of distinctive single-engine biplane amphibians with a 'shoe-horn'-type fuselage/hull shape. These were built in both military and civil models, and the first aircraft was flown in 1923. In military service there were a variety of models with several engine options. For the U.S. Navy, they were in the OL (Observation, Loening) categories, the U.S. Army's aircraft being various OA-1 and OA-2 (Observation Amphibian) versions. Two ambulance examples also existed. Approximately 168 or 169 were built for the military, and best-known were several U.S. Army Air Corps OA-1A amphibians that made a goodwill

tour of South America in 1926-1927. Final military models included the OL-9, which arose when Loening had merged with Keystone Aircraft. There were similarly a number of civil models, generally derived from the military versions and introduced in 1927/1928. Several of these were christened 'Air Yacht'. Again various engine options were available, plus some distinct configurations. A number were passenger models for short-haul, 'downtown-to-downtown' commercial services carrying up to six passengers enclosed within the fuselage. Precise numbers of the civil-operated Loenings are difficult to verify, but their numbers were probably far fewer than the military Loenings.

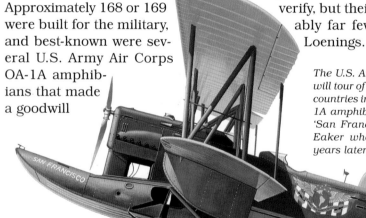

The U.S. Army Air Corps made a goodwill tour of Central and South American countries in 1926-1927 with several OA-1A amphibians. This example, named 'San Francisco', was flown by Ira C. Eaker who rose to high rank many years later.

Specifications – Loening OA-1A

Wingspan	45 ft
Length	34 ft 7 in
Maximum speed	122 mph at sea level
Ceiling	13,500 ft
Range	750 miles
Armament	provision on some aircraft for one fixed forward-firing and one flexible-mounted 0.3 in machine guns
Engine	One Liberty V-1650 inverted inline piston engine, of 425 hp
Crew	Two

Hillson Praga

The very active aviation industry in Czechoslovakia produced many interesting aircraft types during the inter-war years, ranging from military aircraft of most descriptions to light aircraft for the then popular 'sports' or 'touring' activities. During the mid-1930's the Czech company Praga developed a small two-seat light aircraft named the E-114 Air Baby, which went into production in 1934/1935. The Air Baby attracted the attention of buyers across Europe. In England, the Manchester-based company F. Hills & Sons Ltd. negotiated successfully to obtain licence-manufacturing rights, and the Air Baby went into production in Manchester as the Hillson Praga.

Powered by a licence-built Praga engine or other engine options, at least 35 Pragas were built by Hillson. The first was completed during 1936, and the flyaway price was £385. The annexation of Czechoslovakia by Germany ended the production of the Air Baby models, but after World War Two the type returned to production in the newly-reconstituted Czechoslovakia. This time powered by the rather better Czechoslovak Walter Mikron III piston engine, the Air Baby was redesignated E-114M and a number of new examples were built.

The drawing illustrates the post-World War Two Praga E-114M Air Baby layout.

Specifications – Praga E-114M Air Baby

Wingspan	36 ft 1 in
Length	23 ft 4.5 in
Maximum speed	115 mph at sea level
Ceiling	13,452 ft
Range	497 miles
Engine	One Walter Mikron III inline piston engine, of 65 hp
Accommodation	One pilot, one passenger

Boeing P-12

A classic series of biplane fighters, some with fighter-bomber capability, was created by Boeing in the late 1920's and early 1930's. They were the culmination of a line of biplane fighters for the American military that went back to 1923-1924. At that time Boeing was developing what became the FB series for the U.S. Navy, and the PW-9 for the U.S. Army. These aircraft were originally powered by the inline Curtiss D-12 piston engine. Subsequent developments resulted in the U.S. Navy standardising on radial engines for its fighters, and a line of aircraft carrier-based Boeing fighters ensued under the designations F2B and F3B. The Boeing Model 77 F3B of 1928 was a Pratt & Whitney Wasp-powered fighter for the U.S. Navy, and it represented a step in the evolution

towards the famous F4B/P-12 series. The direct forerunners of the F4B/P-12 were two private-venture prototypes, the Models 83 and 89. These two were similar but not identical development aircraft, and both flew during the summer of 1928. Only the Model 83 was arrester hook-equipped (for aircraft carrier operations), but both were initially tested by the U.S. Navy. The Model 89 so impressed U.S. Army officials that the type was ordered into production as the P-12. This was the start of the classic line of P-12 series fighters and fighter-bombers for the U.S. Army Air Corps. At roughly the same time, the U.S. Navy purchased the type as the carrier-capable F4B series (see Pages 218-219). The initial P-12 production aircraft of late 1928 were followed by

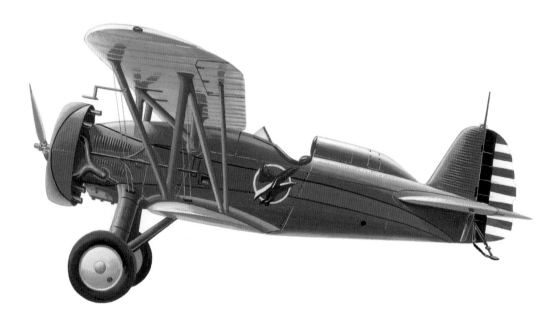

The Boeing P-12E illustrated, with its distinctive metal fuselage construction,
was flown by the U.S. Army Air Corps' 27th Pursuit Squadron of the 1st Pursuit Group.
This unit's falcon fuselage badge was approved as far back as 1924,
and was a symbol of the pride and history of
the unit that it belonged to.

increasingly improved models, the P-12B (90 built), P-12C (96 built), P-12D (35 built), leading to the best of the line, the P-12E (Model 234, 110 built), and P-12F (Model 251, 25 built). The P-12E of 1931 (which equated to the U.S. Navy's F4B-3 and -4) introduced an all-metal semi-monocoque fuselage (pioneered on the private-venture Model 218) to replace the previous part-fabric covered fuselage of earlier models. A tail-wheel (rather than the previous tail skid), retrospectively fitted to earlier P-12s, was introduced during the P-12F production. A total of 366 P-12 of all types was built for the U.S. Army between 1929 and 1932. The type remained in front-line service until 1936.

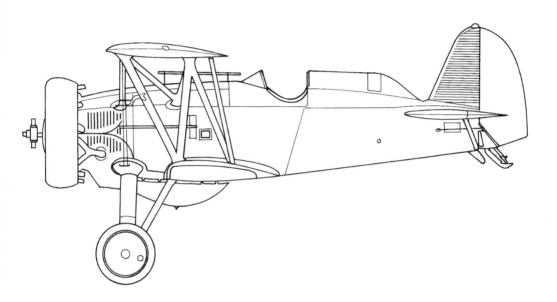

Specifications – Boeing P-12E

Wingspan	30 ft
Length	20 ft 5 in
Maximum speed	187 mph at 6,000 ft
Service Ceiling	27,500 ft
Range	approximately 585 miles
Armament	Two fixed forward-firing 0.3 in machine guns, or one 0.3 in and one 0.5 in machine guns; provision as required for light bomb load
Engine	One Pratt & Whitney R-1340-17 Wasp radial piston engine, of 525-550 hp
Crew	One

Granville 'Gee Bee' Racers

Air racing had become an important aviation spectacle even before World War One, and although most 'racing' aircraft were adapted from standard 'production' types, a number of specialist speed aircraft such as the beautifully-streamlined Deperdussin Monocoque (see page 55) had also been created. The First World War interrupted the spectacle of aerial competition and the technological advances that had come with it, but in the 1920's the concept returned. In the United States, in particular, air racing became a very large spectator sport, with aircraft that were often 'one-off' specials designed specially for the sport. Long-distance races, pylon races and other related categories were created, and a particular folklore grew up around this very

specialised part of aviation. The best-known exponents of this air racing culture were the five Granville brothers, whose Granville Brothers company (often abbreviated to 'GB' or 'Gee Bee'), came to symbolise the almost mythological status that this aerial sport came to represent. The original company began in 1925 and grew into an important organisation in Springfield, Massachusetts. Monoplane layouts began to predominate the design of purpose-built racing aircraft at the end of the 1920's and early 1930's, and very influential was the Travel Air 'Mystery Ship'. This aircraft established a trend, and the first sporting GB products reflected this and included the single-seat Models 'X', 'E' and 'D' monoplanes, and two-seat Model 'Y'. The first of the famous

NR 2101 'Race 7' was the 'Gee Bee' R-2 Super Sportster. This particular aircraft did not win any major races, and crashed in 1933.

194

single-seat racing barrels was the GB Model 'Z'. In this aircraft, as in the Travel Air 'Mystery Ship', the cross-section of the fuselage was enlarged to match the diameter of the aircraft's radial engine. The Model 'Z' flew on 22 August 1931, and named 'City of Springfield' it gained a number of big race successes including the prestigious Thompson Trophy of 1931 – before disintegrating while making an attempt on the world landplane air speed record. Two Model 'R' Super Sportsters followed. These red and white barrels, the R-1 and R-2, with the pilot moved back to the tail, established the 'Gee Bee' legend. The R-1 was flown by the famous aviator 'Jimmy' Doolittle to victory in the 1932 Thompson Trophy race. Both the 'R' series were extensively raced, reconfigured, and both were destroyed in spectacular crashes. An R-1/R-2 hybrid was built from the wreckage, and this too eventually crashed, killing its pilot. The Granville brothers went bankrupt in 1933-1934, their final aircraft, named 'Q.E.D.' failing in its entry in the 1934 England to Australia air race. It later set a Mexico City to New York City non-stop speed record, but its Mexican pilot was killed when it crashed on its homeward journey.

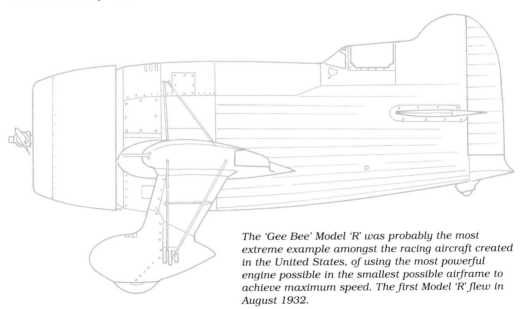

The 'Gee Bee' Model 'R' was probably the most extreme example amongst the racing aircraft created in the United States, of using the most powerful engine possible in the smallest possible airframe to achieve maximum speed. The first Model 'R' flew in August 1932.

Specifications – Granville Brothers 'Gee Bee' Model R-1 (1932)

Wingspan	25 ft
Length	17 ft 9 in
Maximum speed	approximately 300 mph at sea level
Maximum take-off weight	3,075 lb
Engine	One Pratt & Whitney Wasp radial piston engine, of 750-800 hp
Crew	One

Fairey Flycatcher

The end of World War One had resulted in a huge run-down of the large military aviation elements that had been established during the war. The Royal Air Force had been created in Britain on 1 April 1918, and had absorbed most of the naval aviation contingent of the Royal Naval Air Service. It was not until the 1920's that a rejuvenated Fleet Air Arm was established, and by that time a new generation of combat aircraft had started to appear. In 1922 Britain's Air Ministry issued Specification 6/22, requiring the creation of a new single-seat fighter for aircraft carrier and shipboard operation, able to operate on wheels, floats (seaplane), or wheeled floats (amphibian). Two companies, Fairey and Parnall, eventually built aircraft to this specification. The Parnall design, the Plover, was produced in only small numbers and served in 1923/1924. The Fairey design was the Flycatcher, and this aircraft became a classic inter-war

fighter type. Three prototypes were built, to test the wheel, seaplane and amphibian layouts, and the first aircraft flew in 1922. Production commenced in 1923, and altogether 193 examples were built (plus the three prototypes). The first of these entered service in 1923, replacing short-lived Nieuport Nightjar biplane rotary-engined fighters, and the type served with naval units at home and overseas until 1934. By then, newer biplane fighters such as the Hawker Osprey and Nimrod were entering or had entered service. The Flycatcher was used as a fleet fighter, but it could also be used for spectacular vertical dive-bombing. Flycatchers served as floatplanes aboard the flying-off platforms on the turrets of capital ships, but most notably they were operated from British aircraft carriers such as H.M.S. Courageous. On some of these ships the Flycatchers had their own hangar and flight deck at the bows of the vessel. They were capable of land-

ing without the need of arrester wires, possessing a special camber-changing mechanism on the wings to shorten take-offs and landings. The type served only with Britain's Fleet Air Arm, but it was well-liked by its pilots and its mixed metal and wood construction with a fabric covering was strong – even the float-plane examples were capable of aerobatics.

Specifications – Fairey Flycatcher

Wingspan	29 ft
Length	23 ft
Maximum speed	133 mph at 10,000 ft
Service Ceiling	19,000 ft
Endurance	3 hr
Armament	Two 0.303 in machine guns, up to 80 lb of bombs carried externally
Engine	One Armstrong Siddeley Jaguar III or IV radial piston engine, of 400 hp
Crew	One

Fokker Universal

Following the re-establishment of his aviation interests, in new premises in Holland after World War One, Anthony Fokker oversaw the design and manufacture of a succession of comparatively widely-produced and extensively-operated civil aircraft types, such as the F.VII (see pages 174-175). Some of these models were exported to the United States, resulting in a major sales organisation being developed in America to market and promote Fokker's civil aircraft line. Eventually this grew into a full design and manufacturing corporation in the United States, in parallel with but technically separate from Fokker's Dutch-based activities. One of the names used for this Stateside-based organisation was Atlantic, the Atlantic Aircraft Corporation being formed in 1924, resulting in some of the Fokker products from this period during the 1920's being known as Atlantic-Fokkers. The first all-

American product of this arrangement was the Universal line of small passenger aircraft. These could be operated on wheels, skis or floats, and they became well-used especially but not exclusively in the harsh environment of the remoter regions of Canada and the United States. A high-wing monoplane with a strut-braced wooden semi-cantilever wing, the original Universal gained its U.S. type certificate in June 1927. It could seat up to six passengers, and its pilot was placed in an open cockpit beside the wing leading edge. The Universal was originally designed for the 200 hp Wright J-4 Whirlwind radial engine, but the J-5 of 220 hp and later models powered many of the subsequent production aircraft. Approximately 40 of the original Universals were built before a developed model arose. This was the Standard Universal (type certificate issued in June 1929). The Standard Universal seated its

This early Universal was registered in Canada to Western Canada Airlines. Note the open cockpit and ski undercarriage. Universals were rugged aircraft that often operated in austere and demanding conditions.

two crew members in a fully-enclosed cockpit, and included the more powerful 300 hp Wright J-6 Whirlwind radial engine. Further development had by then already led to the slightly larger Super Universal, of late 1927 to early 1928, which had a fully cantilever wing, modified undercarriage and again an enclosed cockpit for its two crew. It could carry six passengers and was powered by a 400-420 hp Pratt & Whitney Wasp radial engine. The first two Universals that conformed to this standard were built in late 1927. In addition to commercial use, this particular Universal model gained important export success in Japan. The type was additionally built in Japan by Nakajima, for both civil and military service. The power plant of these Japanese aircraft was invariably the Nakajima Kotobuki radial, based on the British Bristol Jupiter engine. 47 are known to have been made in Japan between 1931 and 1936, presumably for civil operation, in addition to a number of military examples.

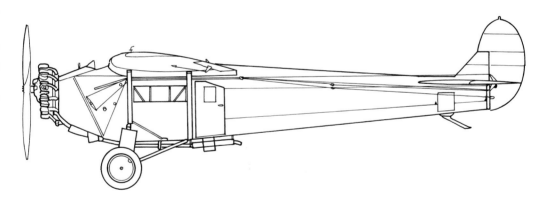

The layout represented here is of an early Fokker Universal, with an open cockpit for its pilot. Aircrew at that time often had to be hardy individuals!

Specifications – Fokker Universal (original configuration)

Wingspan	47 ft 9 in
Length	33 ft 3 in
Maximum speed	118 mph at sea level
Service Ceiling	12,000 ft
Range	approximately 500 miles
Engine	One Wright J-4 Whirlwind radial piston engine, of 200 hp
Accommodation	One pilot, plus up to six passengers

Lockheed Model 10 Electra

The American Lockheed company had achieved great success with such famous aircraft as the Vega and Sirius (see pages 144-145), but by the early 1930's the company was in serious financial trouble. It was taken over during 1932 by a new team. The first design from the 'new' Lockheed Aircraft Co. was the Model 10 Electra (following on from the previous Model 9 Orion single-engine small airliner), and in contrast to former Lockheed types the Model 10 was all-metal. A streamlined cantilever twin-engine airliner for ten passengers with a retractable undercarriage and twin-tail configuration, the Electra continued the tradition of naming Lockheed aircraft after celestial bodies. The first aircraft flew on 23 February 1934, and its type certificate was issued in August 1934. The Model 10 was bought by several airlines, launch orders coming from Northwest Airlines and Pan American. The Model 10A used the Pratt & Whitney Wasp Junior radial engine, the Model 10C was Wasp-powered, and the Model 10E was powered by a higher rated Wasp radial. 149 machines of all types were built in total, for airlines or private buyers, plus some limited military orders (some under the C-36 designation for the U.S. Army Air Corps). The Model 10 fitted in well at the smaller end of the new all-metal airliners that were then appearing such as the Boeing Model 247 and the Douglas DC-2, and was cheaper. Many U.S. civil-operated Electras were impressed (requisitioned) for military service during World War Two, and later some served with smaller civil operators in several overseas countries. Further development led to the reduced-size twin-engine Model 12 Electra Junior, aimed at smaller airlines and the embryonic executive market. Able to carry six passengers, most were powered by Wasp Junior radial engines. Only 130 were built, and many of these were bought by military customers. They included 36 for the Dutch East Indies, most of which

The painting depicts Amelia Earhart's Electra 10 in flight.

were destroyed in the desperate fighting after the Japanese attacked the Dutch East Indies in December 1941. The most famous of the Electras, however, was the special long-range Model 10E used by well-known American aviator Amelia Earhart. She had already performed many successful long-distance flights and other achievements when she attempted a round-the-world flight in May 1937. The aircraft used was a Model 10E Electra registered as NR-16020. Sadly, Earhart and her navigator Fred Noonan disappeared near Howland Island in the Pacific Ocean on 2 July 1937.

The colour photograph shows a preserved Electra in the United States (Photo: John Batchelor).

Below:
The cutaway diagram shows the interior of Amelia Earhart's specially-configured long-distance Electra 10E.

Specifications – Lockheed Model 10A Electra

Wingspan	55 ft
Length	38 ft 7 in
Maximum speed	205 mph at 5,000 ft
Service Ceiling	19,400 ft
Range	approximately 800 miles
Engine	Two Pratt & Whitney Wasp Junior SB-series radial piston engines, of 450 hp each
Accommodation	Two crew, up to 10 passengers

Hughes H-1

No history of aviation in the inter-war period would be complete without the inclusion of American multi-millionaire Howard Hughes. A successful film producer and businessman of great fame, Hughes made a huge contribution to civil aviation in the United States particularly through his work with Trans World Airlines (T.W.A.). He also achieved a number of important aviation feats. He was responsible for a ground-breaking aircraft, the first from his Hughes Aircraft Co. which was created in 1936. This remarkable aircraft was the Hughes H-1, often known as the Hughes Racer although its real achievements only came in two individual and very personal records gained with Hughes himself at the controls. Hughes had a background in aviation engineering, having studied aeronautical engineering in California. The Hughes H-1 was the outcome of collaboration with a number of talented aircraft engineers and designers including designer Richard Palmer. The H-1 was built for speed, and was a beautifully streamlined cantilever wing monoplane with a retractable undercarriage. Its fuselage was a flush-riveted metal mono-coque, with a tightly cowled radial engine, wooden wings, and fabric-covered control surfaces. The whole aircraft was finished to a very high standard to gain the greatest possible speed advantage. It was rolled out in August 1935, and on 13 September 1935 Hughes flew the aircraft at a small airstrip near Santa Ana, California, to break the world speed record for this class of aircraft at 352.388 mph. The H-1could be flown with a short-span wing of some 25 ft, or a longer span wing of 31 ft 9 in. In January 1937 the aircraft, equipped with the long span wing, was flown by Hughes to set a transcontinental speed record from Los Angeles to Newark, New Jersey, in just over seven hours and 28 minutes. This beat his own record, established in a special Northrop Gamma the previous year. Hughes in fact achieved several headline-making flights in various types of aircraft, and later went on to make the enormous H-4 flying boat during and after World War Two. As for the H-1, this aircraft later found its way to the National Air and Space Museum in Washington, D.C. Between 1998 and 2002 a replica of

The Hughes H-1 was a beautifully clean, streamlined aircraft that achieved great fame during the later 1930's.

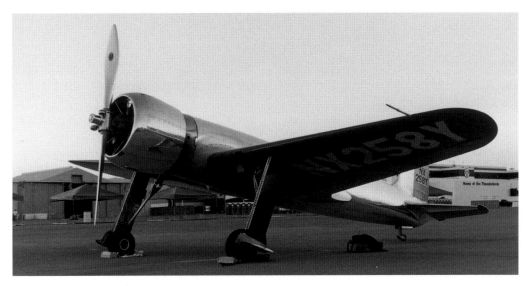

This fabulous replica of the Hughes H-1 was built by James Wright and colleagues in the United States, making its first flight in 2002. Sadly Jim Wright was killed when the aircraft crashed in 2003 (Photo: Malcolm V. Lowe).

the H-1 was built, and flown in the United States by Jim Wright. A very close representation to the original H-1, this beautiful replica was sadly destroyed in a fatal crash in 2003.

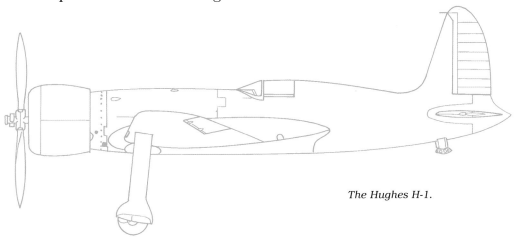

The Hughes H-1.

Specifications – Hughes H-1

Wingspan	31 ft 9 in (sometimes 32 ft quoted)
Length	28 ft 2 in
Record-breaking speed	352.388 mph at sea level
Range	at least 2,490 miles
Engine	One Pratt & Whitney SA1G series Twin Wasp Junior radial piston engine, of 1,000 hp
Crew	One

Curtiss O-1 Falcon Series

Gaining almost legendary status in the United Stated during the later 1920's and into the 1930's, the Curtiss Hawk series of single-seat fighters and Falcon family of two-seat observation and attack models were important front-line aircraft for the U.S. Army Air Corps following its creation in 1926. The Falcon series began life in 1923-1924 with an initially unsuccessful competitor in an observation aircraft competition. Production began in 1925 when this initial model was re-engined with a 510 hp Packard engine, and thus commenced a successful line of O-1 observation two-seat aircraft that continued to the O-1G of 1931. This rugged, purposeful aircraft was armed with one fixed forward-firing machine gun, with twin machine guns for the observer in the rear seat. Some individual models were configured for V.I.P. transport or dual-control training. In parallel was a series of A-3 attack aircraft and light bombers, some being armed with (for their time) a formidable four-gun forward-firing armament, together with the guns for the second crew member in the rear seat. In addition, 200 lb of bombs could be carried under the wings. These A-3 models were powered by the Curtiss V-1150 engine, and did away with the camera equipment of the O-1 series. The O-11 was a development of the O-1 line with a 420 hp Liberty engine, making it one of the fastest of the family with a top speed of 146 mph. A U.S. Navy spin-off, the F8C line, was developed from this series with a Pratt & Whitney R-1340 Wasp radial engine – these were the start of an equally famous line of Helldiver fighter/observation/attack aircraft. A further model for the U.S. Army Air Corps, the O-39, was built in 1931. As with other Falcon types,

The Curtiss O-1/A-3 were large ungainly-looking aircraft that nonetheless gave sterling service in the inter-war years.

there was some cross-over with the design and fitments of the Curtiss P-1/P-6 Hawk series. Total production of the O-1 line exceeded 100, as did the A-3, together with 10 of the O-39. Over 100 examples of the F8C were bought by the U.S. Navy. A number of different engine options were tried out for the overall O-1 series, but most models retained the distinctive swept upper wing planform of the series. In addition to the U.S. military variants, there were several export customers including Colombia (with floatplane models included) and Peru – these aircraft are believed to have seen action on opposing sides when the two countries clashed with each other in 1932. Chile and Brazil also used Falcons, and a line of civil Falcons was developed for American domestic use. There were several mail-planes, plus a single special example for the famous aviator Charles Lindbergh.

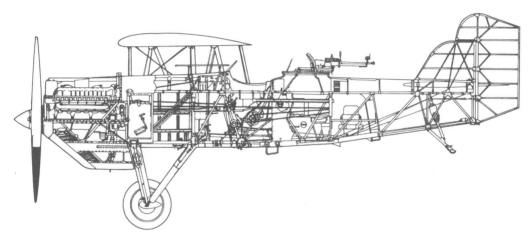

The inner workings of a Curtiss O-1/A-3 series aircraft.

Specifications – Curtiss O-1E Falcon

Wingspan	38 ft
Length	27 ft 2 in
Maximum speed	141 mph at sea level
Service Ceiling	15,300 ft
Range	630 miles
Armament	Three 0.3 in machine guns (one fixed forward-firing, two flexible ring-mounted in rear cockpit)
Engine	One Curtiss V-1150-5 inline piston engine, of 430-435 hp
Crew	Two

Breguet 19

Creator of the famous and widely-produced Breguet 14 of World War One (see pages 104-105), the French Breguet company produced a worthy successor during the 1920's called the Breguet 19. This aircraft turned out to be just as successful and widely manufactured in France and also several other countries, notably Spain, Belgium and Yugoslavia. The exact numbers built remain open to debate, but the Breguet 19 was another contender alongside the Potez 25 (see pages 160-161) for the accolade of being the most widely-produced aircraft in the inter-war period. The prototype Breguet 19 (sometimes written XIX) flew in March 1922, and the type entered service with the French air force in 1924 as the Breguet 19A2 armed reconnaissance aircraft, and as the 19B2 bomber in 1926. In military service the Breguet 19 was highly successful, and orders from customers in Europe and South America were plentiful. The type fought in several wars, notably on both sides in the Spanish Civil War, and some were still in Yugoslav service at the start of hostilities with Germany in 1941. However, it is as a record-breaking and super long-range aircraft that the Breguet 19 is best remembered. The type was rugged, being of basically all-metal structure, mainly fabric covered, and it had great range and endurance possibility with the fitting of additional fuel tanks. Special long-range models were developed, starting with the Breguet 19 Grand Raid, and moving on to the Bidon, and thence to the most spectacular, the Super Bidon. Two of the latter were built, one in France and one in Spain,

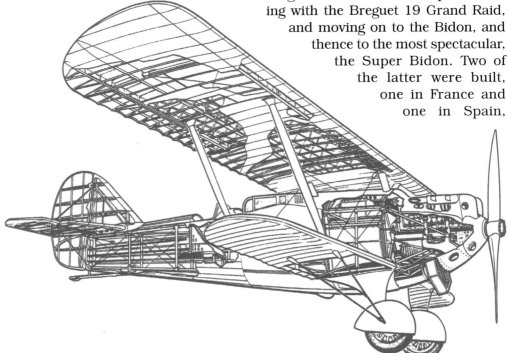

The Breguet 19 was a wonderfully rugged aircraft, of basically all-metal structure. The flights by Costes and Bellonte in the Super Bidon from Paris to New York, and Paris to Tsitsihar (sometimes written Tsitsikar) were world-famous exploits.

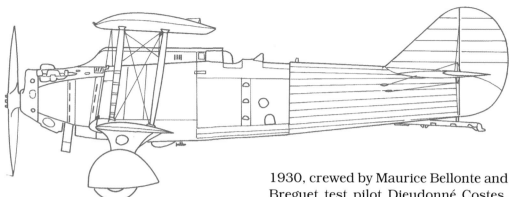

with increased wingspan and alterations for long-distance flight. The French example, doped bright red and named the 'Point d'Interrogation' (Question Mark) or simply '?', flew several headline-making flights. It was the first aircraft to fly from Paris to New York non–stop, in September 1930, crewed by Maurice Bellonte and Breguet test pilot Dieudonné Costes. Between 27-29 September 1929, it established a world straight line non-stop distance record, Costes and Bellonte leaving Paris and flying until they ran out of petrol, at Tsitsihar in Manchuria. This represented a distance of 4,912 miles, a staggering amount in the days before modern flight aids and in-flight refuelling.

A French air force Breguet 19. The French used the type as a bomber, reconnaissance aircraft, and rather surprisingly also as a night fighter.

Specifications – Breguet 19 Super Bidon

Wingspan	60 ft
Length	35 ft 2 in
Maximum speed	151.3 mph 6,562 ft
Range	approximately 5,406 miles
Service Ceiling	22,000 ft
Engine	One Hispano-Suiza 12Nb inline piston engine, of 650 hp
Crew	Two

Hawker Horsley

Specification 26/23 of November 1923 drawn up by Britain's Air Ministry laid down requirements for a two-seat medium day-bomber, which in the comparative austerity of the 1920's was likely to be built in comparatively small numbers. The Specification was eventually amended to also cover the carriage of a torpedo in addition to bombs. Four British companies came up with proposals to meet the requirement, the winner being Hawker's large two-seat Horsley biplane. The prototype flew unsuccessfully in December 1924, with more successful flight testing proceeding from about March 1925 onwards. Production orders led to several batches, the initial series aircraft being of predominantly wood construction. These were followed by Mk.II aircraft of mixed wood and metal construction, and later a selection of Horsleys with all-metal structures were constructed, sometimes called Mk.III machines although there is confusion over mark allocations to production Horsleys. The first Royal Air Force squadron to operate the type was No.11 Squadron, which received

its first Horsley II in January 1927. In 1928 the Horsley was cleared as a torpedo-bomber, with 'all-metal' Horsleys being delivered from 1929 onwards. Most served in Britain although some R.A.F. aircraft also operated in Singapore. In 1929 Hawker received an order for six aircraft for the Greek navy, five of these being torpedo-bombers while the sixth is believed to have been used as a V.I.P. aircraft. Some R.A.F. aircraft operated as target-towers in the early 1930's for training, but by early 1934 all British-based Horsleys had been withdrawn from service, while those in Singapore were replaced in 1935. Two examples of a developed three-seat model, the Dantorp, were purchased by the Danish navy, which operated them on floats. Total production of all Horsleys, including prototypes and the export aircraft, was approximately 138, with the final R.A.F. Horsley being completed in late 1931. Perhaps the most important work that was carried out by the Horsley was as an engine test-bed, several aircraft being used for this purpose including signifi-

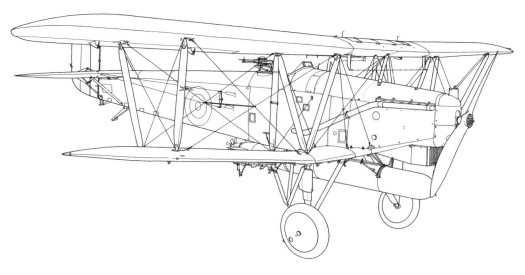

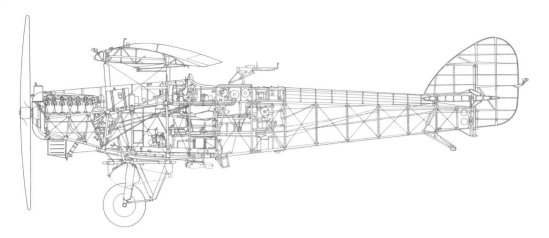

cant development work on the excellent Rolls-Royce Merlin – which in later years was to become one of the world's most significant aero engines.

Serial number J7721 was the second prototype of the Hawker Horsley, and it illustrates well the rather heavy lines of this 1920's vintage day-bomber and torpedo-bomber (Photo: Hawker Aircraft Ltd.).

Specifications – Hawker Horsley Mk.II

Wingspan	56 ft 5.75 in
Length	38 ft 10 in
Maximum speed	125 mph at 6,000 ft
Endurance	approximately 10 hr
Service Ceiling	14,000 ft
Armament	Two 0.303 in machine guns (one fixed forward-firing, one flexible ring-mounted), up to some 1,500 lb of bombs or one 18 in torpedo
Engine	One Rolls-Royce Condor IIIA inline piston engine, of 665 hp
Crew	Two

Beech Staggerwing

One of the great producers of light aircraft in the United States was Walter Beech. Already with a pedigree of light and small commercial aircraft design and manufacture behind him, Beech formed his own company in 1932. The very first Beechcraft aircraft was an attractive, fast biplane for private owners, the Model 17 known as the 'Staggerwing'. The aircraft derived its name from its unusual backwards-stagger biplane wing arrangement. This was claimed to give the aircraft good stall recovery characteristics, and a good forward view for the pilot, but it was never a layout that was particularly favored by other aircraft designers. Nevertheless the Staggerwing proved to be a great success and a good starting point for the Beech Aircraft Co., and it was manufactured in a large number of versions. The first Model 17 flew on 4 November 1932. This aircraft had a fixed undercarriage in which, unusually, its main wheels could be partly retracted into large

trouser fairings. Subsequent refinement of the basic design led to the installation of a fully retractable main undercarriage on the B17 models of 1934/1935 – an innovation that was not even a feature of some front-line military aircraft at that time. The Staggerwing also offered a very high performance for a civil aircraft that was comparable with that of various front-line military aircraft. Early Staggerwings were successful in a number of air races and speed dashes. The Staggerwing subsequently went through several progressively refined models that sold well enough for Beech to become established as a major supplier of light aircraft for the U.S. civil market. Production continued up to, during, and after World War Two, the last Model G17S being built in 1948 (although a final aircraft was pieced together from spare parts in 1949). The Staggerwing also proved to be a useful fast transport for military use. Even before U.S. involvement began in World War Two, the

The 'business end' of a preserved Beech Staggerwing. Several engine options were made available for the Model 17 during its production run, and the type's performance was on a par with that of some military aircraft at the time of its introduction in the mid-1930's.

A civil registered Beech Staggerwing. The original Model 17 gained its type certificate in December 1932, and it is generally agreed that 356 civil Staggerwings were built, in addition to military orders.

Staggerwing had been ordered in small numbers by the U.S. Navy as the GB-1, while the U.S. Army Air Corps had bought a handful for military attaché transport at overseas Embassies. During World War Two the Staggerwing was built for the U.S. Navy principally as the GB-2, and for the U.S.A.A.C./U.S.A.A.F. as the UC-43, in addition to requisitioned civil machines. The military name Traveler was adopted, this name also describing British military examples (as Traveller), some 105 being supplied in particular for Royal Navy use in light transport/liaison duties. In addition, a variety of other countries used the Model 17 as military transports. Approximately 781 Model 17 were built in total.

Specifications – Beech Traveller Mk.I (Royal Navy)

Wingspan	32 ft
Length	26 ft
Maximum speed	198 mph at sea level
Service Ceiling	25,000 ft
Maximum take-off weight	4,250 lb
Range	700 miles
Engine	One Pratt & Whitney R-985-50 (or similar sub-type) Wasp Junior radial piston engine, of 450 hp
Accommodation	One pilot, up to four passengers (usually three)

Short Scylla

The British company Short Brothers was renowned for its seaplanes and flying-boats, and had found particular fame during World War One with its Type 184 and other seaplane designs (see pages 84-85). During the later 1920's and 1930's the company designed and built a well-known selection of flying-boats for military and civil operation, and achieved lasting fame with its 'Empire' flying-boats – and the unusual Short-Mayo composite aircraft (see pages 266-267). The company also produced several landplane designs, one of these being to the request of Britain's principal international airline Imperial Airways. In the early 1930's this airline was running short of aircraft on its short-haul routes in Europe. The airline approached Short in early 1933 to design and produce a limited-run of new 39-passenger biplanes. A rapid solution to meeting the order was to build a landplane airliner based to an extent on the already-existing Short S.17 Kent (Scipio Class) flying-boat airliner. The new project eventually took the designation L.17, and design and manufacture took place quickly – the first L.17 flew on 26 March 1934. Using some of the wing design and powerplant layout of the Kent flying-boat, but with a completely different fuselage and fixed landplane undercarriage, the new airliner gained the name Scylla after the name bestowed on the first example to fly. The other was named Syrinx. The engine layout consisted of four Bristol Jupiter radial engines. Imperial Airways quickly put the new airliner into

G-ACJJ was one of the two Short L.17 Scylla airliners that were built.
It was named 'Scylla'. No further orders were received by Short Brothers for this
type of aircraft (Photo: Short Bros.).

service, with the inauguration of Scylla passenger services between London-Croydon and Paris-Le Bourget on 16 May 1934. Syrinx first flew during that month, and the two aircraft were soon successfully employed on Imperial Airways short-haul European services. The Scylla was a big aircraft to handle on the ground, and in October 1935 Syrinx was blown over by a violent gale at Brussels. Subsequently rebuilt, it received four more powerful Bristol Pegasus XC radial engines, and a refined interior. Both aircraft served reliably until the start of World War Two, when they were evacuated from Croydon to Whitchurch, Bristol, and were used on a variety of war-related tasks. Scylla was blown over and wrecked in Scotland during 1940, while Syrinx was scrapped in that year.

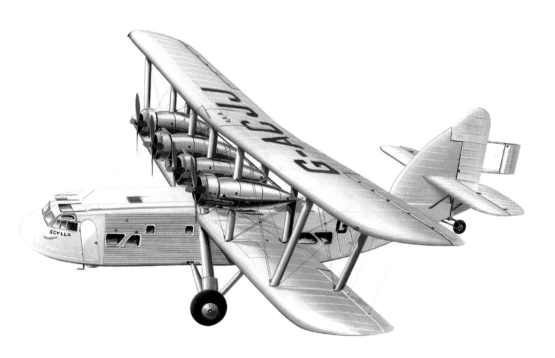

Specifications – Short Scylla

Wingspan	113 ft
Length	83 ft 10 in
Maximum speed	137 mph
Service Ceiling	approximately 20,000 ft
Range	approximately 500 miles
Engine	Four Bristol Jupiter XFBM radial piston engines, of 555 hp each
Accommodation	Two to three crew, up to 39 passengers

Douglas DC-1, DC-2 and DC-3

The Douglas DC-3 belongs to the select group of aircraft that became a legend in their own lifetime and have gained justified status as some of history's truly great aircraft. During a career that began in the 1930's and can be said to still exist today, the DC-3 has served just about everywhere in the world, seen important service in several major wars and countless small ones, and has been developed into a number of significant versions. It all began with American Donald Douglas' aircraft company that had started so well with the Douglas DT and Douglas World Cruiser biplanes, as shown on pages 146-147 and 152-153. In 1932 the major airline T.W.A. was soon going to require a replacement for its existing Fokker airliners. At that time the revolutionary Boeing Model 247 airliner (see pages 294-295) was under development, but most of the somewhat limited production of that type was destined for Boeing's associated air-

lines which grew into United Air Lines. T.W.A. therefore issued a specification for an all-metal 12-seat airliner to fulfil its own needs. Douglas responded with a design that was to grow into the legendary DC-3. Fortunately Douglas' plans were for a twin-engined airliner (T.W.A. had wanted a tri-motor layout). The result was a beautifully clean, streamlined all-metal aircraft named the DC-1 (Douglas Commercial No.1). Powered by two Wright Cyclone radial engines, this aircraft first flew on 1 July 1933. It was an immediate sensation, and production began of a slightly lengthened development with more powerful engines known as the DC-2. This was the first mass-produced Douglas airliner, and it was a great success in civil and military service, with almost 200 being built. In 1934 American Airlines requested Douglas to develop a larger, 'sleeper' model of the DC-2. The result was the D.S.T. (Douglas Sleeper Transport), the first of the

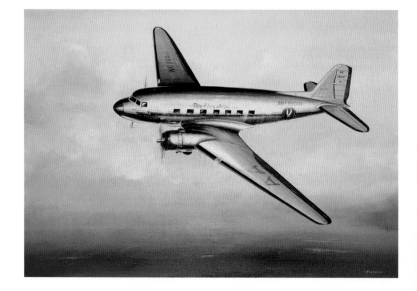

Many significant airlines operated the DC-3, including this example of American Airlines.

The prototype DC-3 flew on 17 December 1935, just 32 years after the first successful flight of the Wright brothers (Photo: Douglas).

DC-3 line. It featured a redesigned fuselage with sleeping accommodation for 14 night passengers, and it quickly became obvious that this new development of the DC-2 was an excellent aircraft. Further development led to DC-3 models with conventional seating for day passengers that by the start of World War Two were already well established with civil airlines and were destined to find many military roles. In U.S. Army service the DC-3 was designated C-47 and C-53, and these types served with distinction in World War Two – as described in much more detail in the next volume of this work.

Specifications – Douglas DC-3

Wingspan	95 ft
Length	64 ft 5.5 in
Maximum speed	231 mph at 8,500 ft
Service Ceiling	24,100 ft
Range	Up to 2,125 miles
Engine	Two Pratt & Whitney S1C3G Twin Wasp radial piston engines, of 1,050 hp each (other options available)
Accommodation	Two to three crew, normally 21 to 24 passengers

Bristol Bulldog

During the inter-war period, the appearance of a number of bomber types with performance better than contemporary fighters of the day caused accelerated attempts to bring fighter capability up to the new mark. One such type was the Fairey Fox single-engine biplane bomber, whose appearance in 1925 displayed how far Royal Air Force fighters were potentially lagging behind the performance of new bomber types. A response was the issue by Britain's Air Ministry of several specifications calling for a comparatively high performance day or night fighter armed with two machine guns and (preferably) an air-cooled radial engine. Several potential contenders were created by British companies to meet Specification F.9/26, the best two being the Hawker Hawfinch and the Bristol Bulldog. The prototype

Bulldog flew in May 1927, and it was a developed model with a lengthened fuselage that entered production as the Bulldog Mk.II. Powered by a Bristol Jupiter VII radial engine (Bristol therefore made both the aircraft and its engine), the type entered service with the R.A.F.'s No.3 Squadron in May/June 1929. Altogether 92 of this initial type were built, but the major production version was the Bulldog Mk.IIA. This model was powered by the improved Jupiter VIIF, and had higher operating weights. 268 Mk.IIA were built, and the Bulldog went on to become one of the principal R.A.F. fighters, particularly for home defence, into the mid-1930's. A trainer version, the two-seat Bulldog TM, was also manufactured, 59 being built. The final production model was the Bulldog Mk.IVA, which was re-engined with

An R.A.F.-operated Bulldog Mk.IIA. Although enjoying better performance over the fighters that went before it, the Bulldog still retained much of the layout and armament of the late World War One era British fighters.

The Bristol Bulldog Mk.IIA. Its performance was better than the Fairey Fox that had been a contributing reason for its creation.

the Bristol Mercury radial engine. 17 were supplied to Finland, which used them in combat during the Winter War against Russia in 1939-1940; they could be flown on skis, and were operated with distinction by their Finnish pilots. In fact there were several export customers for the Bulldog, while Nakajima completed two in Japan. In front-line R.A.F. service the Bulldog persisted until 1936-1937, but some two-seaters continued as R.A.F. trainers into 1939.

Specifications – Bristol Bulldog Mk.IIA

Wingspan	33 ft 10 in
Length	25 ft 2 in
Maximum speed	178 mph at 10,000 ft
Service Ceiling	29,300 ft
Range	approximately 275 miles
Armament	Two fixed forward-firing 0.303 in machine guns, four 20 lb bombs if required below lower wings
Engine	One Bristol Jupiter VIIF radial piston engine, of 490 hp
Crew	One

Boeing F4B

The classic line of Boeing F4B fighters and fighter-bombers for the U.S. Navy and Marine Corps was developed in parallel with the U.S. Army Air Corps' P-12 series (see pages 192-193). The private-venture Boeing Models 83 and 89 development aircraft impressed U.S. Navy evaluation personnel sufficiently for a derived version, the F4B-1, to be ordered into production, combining the best features of both. All subsequent U.S. Navy models were equipped with an arrester hook and were aircraft carrier-capable, and they also had emergency floatation bags installed in the upper wing. The F4B-1 (27 built, first flight May 1929) was similar to the U.S. Army's P-12 and P-12B models, with tripod-type main undercarriage legs. This was followed by the F4B-2 (Model 223), which fea-

tured the definitive main undercarriage arrangement of a hinged cross-axle type. This model was similar to the U.S. Army's P-12C and P-12D, and 46 were built. It did, however, feature a tailwheel which did not become standard on U.S. Army P-12s until some time later. Some of the F4B-2 models had an uncowled Wasp radial engine, while others featured a neat Townend ring cowling. In similar fashion to the U.S. Army's P-12 line, the next development was the introduction of an all-metal semi-monocoque fuselage as pioneered on the Model 218, which led to the F4B-3 and F4B-4 series (both called Model 235). These were the equivalents of the U.S. Army's P-12E. 21 were built as the F4B-3, and 92 as the F4B-4, the latter having revised vertical tail surfaces of

A Boeing F4B-2 in full U.S. Navy regalia and the markings of Navy Fighting Squadron 5 (VF-5). Note the tailhook and small underwing bomb racks.

The streamlined, semi-monocoque fuselage of the F4B-3 and F4B-4 models is well shown by this F4B-4 of U.S. Navy squadron VF-2. This was a colourful period in inter-war aviation.

increased chord. The final 45 F4B-4 also had an altered headrest, which included a liferaft. The improved vertical tail design was retrofitted to some earlier aircraft. In addition, one extra F4B-4 was built from spare parts by the U.S. Marine Corps at Quantico, Virginia. An export model also existed, 14 for Brazil being diverted from the U.S. Navy's F4B-4 alloca-

tion, eventually replaced by 14 examples with updated radio equipment. Brazil also received nine examples of a hybrid P-12E/F4B-3 variant (Model 267). The first unit to receive the F4B-4 was U.S. Marine Corps squadron VF-10M in July 1932, and the type served the Navy/Marine Corps in front-line units until 1937-1938.

Specifications – Boeing F4B-4

Wingspan	30 ft
Length	20 ft 5 in
Maximum speed	187 mph at 6,000 ft
Service Ceiling	27,500 ft
Range	approximately 585 miles
Armament	Two fixed forward-firing 0.3 in machine guns, or one 0.3 in and one 0.5 in machine guns, provision for bomb load of up to 232 lb beneath the lower wings (also provision under fuselage)
Engine	One Pratt & Whitney R-1340-16 Wasp radial piston engine, of 500 hp
Crew	One

Savoia-Marchetti S.55

During the early 1930's, the Fascist dictatorship of Benito Mussolini in Italy successfully showed itself off with two headline-making mass transatlantic flying-boat formation flights. The aircraft used for these mass flights were Savoia-Marchetti S.55 catamaran twin-engined flying-boats. Led by Italy's aviation minister Italo Balbo, the first flight in December 1930 involved a formation of S.55A on a mass flight to Brazil from Italy, which included a crossing of the South Atlantic. Even more eye-catching was a 24 aircraft (plus one spare) flight by special long-range S.55X flying-boats in July/August 1933 from Italy to the Chicago World's Fair exhibition in the United States, plus the return voyage

to Italy. The S.55 derived from a 1922 Italian air ministry requirement for a torpedo bomber for the Italian navy, able to carry a torpedo, bombs or a mine. The Savoia-Marchetti company, recently formed out of the S.I.A.I. company of 1915, planned on a twin-hulled flying-boat able to carry this payload between the aircraft's two fuselages. This basic layout was used for both the S.55, and its larger successor, the S.66. Both were twin-fuselage (hull) catamaran flying-boats with a clean cantilever wing structure, a thick centre section joining the two hulls, and the tailplane carried on booms stretching back from the two hulls. The S.55's basic construction was wood, with

Despite its clumsy engine installation, the S.55 flying-boat for its time was a very advanced, clean design. Shown is an Italian military S.55. Balbo's mass flight from Italy to Chicago in 1933 utilised the S.55X model.

some fabric-covered metal framed control surfaces. Its two engines were pod-mounted back-to-back above the wing centre section. Design work began in 1923 and the first S.55 flew in August 1924. Initially military orders were not forthcoming and the early production aircraft went into airline service with Italian airlines in the Mediterranean area. A crew of four and up to eight passengers could be carried, there being a separate passenger cabin in each fuselage. Military orders were eventually forthcoming, and the S.55 was manufactured in Italy to approximately 240 examples, plus one in the United States. Approximately 24 of the three-engined pusher S.66 were built for airline use, some being requisitioned for military operation early in World War Two.

A poster commemorating the 1933 mass flight by S.55X flying-boats from Italy to the Chicago World's Fair.

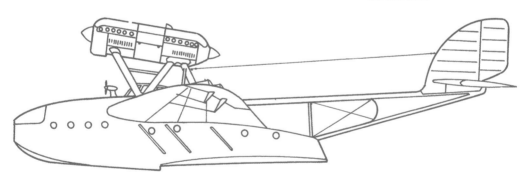

Many S.55 flying-boats were powered by versions of the Isotta-Fraschini inline engine, two of these being pod-mounted back-to-back on struts above the aircraft's centre section.

Specifications – Savoia-Marchetti S.55X

Wingspan	78 ft 9 in
Length	54 ft 1.5 in
Maximum speed	165 mph at sea level
Service Ceiling	13,780 ft
Range	2,175 miles plus
Engine	Two Isotta-Fraschini Asso R inline piston engines, of 750 hp each
Crew	Nominally four for transatlantic flight

De Havilland D.H.88 Comet

A celebrated aircraft from a famous company that won the world's greatest ever air race, the de Havilland D.H.88 Comet was one of the best-known of Britain's civil aircraft of the 1930's. To celebrate the Centenary of the establishment of the state of Victoria in Australia, Sir MacPherson Robertson instigated what is usually abbreviated to the 'MacRobertson' air race from just outside London, England, to Melbourne, Australia, set for October 1934. In Britain at that time there were few possible realistic contenders, so the de Havilland company set about designing a racing aircraft for which potential buyers had to place an order by a February 1934 deadline. Three orders were forthcoming, and de Havilland rapidly designed and built the three aircraft. The first one flew on 8 September 1934. A beautifully streamlined, low-wing cantilever twin-engined monoplane of all-wood construction with stressed-skin wood covering, the D.H.88 had a manually-activated retractable undercarriage, wing flaps,

and somewhat crude variable-pitch propellers – these features and its performance made it one of the most advanced aircraft of its day. Its fuselage contained three fuel tanks to give it a long range – there were only five scheduled stops on the race route. The race itself proved to be a huge success for the Comets. Twenty aircraft started the race on October 20th and only nine finished including two of the Comets. They placed overall first and fourth. The winners were Charles Scott and Tom Campbell Black in the Comet named 'Grosvenor House', G-ACSS, purchased for the race by A.O. Edwards, managing director of the Grosvenor House Hotel in London. They won the speed classification in the race, with a Dutch-manned Douglas DC-2 coming second, but instead being awarded the handicap prize for the race, putting Roscoe Turner's Boeing Model 247 into second (see pages 294-295). Another Comet, that of Owen Cathcart-Jones and Ken Waller, struggled into fourth place. They flew straight

The famed winner of the prize money and trophy for the 'MacRobertson' England to Australia air race was this D.H.88 Comet racer, G-ACSS 'Grosvenor House'.

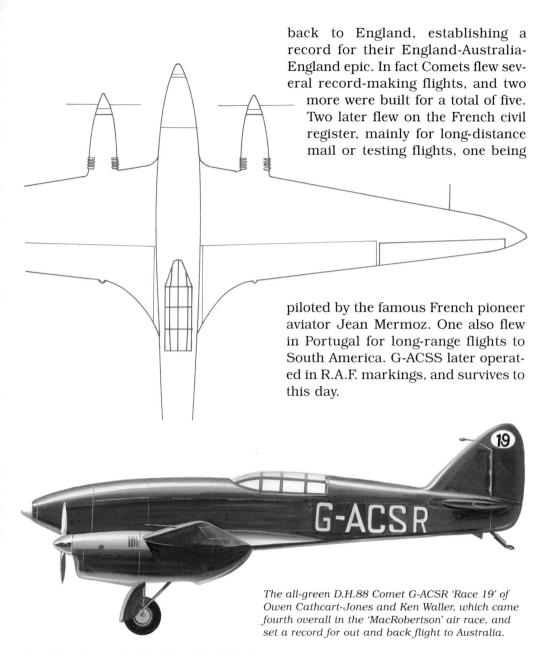

back to England, establishing a record for their England-Australia-England epic. In fact Comets flew several record-making flights, and two more were built for a total of five. Two later flew on the French civil register, mainly for long-distance mail or testing flights, one being piloted by the famous French pioneer aviator Jean Mermoz. One also flew in Portugal for long-range flights to South America. G-ACSS later operated in R.A.F. markings, and survives to this day.

The all-green D.H.88 Comet G-ACSR 'Race 19' of Owen Cathcart-Jones and Ken Waller, which came fourth overall in the 'MacRobertson' air race, and set a record for out and back flight to Australia.

Specifications – de Havilland D.H.88 Comet

Wingspan	44 ft
Length	29 ft
Maximum speed	235 mph 1,000 ft
Range	approximately 2,925 miles
Service Ceiling	19,000 ft
Engine	Two de Havilland Gipsy Six R inline piston engines, of 225 hp each
Crew	Two

223

Curtiss SBC Helldiver

The long association that Curtiss had established with naval aviation in the United States began before World War One, and throughout the 1920's and 1930's Curtiss continued to supply the U.S. Navy with a variety of front-line and training aircraft. The SBC Helldiver biplane grew out of a myriad of changing requirements and differing emphasis during which the U.S. Navy eventually altered its early 1930's fighter requirement into the need for a scout bomber able to carry out dive bombing missions. Curtiss had originally aimed a parasol-wing monoplane design at the initial Navy requirement for a carrier-based fighter as the XF12C-1, but through a somewhat tortuous process of evolution reverted to a biplane layout for the scout bomber requirement, nevertheless with a retractable undercarriage. Given the Navy designation SBC (Scout Bomber Curtiss, or Curtiss Model 77), the new aircraft eventually entered production as the SBC-3. A total of 83 were ordered in the summer of 1936 for aircraft car-

rier operation, and squadron deliveries were made the following summer. The name 'Helldiver' was given to the new aircraft, carrying on a tradition that had commenced with the Curtiss Falcon-derived F8C series (see pages 204-205). The SBC-3 was powered by a Pratt & Whitney R-1535 Twin Wasp Junior radial, but the next model, the SBC-4, featured a more powerful Wright Cyclone. 174 production models were ordered, with delivery starting in the first half of 1939. These SBC-4 served with both the U.S. Navy and Marine Corps. Some were still operational early in America's participation in World War Two, but the type was rapidly phased out of front-line service in favour of more modern aircraft – although some continued in second-line tasks. However, Marine Corps Helldivers operated for some time after the Japanese attack on Pearl Harbour, Marine Observation Squadron VMO-151 using the type for anti-submarine patrols while operating over American Samoa for a time in 1942. 50 Helldivers were

A Curtiss SBC-3 Helldiver from scouting squadron VS-5 of the U.S. Navy.

intended for delivery to France, but these did not see combat – instead, a handful were taken over by the British and used as trainers with the name Cleveland.

Specifications – Curtiss SBC-4 Helldiver

Wingspan	34 ft
Length	28 ft 1.5 in
Maximum speed	234 mph at 15,200 ft
Service Ceiling	24,000 ft
Armament	Two 0.3 in machine guns (one fixed forward-firing, one flexible mounted in rear cockpit), one 500 lb bomb
Engine	One Wright R-1820-34 Cyclone radial piston engine, of 900-950 hp
Crew	Two

Northrop Gamma

The relative success of the all-metal Northrop Alpha passenger/cargo monoplane (see pages 162-163) encouraged John K. Northrop to continue the development of all-metal commercial aircraft tailored to fast passenger/cargo operations over long distances. In January 1932 his Northrop Corp. was formed, and the first major wholly new product of this company was the Northrop Gamma. Like the Alpha it was a beautifully streamlined all-metal low-wing monoplane, and the first Gamma flew later that year. The Gamma was of metal stressed skin construction, and unlike the Alpha it seated its single pilot in a heated, enclosed cockpit. There was no provision for passengers, the type being developed specifically for fast freight and mail carrying. The Gamma 2-D model could haul a payload of 1,300 lb, in two fuselage cargo holds. Most of the Gammas that were built for American buyers were tailored to the individual specifications of the customer. The three 2-D constructed were for the airline Transcontinental and Western Air, and carried mail and cargo on the Los Angeles to Newark route. However, by the mid-1930's freight-only carriage was proving not to be as lucrative as in previous years. One of TWA's Gammas was later used for high-altitude research work. Eight Gammas were built for American customers, but export successes were also achieved, and two aircraft found their way to Britain. One of these was used as an engine test-bed by the Bristol Aeroplane Co. A modified version achieved relative export success to China, where it was used as a light bomber able to carry 1,600 lb of bombs. Some were locally produced in China. A related Northrop product was the Delta airliner. The most celebrated Gamma was that of the Polar explorer Lincoln Ellsworth. A Gamma 2-B, the aircraft concerned was able to operate as a floatplane, but for its Antarctic flying it was fitted with skis. After a number of false

Lincoln Ellsworth's Gamma for the trans-Antarctic flight could be fitted with twin floats as here, or skis.

*The Northrop Gamma 'Polar Star' that was used for the trans-Antarctic flight
was specially converted into a two-seater.
Illustration: John Batchelor © Boeing Corporation.
Lincoln Ellsworth's Gamma for the trans-Antarctic flight could be fitted with twin floats
as here, or skis.*

starts, Ellsworth and English pilot Herbert Hollick-Kenyon successfully flew over the South Pole in a genuine traverse of the Antarctic in November 1935. Their Gamma, registered NR-12269, was appropriately named 'Polar Star'.

Specifications – Northrop Gamma Model 2-D

Wingspan	47 ft 10 in
Length	31 ft 2 in
Maximum speed	224 mph at 7,000 ft
Service Ceiling	20,000 ft
Range	1,700 miles
Engine	One Wright SR-1820-F3 Cyclone radial piston engine, of 710 hp
Crew	One

De Havilland D.H.91 Albatross

First flown on 20 May 1937, the beautiful de Havilland D.H.91 Albatross was a representation of the years of progress that had taken place on the streamlining of aircraft and the advances in aerodynamics that allowed such efficient shapes to be created. The first two Albatrosses built were long-range models with range enough to cross the Atlantic Ocean. They were ordered to an Air Ministry Specification in 1936. Design work on the D.H.91 was carried out by some of the team who had designed the spectacular D.H.88 Comet racing aircraft (see pages 222-223). The Albatross was principally of wood construction, with a stressed skin covering, and its engines comprised four sets of paired de Havilland Gipsy engines. Five 22-passenger Albatross were also ordered, by Imperial Airways. These were delivered from October 1938 onwards, initially for acceptance trials, and the first entered service in November. At first they flew ad hoc route testing missions, but soon regular services were being flown, notably on the scheduled run from London-Croydon to Paris. The original two long-range Albatross also eventually entered service. In December 1938 two of the Imperial Airways aircraft flew mail to Egypt from London. Although capable, the Albatross fleet suffered a number of problems including undercarriage retraction difficulties of the electrically-actuated undercarriage. No further sales were made before World War Two commenced, the conflict finally ending the civil sales prospects of the type. Imperial Airways' aircraft were moved from Croydon to Whitchurch, Bristol, after the war started. At the same time some new routes began, one service linking in stages as far as Karachi. Routes were also opened to Ireland and Portugal, to link with long-range flying-boat services. By then B.O.A.C. had grown out of the famous airline Imperial Airways to become Britain's national flag carrier. The two long-range Albatrosses were impressed into military service during 1940, and were used on an air route to Iceland, both being written off there. The remaining aircraft were broken up in 1943.

The graceful lines of D.H.91 'Frobisher' (G-AFDI), contrast strongly with the biplane Handley Page H.P.42 in the background.

The beautifully graceful lines of the de Havilland D.H.91 Albatross are well shown in this painting of G-AEVV, one of the two long-range Albatross models.

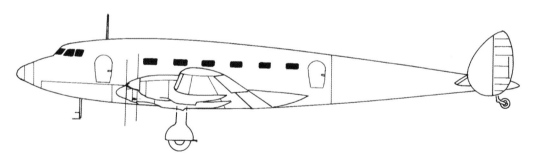

This side view shows the standard D.H.91 Albatross layout – the long-range models had fewer fuselage windows than this.

Specifications – de Havilland D.H.91 Albatross (standard model)

Wingspan	105 ft
Length	71 ft 6 in
Maximum speed	234 mph at 8,750 ft
Service Ceiling	17,900 ft
Range	1,040 miles, transatlantic capability in long-range model
Engine	Four de Havilland Gipsy Twelve inline piston engines, of 525 hp each
Accommodation	Four to five crew, up to 22 passengers

Westland-Hill Pterodactyl

The unusual tail-less series of monoplanes built by the British company Westland in the late 1920's and early 1930's was inspired by designer Geoffrey Hill (later Professor). Hill had been involved in various studies into aerodynamics, with specific aims including the achievement of safe flight without the pitfalls such as spinning that could befall conventional aircraft. He was not the first to pursue the tail-less aircraft concept; other pioneers such as John William Dunne (see pages 48-49) had also explored ideas similar to this. Hill's work included inspiration from Dunne's experiments, and like some other aviation pioneers he was intent on creating an inherently-stable aircraft. Hill began his practical work on his theories with the construction of a 'flying wing' tail-less glider which he referred to as a Pterodactyl. This flew successfully enough to lead to a 32-34 hp Bristol Cherub engine being installed in the machine. Hill later joined Westland to develop his ideas

further, and several Westland-Hill Pterodactyl aircraft ensued. The first of these was a two-seat side-by-side seating pusher flying wing powered by a single Bristol Cherub (as the IA) or 70 hp Armstrong Siddeley Genet radial (as the IB). It first flew in 1928, and operated successfully if somewhat unconventionally. It was later used for trials into the tail-less concept. The next Pterodactyl to fly was the high-wing Mk.IV, which had a distinctive enclosed cabin accommodation for three (the pilot and two passengers), and featured outer-wing elevons. The wings could be 'swept' by a hinging mechanism to allow for trim differences depending on the load carried. This curious aircraft also flew comparatively successfully from March 1931, and further proved the concepts that Hill had been working on. It led to the best known of the Pterodactyl line, the Mk.V, for which the Air Ministry Specification F3/32 was evolved. The Pterodactyl V was intended as a two-seat fighter, and

Colour drawing shows the Westland-Hill Pterodactyl V, but without a turret in the rear fuselage.

had a 600 hp Rolls-Royce Goshawk steam (evaporative)-cooled inline engine. This was mounted as a tractor installation, rather than the pusher layout of the previous Pterodactyls, and it was intended that an electrically-actuated twin-gun turret be installed in the rear of the fuselage pod. It had a sesquiplane layout with its top wing held by struts above the fuselage. Flight trials from May 1934 revealed a number of problems, and eventually the Pterodactyl V did not exhibit sufficient improvement over conventional contemporary fighters to justify further development. Other projected tail-less designs included a flying-boat and an airliner, but these were not built.

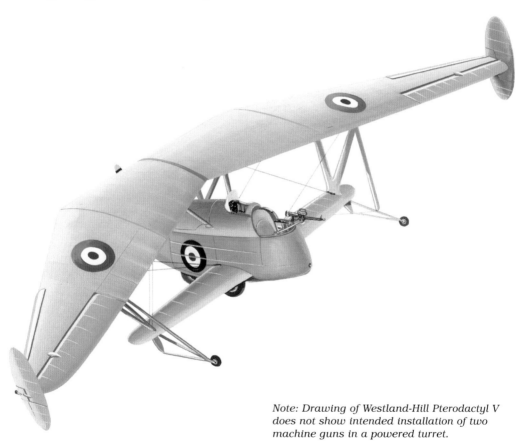

Note: Drawing of Westland-Hill Pterodactyl V does not show intended installation of two machine guns in a powered turret.

Specifications – Westland-Hill Pterodactyl Mk.V

Wingspan	46 ft 8 in
Length	21 ft
Maximum speed	190 mph at 15,000 ft
Ceiling	30,000 ft
Armament	intended installation of two machine guns in powered turret
Engine	One Rolls-Royce Goshawk inline piston engine, of 600 hp
Crew	Two

Morane-Saulnier M.S.230

Famous for its parasol-wing First World War aircraft such as the Morane-Saulnier Types L and P (see pages 58-59), the French Morane-Saulnier company persisted with the parasol-wing design layout for a variety of post-war programmes. Notable amongst these were the M.S.121 series of fighter prototypes, and the M.S.225 single-seat fighter. The latter was a stop-gap parasol-wing fighter that served into the commencement of the monoplane fighter era in the French air force, 55 being built for French air force service plus others for the French navy and export. Resembling a civil sports aircraft rather than a front-line fighter, one was used for aerobatic demonstrations, while some military examples were employed for aerobatic team displays. The trainer that prepared French pilots for this and other front-line types during the 1930's was another of Morane-Saulnier's parasol-wing aircraft, the famous M.S.230. This two-seat intermediate/transition trainer was built in considerable numbers for the French air force and navy, and saw widespread export use or licence production abroad. The initial prototype flew in early 1929, the lineage of design actually tracing back to First World War Morane-Saulnier types such as the Type AR (which itself persisted in service into the late 1920's as a primary trainer). Large orders for the M.S.230 for French air force and naval aviation resulted in several other manufacturers being brought into the construction programme. Some were built for private flying training and even private individuals, this aircraft like the M.S.225 almost resembling a civil sports aircraft rather than a serious military machine. Licenced production took place in Portugal and Belgium, and there were a number of related models and one-offs including several with different power plant options. Total production is believed to have exceeded 1,100, and the type was still in service in France as a major training type at the start of World War Two.

A classic training aircraft of the 1930's, the M.S.230 was a robust strut-braced parasol-wing monoplane that trained large numbers of pilots in France and several other countries.

A preserved M.S.230Et2 trainer, photographed in Paris some years ago. The M.S.230 was an exceptional training aircraft (Photo: John Batchelor).

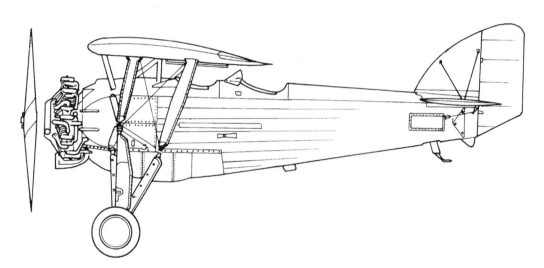

The instructor sat in the rear seat, with the pupil pilot in the forward cockpit in the M.S.230.

Specifications – Morane-Saulnier M.S.230

Wingspan	35 ft 1.25 in
Length	22 ft 10.75 in
Maximum speed	127.4 mph at sea level
Service Ceiling	16,405 ft
Maximum take-off weight	2,535 lb
Engine	One Salmson 9Ab radial piston engine, of 230 hp (other options available)
Crew	Two

Avro Tutor

The well-liked and long-lived World War One-vintage Avro 504 (see pages 82-83) continued for many years after the war in service as a basic trainer with Britain's Royal Air Force in the form of the Avro 504N. Production of the 504N continued until 1932, but by then the question of a replacement was being addressed. The aircraft that fulfilled this requirement was another Avro product, the Tutor series of basic trainers. To begin with the Avro 621 biplane, which flew in 1929, was ordered into limited production for the R.A.F. under Specification 3/30. This aircraft is sometimes called the Mongoose Trainer due to its 155 hp Armstrong Siddeley Mongoose radial engine. By a process of evolution, including the adoption of the Armstrong Siddeley Lynx radial and a tailplane alteration, the 621 design evolved into the Tutor basic trainer which was ordered into large-scale production for the R.A.F. in June

1932. It was built to Specification 25/32, an initial batch of Lynx Trainers being built before the first actual Tutor Mk.I aircraft appeared from early 1933. These aircraft equipped all the major R.A.F. basic training units in Britain, the R.A.F. College at Cranwell, and the Central Flying School, as well as serving with one basic training unit in Egypt. In addition to the standard two-seat trainer, several single-seaters were built, these being special aerobatic aircraft for a formation display team at the annual R.A.F. display at Hendon in north London. In addition, 14 float-plane Sea Tutors were built for the R.A.F. Eventually the Tutor was replaced in its basic training role by the de Havilland Tiger Moth while the monoplane Miles Magister also took over part of its role in the R.A.F. for better lead-in training for fighter pilots moving on to monoplane front-line fighters. Total production for the

Serial number K6100 was one of the later Avro Tutors that was built for the R.A.F., and it shows a typical colourful trainer yellow colour scheme.

The 'business' end of an Avro Tutor. This particular aircraft is preserved by the Shuttleworth Trust at Old Warden north of London.

R.A.F. appears to have been 414 or 417 of all types, including the original Mongoose-powered aircraft. Avro also successfully sold the Type 621 and Tutor abroad, Greece, China, Ireland, Poland, South Africa, Denmark and Canada all receiving examples, while licence production took place in Poland (as the PWS-18) and South Africa. A number of Tutors were also made for civil customers, and some spin-off models addition-ally ensued. These included the two/three seat Avro 626 trainer (Prefect in R.A.F. service, nearly 200 built, including licenced production in Portugal); and the Avro 637, an armed model for Chinese service.

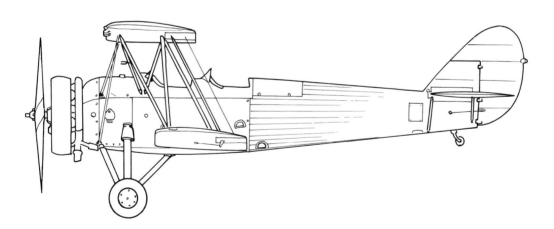

Specifications – Avro Tutor Mk.I

Wingspan	34 ft
Length	26 ft 6 in
Maximum speed	122 mph at sea level
Range	250 miles
Service Ceiling	16,200 ft
Engine	One Armstrong Siddeley Lynx IVc radial piston engine, of 215 hp
Crew	Two

Grumman F3F

One of the great names in U.S. naval aviation manufacture was that of Leroy Grumman. The original Grumman company was created in 1929, and the first aircraft that Grumman supplied to the U.S. Navy was the FF two-seat fighter and SF two-seat scout/armed reconnaissance aircraft. These biplanes had excellent performance compared to contemporary types, and the FF was the first U.S. Navy fighter to have a retractable undercarriage. As explained on Pages 250-251, the long-established biplane layout continued to have many enthusiasts even in the age of the first all-metal monoplane fighters. The FF series, plus the F2F and F3F that followed it, were some of the best biplane fighters of their time, featur-ing as they did the increasingly important innovation of a retractable undercarriage and an enclosed cock-pit. The prototype XFF-1 flew in late 1931, and the production FF-1 saw important U.S. Navy service together with its scout equivalent, the SF-1. Licence production took place in Canada as the Goblin, while other examples flew in the Spanish Civil War. Continuing and logical development saw the FF's two-seat layout transformed into a single-seat fighter configuration, leading to the F2F. The first example flew in October 1933, and this model proved to be the start of a famous line of Grumman naval fighters that continued into World War Two. The F2F-1 production model entered service in 1935, with over

The photographs show the interior of an F3F, probably an F3F-1 (Photos: Grumman Corporation).

236

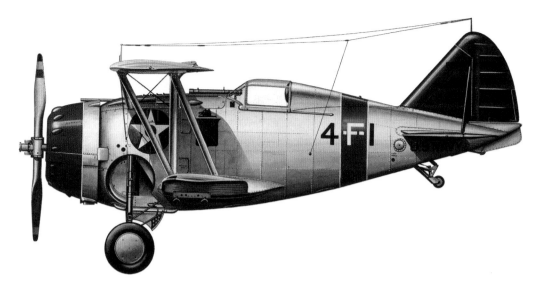

The Grumman F3F series were portly little fighters that were of excellent performance. Few retractable undercarriage biplane fighter types existed. Grumman built a related private-venture one-off, the high-performance Grumman 'Gulfhawk'.

fifty being built. Continuing development led to the F3F, with a lengthened fuselage and greater wingspan. The prototype flew in March 1935, and the first of 54 production F3F-1 entered service in 1936. This model was powered by a Pratt & Whitney Twin Wasp Junior radial, but the next production version, the F3F-2, featured a Wright Cyclone radial. 81 F3F-2s were built, and they were followed by the slightly improved F3F-3, of which 27 were constructed. The F3F also served with the U.S. Marine Corps in addition to the U.S. Navy, and at the outbreak of World War Two the F2F and F3F were the most important fighters for both of these services. Continuing development, this time with the adoption of the all-metal monoplane structure, led to the excellent Grumman F4F Wildcat fighter of the early Second World War period.

Specifications – Grumman F3F-3

Wingspan	32 ft
Length	23 ft 2 in
Maximum speed	264 mph at 6,000 ft
Service Ceiling	33,200 ft
Range	approximately 980 miles
Armament	Two fixed forward-firing 0.3 in machine guns, or one 0.3 in and one 0.5 in machine guns
Engine	One Wright R-1820-22 Cyclone radial piston engine, of 950 hp
Crew	One

Dornier Wal

In the post-World War One era the German company Dornier had successfully pioneered a series of all-metal transport aircraft that had commenced with the Dornier Komet (see pages 140-141). The company had also successfully developed a number of all-metal flying-boats and amphibians, and had built the enormous Dornier Do X as described on Pages 158-159. Additional work in the early 1920's led on to the smaller and highly-successful Dornier Do J Wal (Whale) series. The ancestor of the Wal flew in November 1922, drawing its inspiration from an all-metal flying-boat which was being developed at the end of World War One. Germany's defeat led to that design being ended. To get around post-war restrictions imposed by the victorious Allies, the Dornier company established in 1922 an Italian equivalent company to build Dornier fly-

ing-boats under licence. Production began at once and the Wal grew during the following years into a widely-used flying-boat that was developed into a number of different sub-types. It was considered for Luftwaffe service after the Nazis came to power in Germany, with the Do 15 duly serving. Other military users included Italy and Spain. In commercial service, passenger-carrying Wals operated with a variety of airlines in Europe and South America. Eight to ten passengers plus a crew of two could be carried. The most notable amongst the civil Wals were the transatlantic mail-carrying Wals of Deutsche Luft Hansa. These were used on mail flights from Germany to South America, and employed staging ships including the S.S. Westfalen for their mid-Atlantic stops. These boats acted as refuelling points for the Wals. Once replenished the aircraft could then be

The black & white photographs show Deutsche Luft Hansa Wals and the staging ship S.S. Westfalen.

catapulted from the ship to continue its journey. This novel approach to bridging the Atlantic gap worked well, and over 300 crossings are said to have been made. Wals also featured in a

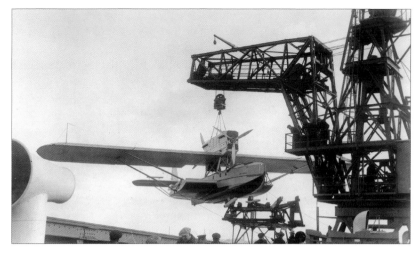

number of pioneering flights, and were used by Polar explorer Roald Amundsen in an attempt to reach the North Pole by air. More successful was the attempt by Wolfgang von Gronau for a transatlantic flight in August 1930 – the first ever such east to west North Atlantic crossing by a flying-boat. He repeated the feat in 1931 in another Wal. Approximately 300 Wals in total were built. A later development of the Wal was the four-engined (two in tandem) Do R Super Wal.

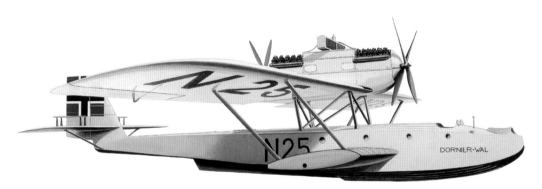

Two Dornier Wals were used by Norwegian Polar Explorer Roald Amundsen in an unsuccessful attempt to reach the North Pole by air.

Specifications – Dornier Do J Wal (von Gronau transatlantic Wal)

Wingspan	76 ft 1.5 in
Length	59 ft 8.5 in
Maximum speed	140 mph at sea level
Service Ceiling	9,842.5 ft
Range	1,367 miles plus
Engine	Two BMW VI inline piston engines, of 600 hp each
Accommodation	Two crew, up to eight or ten passengers in passenger-carrying models

Piper Cub

Definitely a contender for the title of best-loved and most widely-used light aircraft of all time, the ubiquitous Piper Cub family can trace its origins back to the early 1930's, and yet many of this type are still flying today. The Cub originated with the American Taylor company of the Taylor brothers, the original Taylor E-2 Cub of 1930-1931 being the first of the line. A succession of Taylor Cubs ensued, before the rights to the design passed to the Taylor brothers' secretary and treasurer William T. Piper. Piper's own company was formed in 1937, and the name Piper ever since has been associated with excellence in light aircraft, the first of many Piper types being the Cub itself. The original Piper Cub was the J-3 of 1937, built in a number of models

mainly relating to the different engines that could be fitted. The best known of these is the J-3C, powered by a Continental flat-four piston engine. Featuring tandem seating for two, the Cub was a true lightweight of mixed construction. The fuselage was of welded steel tube, fabric covered, the wings of metal ribs with wooden spars and fabric covering. The whole aircraft was simple to build, fly and maintain, and was at once a tremendous success. Many sources claim that 737 were built in the first year of manufacture alone. Military interest resulted in evaluation during 1941 for the artillery-spotting role. The Cub proved to be highly suitable for this and other military tasks, and was ordered in large quantities mainly for the U.S. Army/U.S. Army Air Force,

The Piper Cub is arguably the world's best-known light aircraft. Many production aircraft for civil customers were coloured yellow, with the Cub motif on the vertical tail. Once the preserve of the rich, flying was brought to a far wider audience in the United States by this aircraft.

A Continental-powered Cub of the U.S. Army.
Well over five thousand Cubs of various types were purchased for the U.S. military.

and smaller numbers were also used by the U.S. Navy. The original mass-produced military model was the O-59 series. A change of designation resulted in the celebrated L-4 line of liaison and artillery spotter aircraft, including new-build and impressed (requisitioned) ex-civil examples. Total production for the U.S. military reached over 5,500. Some of the impressed aircraft were of the developed J-4 type Cub. An un-powered, glider training derivative also existed as the TG-8. Cubs proved invaluable during World War Two, and post-war Cubs were used by air arms around the world. Further development led to

the uprated post-war PA-18 Super Cub. Military Super Cubs were the L-18 and L-21, and Piper's own production of the Super Cub only ceased in the early 1980's.

Specifications – Piper J-3C-40 Cub

Wingspan	35 ft 2.5 in
Length	22 ft 3 in
Maximum speed	92 mph at sea level
Service Ceiling	12,000 ft
Range	260 miles
Engine	One Continental A-40-4 flat-four piston engine, of 40 hp (many other options available)
Accommodation	One pilot, one passenger

241

Dewoitine D.500 Series

At the time of its creation the Dewoitine D.500 was a revolutionary fighter, and it combined a number of old with some significant new features. New was the streamlined low-wing all-metal monoplane configuration with a powerful engine containing in some models an engine-mounted cannon firing through the propeller hub. Old features included the fixed undercarriage and open cockpit. Although the D.500 was in the vanguard of forward-looking fighter design when it first flew, such was the very fast pace of fighter development during the 1930's that it was obsolete by the time that the final production examples of the developed D.510 entered service. Designed in response to a number of French military specifications for a modern fighter replacement for Nieuport biplane fighters then in service, the prototype D.500 flew on 18 June 1932. There were many contenders to meet the French requirements, but the D.500 beat them all and was ordered into production in November 1933. Initial orders were for the D.500 fitted with an Hispano-Suiza 12Xbrs inline engine of 690 hp and twin synchronised machine guns in the fuselage plus (later) two wing-mounted machine guns; and the rather better D.501 with improvements including an engine-mounted cannon firing through the propeller hub. There are several differing views of production figures, but it appears that total production of the D.500/D.501 series by several French factories for the French air force was approximately 271 examples. The first aircraft entered service in June/July 1935, and these were amongst the first if not the first cannon-armed single-seat monoplane fighters in service anywhere in the world. Three were ordered by Venezuela, and Lithuania eventually received 14. A

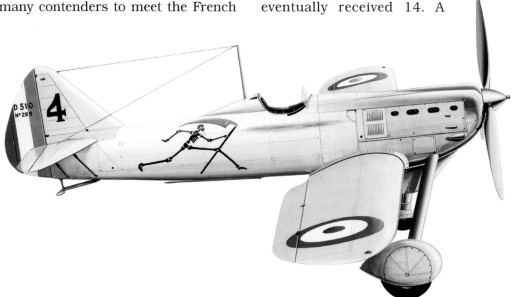

The Dewoitine D.510 was already getting behind the times when it entered service with the French air force. This example bears the markings of the French fighter unit GC II/1.

A Dewoitine D.500 of the French air force's Groupe de Chasse I/4 (1ère Escadrille). A remarkable fighter when it first flew, the D.500 was very quickly overtaken by fighter development in several other countries.

developed model was the D.510, with a more powerful Hispano-Suiza 12Ycrs inline engine of 860 hp, an engine-mounted cannon also being fitted to this model. The first prototype flew in August 1934. The new engine gave the D.510 marginally better performance over the previous models, and with other alterations the D.510 was ordered into production for the French air force, deliveries beginning in November 1936 by which time the design was seriously lagging behind fighter development in other countries. Production for the French air force by several manufac-

turers (including under the newly-nationalised aviation industry in France) totalled some 112 examples. Of these, 24 were diverted to China. A cancelled Turkish order yielded one-off examples to Britain and Soviet Russia for trials work, two went to Japan and two were delivered to Republican forces during the Spanish Civil War. Some D.510 were still in French service at the time of the German invasion of France in May 1940, mainly in second-line or local defence duties, or in the French overseas territories.

Specifications – Dewoitine D.501

Wingspan	39 ft 8 in
Length	24 ft 9.5 in
Maximum speed	228 mph at 16,405 ft
Service Ceiling	33,465 ft
Range	540.6 miles
Armament	One 0.787 in cannon engine-mounted, two fixed forward-firing wing-mounted 0.295 in machine guns
Engine	One Hispano-Suiza 12Xcrs (Type 76) inline piston engine, of 690 hp
Crew	One

De Havilland D.H.89 Dragon Rapide

One of the best-known and best-loved light transport aircraft of the inter-war and World War Two era, the D.H.89 Dragon Rapide was yet another superb product from the prolific British de Havilland company. The Dragon Rapide owed its parentage to the earlier D.H.84 Dragon, which had been developed to meet the requirement of a small British airline for a light transport to fly air services from England to France. The Dragon was comparatively successful, but further development led to the superlative Dragon Rapide. The Dragon Rapide owed some of its parentage to the larger four-engined D.H.86 airliner, which first flew in January 1934. The first flight of the initial D.H.89 was made on 17 April 1934, and it initially bore the name Dragon Six. Deliveries began later in 1934, and the subsequent years saw large-scale production and the appearance of a small number of specific models. The basic seating was for six to eight passengers, but an armed military derivative was also developed. This model lost out in a competition for a general reconnaissance and coastal patrol aircraft for Royal Air Force service, but Lithuania and Spain purchased small numbers of a developed armed model. However, in later years the Dragon Rapide saw much military service in Britain. Initial deliveries were made before World War Two for wireless (radio) training, but the start of the war resulted in large orders for both navigation and wireless trainers (named Dominie Mk.I), and communications (Dominie Mk.II). Many civil-operated Rapides were also impressed (requisitioned) for military service. Over 500 are believed to have been built to military contracts in this way, and these two types were widely operated by the R.A.F., with 65 being employed by the Royal Navy. Small numbers were used by the U.S. Army Air Force in Britain. Post-war, some retired military aircraft were supplied to other countries, notably Belgium, while many were made available to civil operators. This began a second golden age for the aircraft in

One of the chief users of the Dragon Rapide post-World War Two was British European Airways. This airline operated the type into the 1960's.

When the King's Flight was formed to give Britain's Royal Family a yet more luxurious way of getting around, amongst the first aircraft were Dragon Rapides. The photograph shows a preserved Dragon Rapide painted specially as one of the first King's Flight aircraft (Photo: John Batchelor).

civil use, with large operators like British European Airways (B.E.A.) and many smaller companies using the Dragon Rapide. Production eventually ceased in 1945 (although two were put together in 1947 from spares), manufacture having been shared between de Havilland and Brush Coachworks. In total 728 were built, and a number of these aircraft are still flying, some earning their keep through joy-riding and sight-seeing.

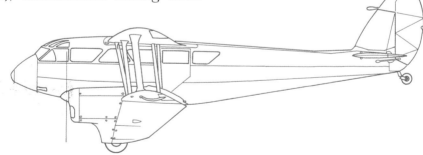

Specifications – De Havilland D.H.89 Dragon Rapide

Wingspan	48 ft
Length	34 ft 6 in
Maximum speed	165 mph at 1,000 ft
Service Ceiling	19,350 ft
Range	approximately 520 miles
Engine	Two de Havilland Gipsy Six inline piston engines, of 205 hp each
Accommodation	One pilot, normally six to eight passengers

Boeing P-26

A number of fighter designs appeared during the first half of the 1930's that included revolutionary features that pointed to the future, while nevertheless retaining aspects that were a throwback to the increasingly obsolete biplane fighters of the late 1920's and early 1930's. One such aircraft was the Boeing P-26, which, like the Dewoitine D.500 series (see pages 242-243), was a curious mixture of old and new. Its all-metal, monoplane structure pointed to the future, but its wire-braced wing, spatted fixed undercarriage and open cockpit were definitely not features of future fighter design. The American Boeing company was a leading exponent in the early 1930's of all-metal, monoplane aircraft, and created amongst others the Y1B-9 bomber for the U.S. Army Air Corps, and the Boeing Model 247 airliner (see pages 294-295). Also produced by Boeing at that time was a small fighter prototype which included some of these advanced features and known initially by the company

designation XP-936 (Model 248). The first of three 'prototype' aircraft flew on 20 March 1932. All three were partly financed and equipped by the Army Air Corps, and they eventually took on the official designation P-26. U.S.A.A.C. interest in the type resulted in a contract in January 1933 for 111 production aircraft designated P-26A (Model 266). This order was later increased to 136 examples. Several improvements were incorporated during production, including a taller headrest to avoid pilot injury in the event of the aircraft rolling over, a radio and floatation gear. Deliveries of production aircraft began in December 1933 and the type entered service the following year – making it one of the first all-metal production monoplane fighters in service anywhere in the world. Initially based in the continental United States, U.S.A.A.C. P-26As were later based as far afield as Panama and Hawaii – the last in serv-

The P-26A was generally named 'Peashooter', and was the U.S.A.A.C.'s first monoplane fighter.

A classic photograph from the era when monoplane fighters were just starting to enter service, a neat formation of 34th Pursuit Squadron P-26A aircraft displays the skill of their pilots (Photo: Boeing Corporation).

ice being relinquished as late as 1942. Of the 25 final production aircraft, two were completed as P-26B with a fuel-injected Wasp radial engine, the remaining aircraft being to an improved standard and called P-26C. An export version, the Model 281, was produced with split landing flaps, which were retrospectively fitted to some U.S.-operated aircraft. China received 11 export aircraft, eventually flying these against Japanese forces. One was exported to Spain. Later, several former U.S.-operated aircraft were supplied to the Philippines, some of these flying against Japanese forces when Japan invaded the Philippines late in 1941. Several P-26s also went to Guatemala, which retained them until after World War Two.

Specifications – Boeing P-26A

Wingspan	27 ft 11.5 in
Length	23 ft 10 in
Maximum speed	234 mph at 6,000 ft
Service Ceiling	27,400 ft
Range	635 miles
Armament	Two fixed forward-firing 0.3 in machine guns, or one 0.3 in and one 0.5 in, up to 200 lb of bombs
Engine	One Pratt & Whitney R-1340-27 Wasp radial piston engine, of 600 hp
Crew	One

Polikarpov I-15

While most of the world's major air forces were starting to adopt monoplane fighters as the 1930's wore on, the Soviet Union persisted with several biplane fighter designs. Thus at the start of World War Two the U.S.S.R. had various Polikarpov biplane fighters in service, mainly for ground-attack roles. The I-15, developed from the earlier I-5 biplane fighter of 1930, was the brainchild of Soviet designer Nikolay Polikarpov. The original I-15, referred to as the TsKB-3, flew in late 1933. Manufacture of initial I-15 production models began in 1934, early aircraft having the American Wright Cyclone radial engine although many were powered by the Russian-built M-22 radial. The I-15 featured a cantilever fixed main undercarriage (which could also be fitted with skis), and a prominent 'gull-wing' upper wing whose central portion connected with the fuselage. Further development led to the I-15bis, some-times called the I-152, which featured a conventional straight upper wing and a more powerful M-25V radial engine. Additional design work led to the I-153, which reverted to the upper 'gull-wing' and had a retractable undercarriage. I-15 models flew for the Republican forces during the Spanish Civil War, where they were nicknamed 'Chato'. Russian-operated Polikarpovs were in action against the Japanese over Manchuria before the start of World War Two, and during the 1939-1940 Winter War against Finland. Some captured examples were used by the Finns against Russian forces. A number were also supplied to China. Later, the I-153 in particular saw action during the initial stages of the German attack on the Soviet Union from June 1941.

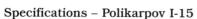

Polikarpov I-153

Specifications – Polikarpov I-15

Wingspan	31 ft 11.75 in
Length	20 ft 0.15 in
Maximum speed	218 mph at 9,843 ft
Service Ceiling	24,672 ft
Armament	Two or four 0.3 in machine guns, provision on some aircraft for small bombs or rockets
Engine	One M-22 radial piston engine, of 480 hp
Crew	One

Junkers Ju 86

The Junkers Ju 86 was designed in 1934 with the purpose of creating a new airliner for Deutsche Luft Hansa, but also with the potential of being used as a bomber. The first prototype flew in late 1934, and Junkers' designers managed to create an aircraft that was useful if unspectacular in both its intended roles. Initial production Ju 86A bombers for the Luftwaffe were delivered during 1936. These were powered by two Junkers Jumo diesel engines. Several more powerful Ju 86D-model examples served with the Condor Legion during the Spanish Civil War. A complete power plant change came about with the Ju 86E, which was powered by two BMW 132 radial piston engines. The last major conventional bomber production model was the Ju 86G, and export orders for the Ju 86K series were gained from a number of countries, including Sweden and South Africa – licenced production also took place in Sweden. In Luftwaffe service the rather better Heinkel He 111 and Dornier Do 17 series had largely taken on the Ju 86's bomber role by the start of World War Two. However, the Ju 86 was later used as a high-altitude bomber and particularly a reconnaissance aircraft. The Ju 86P-1 was the former, the Ju 86P-2 the latter. These were specially-converted Ju 86D models with increased wingspan, and a shortened nose with pressurised crew compartment. They served usefully into 1942, when high-flying Allied aircraft were increasingly able to catch them. A further high-altitude model, the Ju 86R also existed, several being converted from Ju 86P with even longer span wings of over 104 feet.

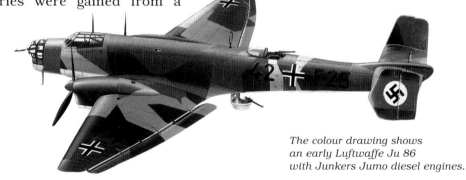

The colour drawing shows an early Luftwaffe Ju 86 with Junkers Jumo diesel engines.

Specifications – Junkers Ju 86D-1

Wingspan	73 ft 9.75 in
Length	58 ft 7.5 in
Maximum speed	202 mph at 9,843 ft
Service Ceiling	19,357 ft
Range	932 miles
Armament	Three 0.312 in machine guns, bomb load of up to 1,764 lb
Engine	Two Junkers Jumo 205C-series diesel engines, of 600 hp each
Crew	Four

Curtiss Hawk III

A well-known family of biplane fighters of the 1920's and early 1930's was the Curtiss Hawk/Goshawk series. They were built in a wide variety of models for the U.S. Army and Navy, as well as a number of export customers around the world. The basic Hawk series (Curtiss Model 34) of the mid-1920's (including the very first model in the U.S. Army's new Pursuit (fighter) category, the P-1) had gained considerable fame and had seen (for those days) significant production. Continuing development led to the Hawk II series (Curtiss Model 35). All these aircraft were biplane, fixed-undercarriage single-seat fighters which for their day were comparatively advanced and capable warplanes. However, by the early 1930's the days of the biplane fighter were starting to be numbered. Monoplanes were beginning to appear more regularly on the drawing boards of an increasing number of aircraft companies around the world. Nevertheless,

the biplane fighter continued to have its exponents, at least until the advanced monoplane fighters of the mid-1930's had had the opportunity to prove their considerable leap forward in performance and capability compared to the biplane fighters. At the American Curtiss company, plans were hatched to wring some more life out of the biplane fighter design by giving it a retractable undercarriage. Already in production was the Curtiss F11C-2 (later BFC-2) series for the U.S. Navy, who had ordered 28 in October 1932. Taking one of these fixed undercarriage aircraft, Curtiss considerably modified it with a deepened lower fuselage and an undercarriage that retracted inwards and upwards into the lower fuselage. The undercarriage had a manual retraction mechanism, and a semi-enclosed cockpit layout was also introduced compared to the basically open cockpit of most of the earlier Hawks. The resulting retractable undercarriage

The only U.S. Navy squadron to fly the Curtiss BF2C-1 (F11C-3) was VB-5B on board the aircraft carrier U.S.S. Ranger in 1934/1935. This was at the height of the wonderfully colourful inter-war period of U.S. Naval aviation.

An evocative photograph of three BF2C-1 from VB-5B. The name Goshawk is sometimes associated with these U.S. Navy bomber/fighter retractable undercarriage biplanes (Photo: U.S. Navy).

fighter, named the XF11C-3, gained a U.S. Navy order in February 1934 for 27 production aircraft. Reflecting a changed thinking about the role of these aircraft, their F11C-3 name was altered to the bomber/fighter BF2C-1 (Model 67A) designation. These aircraft duly served with the U.S. Navy's VB-5B bombing squadron from late 1934, but they were not well-liked and the type was withdrawn after about one year in service. They were Curtiss' last-ever naval fighters for the U.S. Navy. However, the retractable under-carriage fighter gained modest export successes as the Hawk III. China ordered 60, for local assembly in Hangchow, and more may well have been supplied. The Chinese Hawks saw considerable action during the Sino-Japanese war from 1937. Siam (Thailand) ordered 12, plus others assembled locally. They fought against the invading Japanese from December 1941. Argentina ordered 10 during 1936, plus the sole Hawk IV with a fully enclosed cockpit.

Specifications – Curtiss BF2C-1

Wingspan	31 ft 5 in
Length	23 ft 5 in
Maximum speed	240 mph at 11,500 ft
Service Ceiling	25,800 ft
Armament	Two or four 0.3 in machine guns, provision for up to four 116 lb bombs
Engine	One Wright R-1820-04 Cyclone radial piston engine, of 700 hp
Crew	One

Hawker Fury

In a period when new bomber types sometimes proved to have better performance than existing fighters, thus accelerating new fighter design, the Hawker Hart (see pages 256-257) light bomber was a major stimulant to the development of higher performance fighters for the Royal Air Force. The Hawker company (which had created the Hart) had already been working on single-seat fighter designs from the mid to late 1920's. This coincided with the development of a new powerful inline engine by the famous Rolls-Royce company, the predecessor of the generally successful Kestrel engine. By a process of evolution, Hawker's design work led to the Hawker Hornet of 1929, which led directly to the classic Hawker Fury. The Hornet displayed sufficient good performance and handling during official trials that Specification 13/30 was written to

describe a production aircraft based on the Hornet layout. Named Fury, the production aircraft became one of the best-known British fighters of the inter-war period. No prototype as such was built, the first three aircraft of the initial production batch of 21 ordered in August 1930 acting as initial development aircraft. In May 1931 the first Royal Air Force Fury unit, No.43 Squadron, received its first aircraft, and the Fury went on to equip several home-based fighter squadrons. Approximately 118 Fury Mk.I were built for the R.A.F., the type being the first R.A.F. fighter to exceed 200 mph in level flight. A number of export aircraft were built for several customers, notably Yugoslavia, while Persian aircraft were powered by American Pratt & Whitney Hornet radial engines. Further development led to the Intermediate Fury and the High Speed Fury (first flight May 1933), two trials aircraft that led the way to an improved production model, the Fury Mk.II.

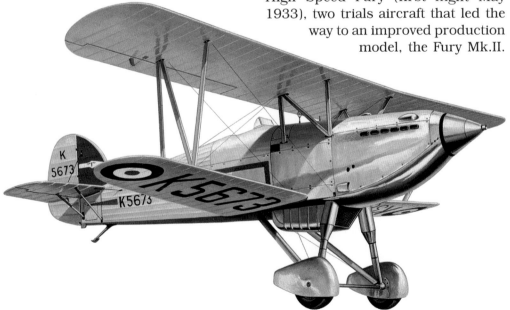

The Hawker Fury was one of the classic British fighters of the inter-war era, with sleek and purposeful lines, although it never flew in combat with the R.A.F. in Europe.

The Hawker High Speed Fury was K3586, and it pioneered some of the features later incorporated on the Fury Mk.II for the R.A.F. (Photo: Hawker Siddeley).

Specification 6/35 was issued to cover production of 23 of this type for the R.A.F., with neat main wheel spats and an uprated Kestrel engine, and they were followed by 75 more. They entered R.A.F. service in numbers during early 1937. The Fury Mk.II was also exported, but the days of biplane fighters were numbered by that time and the Fury had been relegated to training duties in Britain by the early part of World War Two.

Experimental Rolls-Royce engine installation on what appears to be the Hawker High Speed Fury. Note the metal fuselage structure and cabane strut attachment arrangement (Photo: John Batchelor).

Specifications – Hawker Fury Mk.I

Wingspan	30 ft
Length	26 ft 8 in
Maximum speed	207 mph at 14,000 ft
Service Ceiling	28,000 ft
Range	approximately 305 miles
Armament	Two fixed forward-firing 0.303 in machine guns; small bombs if required below lower wings
Engine	One Rolls-Royce Kestrel IIS inline piston engine, of 525 hp
Crew	One

Percival Mew Gull

Edgar W. Percival was an Australian aviation designer, businessman and pilot who had been an aviator during World War One. In 1932 he established the Percival Aircraft Co. in Britain, and a series of light aircraft for private owners ensued. These were all low-wing monoplanes with cantilever wing construction, usually of wood, and they gained comparatively successful sales in the mid to late 1930's. Named Gull, Gull Four, Gull Six, and Vega Gull, some of these were additionally used for long-distance flying. Percival also created a limited series of single-seat racing aircraft called the Mew Gull, and these gained some excellent successes in several important European air races. The original Model E.1 Mew Gull was of all-wood construction, and resembled some of the small racing aircraft that existed in the United States at that time. It first flew in March 1934, but crashed during an air race in France.

In 1935 a completely revised Mew Gull type was unveiled, the Model E.2, and the first aircraft achieved sev-eral good results in the 1935 air racing season. Unfortunately it failed to win the prestigious King's Cup, despite gaining the fastest speeds, due to the event's somewhat archaic handicap rules. Three further Mew Gulls were built in 1936, and one of these managed to finish second to a German Messerschmitt Bf 109 in the Circuit of the Alps race in Switzerland during July 1937. They were followed by a special Mew Gull for Percival himself, the Model E.3H, registered G-AFAA. This aircraft was of reduced wingspan and featured a number of other refinements over the previous aircraft. It achieved a top speed of 252 mph (405.5 km/h) in the 1937 King's Cup air race, which was won on handicap by another of the Mew Gulls that had entered. Mew Gulls were successful in several other important races, including a win in the 1938 King's Cup by Alex Henshaw. Flying the specially-modified G-AEXF, Henshaw also

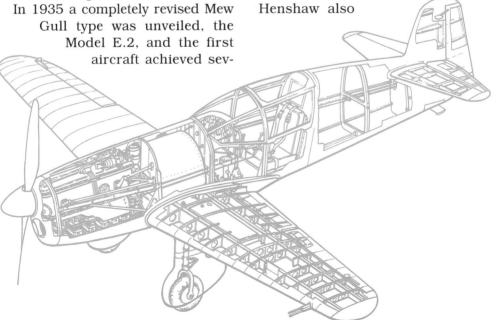

G-AFAA was the special Mew Gull E.3H that was built for Edgar Percival himself to race. It is shown in the exact color scheme in which it was flown in the 1937 King's Cup air race. It achieved a speed of 252 mph (405.5 km/h) during the event, an excellent speed for a private aircraft at that time.

accomplished in February 1939 a headline-making flight. With extra fuel tanks installed and a Gipsy Six Series II engine, the Mew Gull flew from southeastern England on a round trip in stages to Cape Town in present-day South Africa and back. This 12,000 miles (19,312 km) adventure was achieved in just over four days ten hours. Only one Mew Gull, G-AEXF, survived World War Two, but it managed to win a King's Cup race in the 1950's.

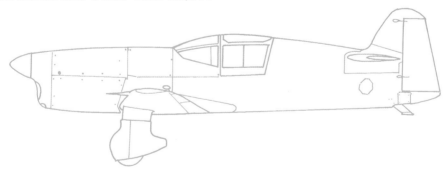

Specifications – Percival Mew Gull Model E.3H

Wingspan	22 ft 9 in
Length	20 ft 3 in
Maximum speed	approximately 252 mph at sea level
Maximum take-off weight	2,125 lb
Engine	One de Havilland Gipsy Six Series II inline piston engine, of 205 hp
Crew	One

Hawker Hart

The Hawker Hart was one of several inter-war bomber types that caused a sensation on its entry into service, by being faster than contemporary fighters in its own armed services. One result of this was the creation by Hawker of the Fury fighter for the Royal Air Force (see pages 252-253), while the Hart became a significant light day bomber and trainer that was also the basis of a number of specific derivatives. Developed to the far-sighted Air Ministry Specification 12/26 for a light day bomber with a maximum speed of some 160 mph, the Hart combined a well-refined and clean biplane design layout with a potentially excellent new engine from Rolls-Royce which ultimately became the Kestrel. The prototype Hart flew in June 1928, and Specification 9/29 covered the manufacture of an initial batch of 15 Hart Mk.I aircraft. This was the start of a production life that eventually led to just over 1,000 examples being built by several man-

ufacturers in a number of distinct versions – an amazing total for the austerity of the early 1930's. The first Hart bombers were delivered to the R.A.F.'s No.33 Squadron in January 1930, where they replaced Hawker Horsleys, and the Hart became the R.A.F.'s standard light bomber of the early to mid-1930's. A trainer version, the dual-control Hart Trainer was also built. So good was the Hart's performance that until newer fighters entered service, only another Hart could catch a Hart, leading to a handful of Hart Two-Seat Fighters being produced. This modification was developed into a distinct two-seat fighter derivative, the R.A.F.'s Hawker Demon. A Hart model for hot and high operations over the Northwest Frontier of India also existed, and separate spin-offs apart from the Demon included the Osprey naval fleet spotter/reconnaissance aircraft, the Audax army co-operation aircraft, the Hardy empire policing aircraft,

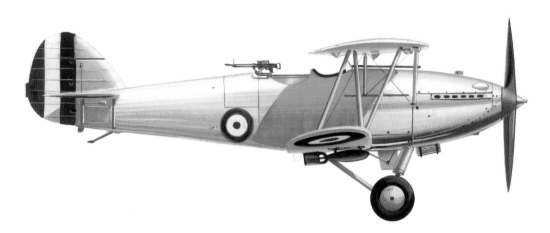

The classic lines of the R.A.F.'s Hawker Hart. Although phased out of front-line R.A.F. service in Europe by World War Two, the Hart gave valuable service to South African and particularly Swedish forces in the early part of the conflict.

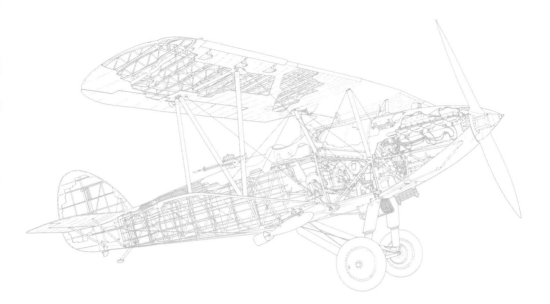

and the Hartbees tropical close-support derivative for South African service. A developed model was the Hawker Hind, which was an interim type between the Hart and the future advanced monoplane Bristol Blenheim and Fairey Battle bombers of the late 1930's/early 1940's. Licenced production of 42 Harts took place in Sweden, these being powered by locally-produced Bristol Pegasus radial engines and seeing action against Soviet forces in the Winter War of 1939-1940.

Specifications – Hawker Hart Mk.I

Wingspan	37 ft 3 in
Length	29 ft 4 in
Maximum speed	184 mph at 5,000 ft
Endurance	approximately 2 hr 45 min
Range	470 miles
Service Ceiling	21,350 ft
Armament	Two 0.303 in machine guns (one fixed forward-firing, one flexible ring-mounted), up to some 520 lb of bombs
Engine	One Rolls-Royce Kestrel IB inline piston engine, of 525 hp (or Kestrel XDR of 510 hp)
Crew	Two

Heinkel He 51

Development work on a number of biplane fighter designs by the German Heinkel company commenced during the mid-1920's with the He 23, and evolved through the He 37 and He 43 types to the He 49, which was the immediate forerunner of the famous He 51. Ostensibly a civil training biplane, the He 49 had a performance comparable with front-line combat aircraft of some countries at that time at around 200 mph. It first flew in November 1932, and development with several He 49 examples led to the first flight of the He 51 in May 1933. This came at a time when the Nazi party had recently taken power in Germany, and the He 51 was destined to become Nazi Germany's first major front-line fighter. Deliveries of the initial He 51A-1 were made to Germany's armed forces in 1934, and when the previously clandestine Luftwaffe (German air force) was officially announced in March 1935 the He 51A was commencing increasingly wide-

spread service. The first major unit to operate the He 51A-1 initial production model was fighter wing JG 132 'Richthofen', named for the famous World War One German fighter ace. Production commenced in early 1936 of the He 51B-1. The He 51B series was a marginally improved model, which also included the floatplane He 51B-2 version. The He 51B-2 could be catapult-launched from warships, but some were shore-based for coastal defence. At least one example was built of the He 51D floatplane with altered, two-bay (two sets of interplane struts) wings, which were pioneered on the He 51B-3. The final major production series was the He 51C. Many of these, fitted with bomb racks, were fully involved in combat in the Spanish Civil War, either with the German-manned Condor Legion or the Spanish Nationalist forces of General Franco. They were found to be lacking when pitted in aerial combat against Spanish Republican Polikarpov I-15 fighters

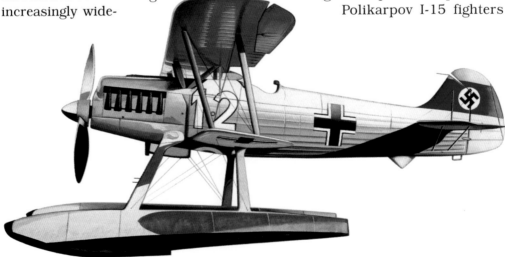

The He 51B-2 was the front-line floatplane version of the basic Heinkel He 51 design, illustrated here by an aircraft of the Luftwaffe's Küstenjagdgruppe 136 at Kiel-Holtenau in late 1936.

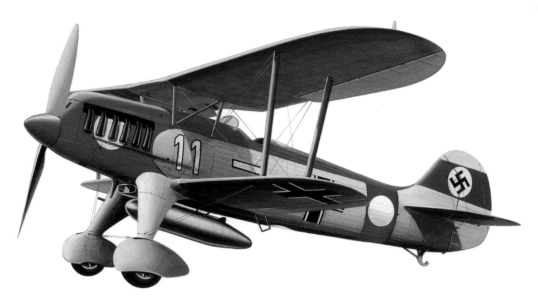

The He 51A-1 was the first major front-line version of the Heinkel He 51 fighter, shown in this beautiful painting by a colourful example from Jagdgeschwader (JG) 132 'Richthofen' of the Luftwaffe in 1936.

(see pages 248), and were relegated mainly to ground attack duties as the war progressed. In Luftwaffe front-line service the He 51 was replaced in 1937/1938 in some cases by the superb monoplane Messerschmitt Bf 109. Some 700 were built by several manufacturers, and the type later served as a trainer well into World War Two.

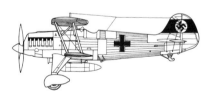

The Heinkel He 51 was one of Germany's last major biplane fighters, and was of all-metal structure covered with fabric. A rugged if largely unspectacular front-line type, it saw much action in the Spanish Civil War.

Specifications – Heinkel He 51B-1

Wingspan	36 ft 1 in
Length	27 ft 6.75 in
Maximum speed	205 mph at sea level
Service Ceiling	25,262 ft
Range	354 miles
Armament	Two fixed forward-firing 0.312 in machine guns
Engine	One BMW VI inline piston engine, of approximately 750 hp
Crew	One

Avia B-534

One of the most important products of the aviation industry in Czechoslovakia between the two world wars, the Avia B-534 was arguably the best fighter to be produced in Central and Eastern Europe during that period. It was the culmination of a design process that had resulted in a number of fighter designs from the Avia company for the Czechoslovak armed forces. The first prototype flew in May 1933, and initial deliveries to the Czech air force commenced in 1935. As originally developed, the B-534 featured an open cockpit, and the first three production series of the type retained this feature. The fourth production series introduced a neat enclosed cockpit, and wheel spats were fitted to later production aircraft. The first series featured two wing-mounted machine guns, but all subsequent production aircraft carried their machine gun armament in the fuselage. This consisted of four fuselage side mounted weapons, but the Bk-534 series had two fuselage side guns, plus a machine gun engine-mounted to fire through the propeller hub. Serial numbers were allocated for the manufacture of some 445 B-534, with 120 serial number allocations for the Bk-534 although not all of these may have been built. The B-534 performed very well in its major peacetime test, when it was the best-performing biplane at the Zurich international aviation meeting in 1937, and only slightly slower than the German Messerschmitt Bf 109 monoplane fighters also present. Unfortunately the B-534 was never allowed to prove itself in combat, due to the ludicrous policy of appeasement pursued by Britain and France which handed Czechoslovakia to Nazi Germany at the Munich 'agreement' in 1938. Czech B-534s were subsequently allocated by Germany to the newly-created Slovak state, and to Bulgaria. Some were used by Germany's Luftwaffe for training, a neat 'teardrop' enclosed cockpit cover being fitted to several of the open cockpit earlier production examples. Slovak and Bulgarian B-534s saw some limited action during World War Two, and a handful flew in the Slovak National Uprising in 1944.

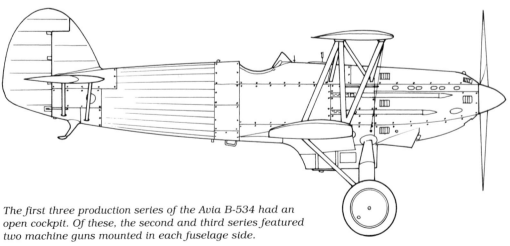

The first three production series of the Avia B-534 had an open cockpit. Of these, the second and third series featured two machine guns mounted in each fuselage side.

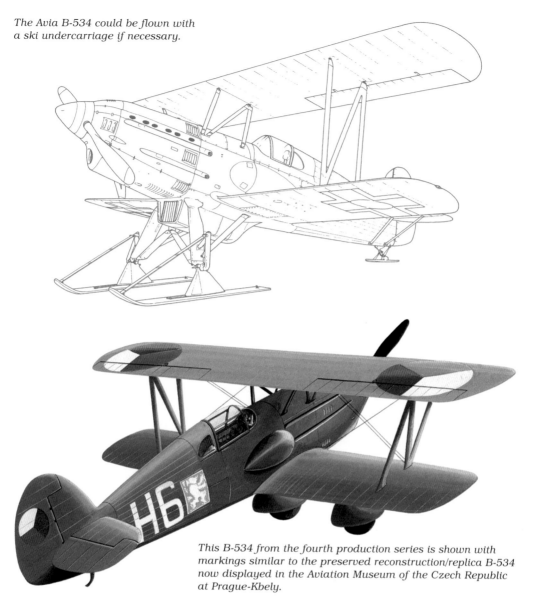

The Avia B-534 could be flown with a ski undercarriage if necessary.

This B-534 from the fourth production series is shown with markings similar to the preserved reconstruction/replica B-534 now displayed in the Aviation Museum of the Czech Republic at Prague-Kbely.

Specifications – Avia B-534 (Fourth Series)

Wingspan	30 ft 10 in
Length	26 ft 7 in
Maximum speed	236 mph at 14,764 ft
Service Ceiling	34,777 ft
Range	373 miles
Armament	Four fixed forward-firing 0.3 in machine guns, provision for small bombs under wings
Engine	One Avia (licence-built Hispano-Suiza) HS 12Ydrs inline piston engine, of 850 hp
Crew	One

Mitsubishi A5M

Created to meet a specification from the Japanese naval aviation in 1934 for a new-generation single-seat land-based fighter to replace increasingly obsolete biplanes, the Mitsubishi A5M represented a huge leap forward when it entered service. A neat low-wing all-metal flush-riveted mono-plane with an inverted gull wing, the prototype looked particularly sleek. However, the gull wing configuration was changed for production aircraft to a conventional low-set monoplane wing with dihedral from the wing roots. The prototype flew in February 1935, and easily met the design requirement for a maximum speed of 217 mph. Though envisaged as a landplane, the need for a carrier-based model led to the A5M being used for Japanese aircraft carrier operations fitted with an arrester hook. The type was ordered into pro-duction as the Navy Type 96 Carrier Fighter Model 1 (A5M1). Several specific further production models followed, all powered by versions of the Nakajima Kotobuki radial engine based on the British Bristol Jupiter engine. In addition to single-seat fighter models, there was also an A5M4-K two-seat trainer version of the major A5M4 production series. The A5M quickly became an important fighter in the Sino-Japanese war during 1937. Significant numbers were still in service at the time of the Japanese attack on Pearl Harbour in December 1941. However, soon out-classed, the type was relegated to sec-ond-line duties from 1942. Later some were used in Kamikaze suicide attacks. The A5M was known to the Allies for identification purposes as 'Claude', and as many as some 1,091-1,094 were built.

Specifications – Mitsubishi A5M4

Wingspan	36 ft 1 in
Length	24 ft 9.25 in
Maximum speed	273 mph at 9,843 ft
Service Ceiling	32,152 ft
Range	746 miles
Armament	Two 0.303 in machine guns, two 66 lb bombs carried externally
Engine	One Nakajima Kotobuki 41 radial piston engine, of 710 hp
Crew	One

Henschel Hs 123

The stocky, strong and relatively powerful Henschel Hs 123 was very much an aircraft of the 1930's, but it gave sterling service to Germany's Luftwaffe during World War Two, actually remaining in front-line service until 1944. The Hs 123V1 first flew in April or May 1935, the type being intended as a dive-bomber. Unfortunately two of the initial aircraft were destroyed in crashes during diving tests, leading to design alterations and strengthening amongst other changes. A sesquiplane aircraft with a small lower wing compared to the upper wing, the Hs 123 carried its bomb load below the lower wings although a fuel tank or bomb could be carried beneath the fuselage. The main production model was the Hs 123A-1, and it was the Luftwaffe's last front-line biplane. Approximately 265 were built, and the first aircraft entered Luftwaffe service in 1936. Several went to Spain to fight in the Spanish Civil War with the Condor Legion. The survivors of these were later turned over to the Nationalist Spanish forces, and a further batch was subsequently supplied to Franco's victorious followers. During 1937 and 1938, 12 were supplied to China. In Luftwaffe service the type was superseded by the legendary Junkers Ju 87 Stuka dive-bomber, but the Hs 123 was nevertheless successfully used in the Polish campaign in September 1939 in the close-support role – mirroring successful service like this in the Spanish fighting. Thus with a new role, the Hs 123 served in the campaigns in the Low Countries and France in 1940, and then from 1941 onwards in Russia. Some were also employed for training. The type served as late as 1944 on the Russian front for various front-line tasks and supply missions. The final Spanish-operated example was retired in 1953.

This is believed to be the Henschel Hs 123V5 development aircraft, possibly photographed at a Henschel factory airfield. (Photo: John Batchelor Collection).

Specifications – Henschel Hs 123A-1

Wingspan	34 ft 5.5 in
Length	27 ft 4 in
Maximum speed	211 mph at 3,937 ft
Range	531 miles
Service Ceiling	29,528 ft
Armament	Two 0.312 in machine guns, up to 992 lb of bombs or equivalent
Engine	One BMW 132Dc radial piston engine, of 880 hp
Crew	One

Martin B-10

During the inter-war period the pace of fighter development was speeded up at several points due to the appearance in service of bombers with performance higher than or at least comparable to contemporary front-line fighters. One of these bomber types was the Martin B-10, and this streamlined bomber with excellent performance, a gun turret, advanced bomb-sight and a retractable undercarriage revolutionised bomber design and equipment. Design work on the Martin Model 123 that eventually grew into the B-10, commenced in the early 1930's. Essentially a private venture, the resulting aircraft was a clean, mid-wing cantilever monoplane with all-metal construction although some areas of the wings and control sur-

faces were fabric covered on production aircraft. Given the experimental designation XB-907, the first aircraft flew in 1932 and immediately displayed a performance on a par with and in some cases superior to that of the fighters then in U.S. military service. Several changes and refinements were made to this initial layout, which improved the aircraft's streamlining, crew accommodation and other issues, and the type received production go-ahead in 1933 as the B-10. Initial front-line deliveries were made to the U.S. Army Air Corps in 1934, the major production model for this service being the B-10B of which 103 (possibly 105) were manufactured. Compared to the lumbering 1920's vintage biplane bombers that had gone before it, the B-10 represented a

The B-10B operated in the colourful period of U.S.A.A.C. aircraft during the 1930's.
The U.S. Army received 154 B-10/B-12 aircraft including prototypes, the B-12 being a developed
model with Pratt & Whitney Hornet engines. There were also some 189 export examples.

Pictured is one of the B-10 or B-12 prototype/development aircraft. The B-10 was the first American-designed bomber to see combat, with either Thai or Dutch East Indies forces operating against the Japanese holding that honour (Photo: Martin).

huge leap ahead in American military capability. The B-10's range and endurance was well demonstrated by a showcase deployment in several stages by ten U.S.A.A.C. B-10s from Washington D.C. to Alaska and back. The B-10 attracted foreign sales from July 1936 onwards, Argentina, Siam (Thailand), Turkey, China and the Netherlands receiving various export models. In Dutch service the Martin Model 139 in its WH-2, WH-3 and WH-3A versions (some with a long single 'greenhouse' canopy instead of the separate crew canopies on U.S.-operated machines) saw considerable gallant if ultimately unsuccessful action against invading Japanese forces in the Dutch East Indies from December 1941/January 1942 onwards.

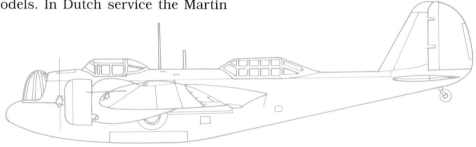

The drawing shows the 'separated' type canopies of U.S. operated B-10 aircraft, some Dutch examples were fitted with a long continuous single canopy.

Specifications – Martin B-10B

Wingspan	70 ft 6 in
Length	44 ft 9 in
Maximum speed	212 mph at sea level
Service Ceiling	24,200 ft
Range	590 miles
Armament	Three 0.3 in machine guns, up to 2,200 lb of bombs or single 2,000 lb bomb
Engine	Two Wright R-1820-33 Cyclone radial piston engines, of 775 hp each
Crew	Three or four

Short-Mayo Composite

During the inter-war period a number of aircraft were built that proved capable of flying very long distances. However, the aircraft that achieved these feats were usually specially-made or converted 'one-offs', often with a single occupant or an intrepid crew made up of aviation pioneers or explorers. Although there were significant developments in the design and performance of commercial aircraft during this period, great range coupled with a commercially-viable payload were two factors that it seemed almost impossible to build into the same aircraft. In an effort to establish a means to achieving this desirable combination, Major Robert Mayo, technical manager of Britain's Imperial Airways, came upon a novel idea. His plan was to mount the aircraft carrying the commercial payload (passengers or cargo) on top of another aircraft. The lower aircraft would contribute the power to get the two combined aircraft into the air and start the journey, with the upper aircraft afterwards taking off in flight from the top of the combination to complete the journey using its own hitherto untouched fuel supply. Although nowadays this scheme might seem strange and more than a little dangerous, at the time it seemed like a good idea, and Short Brothers were approached to build the necessary two aircraft. In the mid-1930's this company was developing what became the excellent Short 'C' Class 'Empire' flying-boats, which combined good (but not massive) range and payload. To meet Imperial Airways' composite-aircraft requirement, Short designed and purpose-built a 'one-off' upper and lower aircraft combination. The lower part of the composite resembled but was not identical to an 'Empire' flying-boat. It

The Short-Mayo Composite was an impressive sight when the two aircraft were mounted together. The combination made its first commercial flight, to Canada from Ireland, in July 1938. In October 1938 'Mercury', after being air-launched, flew non-stop from Scotland to South Africa, an amazing and long-lasting seaplane distance record.

was named the S.21 'Maia', and it first flew in July 1937 – a year after the first 'C' Class flying-boat. The much smaller S.20 named 'Mercury' was the upper, seaplane part of the combination. It first flew in September 1937. The first time that the two took off together was in January 1938, and the first in-flight separation took place on 6 February 1938. Unfortunately delays occurred with the whole program, and eventually it was overtaken by the outbreak of war – and by the much longed-for advances in conventional airliner capability exhibited by the Boeing Model 314 flying boats (see pages 296-297). 'Mercury' was eventually scrapped, while 'Maia' was sunk by German bombs in Poole Harbour, southern England, in May 1941.

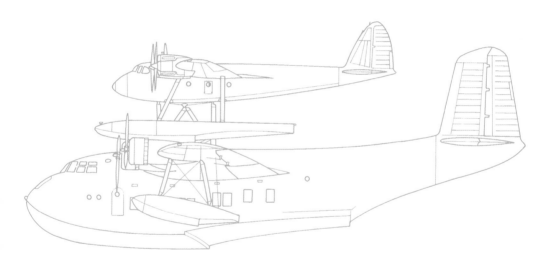

S.21 'Maia' had a wingspan of 114 ft, and a range itself of some 850 miles. The two aircraft proved the potential of the commercial composite, but no further development took place.

Specifications – Short S.20 'Mercury'

Wingspan	73 ft
Length	50 ft 11.5 in
Maximum speed	195 mph at 8,500 ft
Normal in-flight range	Up to some 3,900 miles
Engine	Four Napier-Halford Rapier V inline piston engines, of 340 hp each
Accommodation	Two or three crew, commercial payload of mail or cargo

Dornier Do 18

The outstandingly successful Dornier Wal series (see pages 238-239) established the German company Dornier as a major producer of all-metal flying-boats. In the early to mid-1930's the question of a successor to the Wal was addressed by Dornier, in response to a requirement from the major German airline Deutsche Luft Hansa for a mail carrier with transoceanic range. Aerodynamics had come a long way since the original Wal design work, and the Dornier Do 18 emerged with a clean and refined fuselage that nevertheless retained the Wal's all-metal hull configuration with stabilising sponsons. The original prototype flew in March 1935, characterised by the installation of two 540 hp Junkers Jumo 5 diesel engines. The initial Do 18E aircraft were for Deutsche Luft Hansa, as was the one-off Do 18F.

Between 27-29 March 1938 this aircraft flew non-stop from the English Channel to Brazil, creating a non-stop straight-line seaplane distance record of some 5,214 miles in 43 hours. Luftwaffe interest in the Do 18 resulted in the type being built for German military service, entering service as the Do 18D in the second half of 1938. Over 100 Do 18 of all types were eventually built in a number of military models, including the improved Do 18G. This had more powerful engines and better armament, including a dorsal turret instead of the open gunner's position in the Do 18D. In Luftwaffe service the Do 18 served on coastal maritime reconnaissance and related roles. A Do 18 had the dubious distinction of being the first German aircraft to be shot down by British aviation elements in World War Two: on 26

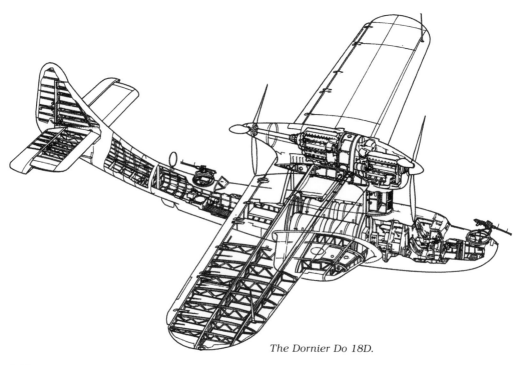

The Dornier Do 18D.

Do 18E D-ABYM 'Aeolus' was operated by Deutsche Luft Hansa (the spelling 'Lufthansa' was in widespread use by World War Two).

September 1939 a Luftwaffe Do 18 was brought down by a Blackburn Skua of No.803 Squadron, Fleet Air Arm. Some Do 18G were later converted for air-sea rescue work (as the Do 18N), and a training version was also built. Further development by Dornier led to the three-engined Do 24 flying-boat.

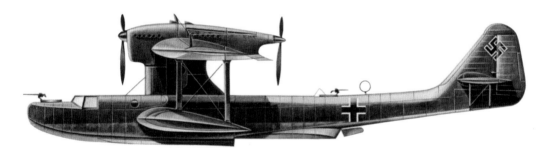

Specifications – Dornier Do 18G

Wingspan	77 ft 9 in
Length	63 ft 1.75 in
Maximum speed	162 mph at 6,562 ft
Service Ceiling	13,780 ft
Range	2,175 miles
Armament	One 0.51 in machine gun, one 0.787 in cannon, two or four 110 lb bombs or equivalent
Engine	Two Junkers Jumo 205D diesel engines, of 880 hp each
Crew	Four

Gloster Gladiator

Destined to be the last biplane fighter to serve with Britain's Royal Air Force, but also the first with an enclosed cockpit, the Gloster Gladiator represented the end of an era in front-line fighter equipment but it nevertheless remained operational in some numbers early in World War Two. The Gladiator's origins went all the way back to 1930, when biplane fighters were still generally regarded as the way ahead. At that time Britain's Gloster company was developing what became the Gauntlet biplane fighter, and the release of the far-sighted Specification F.7/30 had allowed the company to look to a more developed fighter design. The Gladiator emerged from this private-initiative design work, based around the power of a 645 hp Bristol Mercury radial engine and with a radical four-gun armament. The first aircraft, called SS.37, flew in September 1934. Evaluation by the R.A.F. of this first aircraft led to an initial contract for 23 production Gladiator Mk.I air-

craft, ordered in mid-1935. With a more powerful Mercury engine installed, and with the new idea of the four-gun armament standardised, the first deliveries were made in early 1937. Eventually over 480 Gladiators were ordered for the R.A.F., and these equipped a significant number of front-line British-based fighter squadrons. The type was thus still in front-line service at the start of World War Two, although replacement by Hawker Hurricanes and Supermarine Spitfires was well under way. Significant numbers of Gladiators were exported, to such countries as Belgium, China, Greece, Latvia, Lithuania, Norway, Portugal, and Sweden. Production for the R.A.F. additionally included the Gladiator Mk.II, with a different Mercury engine and other changes. A number of naval Sea Gladiators were also made for the Royal Navy, 60 being manufactured with an arrester hook and catapult attachments for

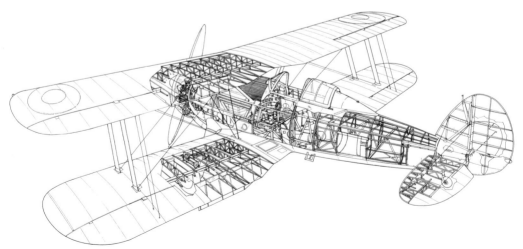

Drawing credit: John Batchelor.

aircraft carrier operation in addition to conversions from some R.A.F. machines. Total Gladiator production stood at some 747 machines including the original prototype. Gladiators saw much action early in World War Two, particularly for the R.A.F. in the Middle East, and over Finland, Greece, Norway, and in the Mediterranean. Against German aerial opposition the type generally fared badly, but against Russian and Italian forces the Gladiator achieved more, most famously in the air defence of the island of Malta.

An atmospheric painting of the colourful 1930's, before the drab days of the Second World War. Two Gladiators, including Mk.I K7985, show off the blue and yellow markings of the R.A.F.'s No.73 Squadron.

The first R.A.F. unit to receive the Gladiator was No.72 Squadron in 1937. A Gladiator Mk.I in the unit's blue and red markings is shown here.

Specifications – Gloster Gladiator Mk.I

Wingspan	32 ft 3 in
Length	27 ft 5 in
Maximum speed	253 mph at 14,500 ft
Service Ceiling	32,800 ft
Range	approximately 430 miles
Armament	Four fixed forward-firing 0.303 in machine guns
Engine	One Bristol Mercury IX radial piston engine, of 830 hp
Crew	One

Focke-Achgelis Fa 61

In the same way that it proved so difficult for so long to create a practical powered man-carrying aircraft, so the development of the helicopter similarly was a long and arduous process. As explained on pages 50-51, many pioneers tried their hand at perfecting the helicopter. It was not until the 1920's that any real steps forward were achieved, but in the 1930's, thanks to the work of Breguet, Focke, Achgelis, Flettner, and Sikorsky, the helicopter began to develop into reality. In mid-1935 the Gyroplane Laboratoire of Frenchmen Louis Breguet and René Dorand had made its first untethered flight, this being a real step towards a practical helicopter. What is often seen as the world's first true technically successful helicopter was the Focke-Achgelis Fa 61. Heinrich Focke, a founder of the German Focke-Wulf aircraft company, had become seriously interested in rotorcraft when Focke-Wulf began licence production of Cierva Autogyros (see pages 148-149). He created the Focke-Achgelis company with his colleague Gerd Achgelis, and the Fa 61 was the first practical expression of their development work. It used a fuselage similar to that of the Focke-Wulf Fw 44 Stieglitz (Goldfinch) biplane training aircraft, but with a tricycle undercarriage and opposite-rotating coaxial three-blade main rotors on outriggers which cancelled out each others' torque. The machine's engine provided drive to these rotors. Importantly, the rotor blades were articulated, allowing cyclic and differential pitch for longitudinal and directional control, with differential collective pitch control of the blades for lateral control (so that the blades could act as the equivalent of an aircraft's ailerons). The Fa 61 first flew on 26 June 1936, and at once began to achieve great advances. It soon started to set international rotorcraft records, and eventually achieved a duration record of just

The Fa 61 looked ungainly, but was the world's first technically successful helicopter. The small propeller on the engine was for cooling – this machine was definitely NOT an autogyro.

over 80 minutes – something that would have been unthinkable in a helicopter only a short time previously. The Fa 61's development was curtailed by the decline into World War Two – although a larger derivative, the Fa 223 Drache (Dragon) was later built in limited numbers.

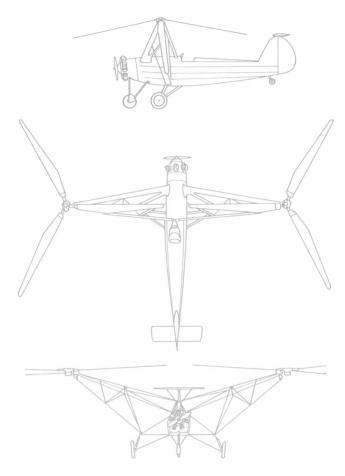

The Fa 61 was a revolutionary machine, and the best looking helicopter up to that time. Amongst its pilots was the famous German female aviator Hanna Reitsch.

Specifications – Focke-Achgelis Fa 61

Rotor diameter (each)	22 ft 11.5 in
Length	23 ft 11.5 in
Maximum speed	just over 76 mph at sea level
Range	143 miles
Maximum take-off weight	2,094 lb
Engine	One Bramo (Siemens-Halske) Sh 14A radial piston engine, of 160 hp
Crew	One

Supermarine Spitfire

Undoubtedly one of the most famous aircraft ever built, and a real contender for the title of best fighter of all time, the fantastic Supermarine Spitfire was the product of an excellent aircraft company – Supermarine; its brilliant Chief Designer – Reginald J. Mitchell; and an equally accomplished aero engine company – Rolls-Royce. Supermarine, Mitchell and Rolls-Royce had collaborated successfully in the series of Schneider Trophy contest aircraft (see pages 172-173) which had been so accomplished in the 1927, 1929 and 1931 Schneider Trophy competitions. These aircraft had successfully advanced the art of design and performance that Mitchell was able to include in his new fighter creation, aided by his talented colleagues at Supermarine. The Spitfire essentially began as a private venture, and was helped along by Air Ministry Specification F.5/34 which required an eight-gun fighter for the Royal Air Force. The Spitfire was actually far more advanced than this specification, and in late 1934 Britain's Air Ministry finalised Specification F.37/34 to cover the construction of a

prototype of Mitchell's new creation. The prototype, serial number K5054, powered by a 990 hp Rolls-Royce Merlin C engine, first flew on 5 March 1936, at Eastleigh airfield near Southampton in southern England. The pilot for this historic flight was Joseph 'Mutt' Summers, the Chief Test Pilot of Vickers Ltd, which had taken over Supermarine in 1928. Originally known as the Type 300 but eventually adopting the name 'Spitfire' ('Shrew' had been considered, and luckily abandoned), the new aircraft was undoubtedly the most advanced fighter in the world at that time. Sadly, Mitchell died before he could see his excellent creation fulfil its destiny in World War Two. Initial orders for production Spitfires were for 310 aircraft, paralleling the Expansion Scheme that was fortunately then developing within the R.A.F. The first deliveries of Spitfire Mk.I aircraft to an R.A.F. front-line unit reached No.19 Squadron at Duxford in August/September 1938. By the time of the outbreak of World War Two in September 1939, there were nine Spitfire-equipped R.A.F. squadrons –

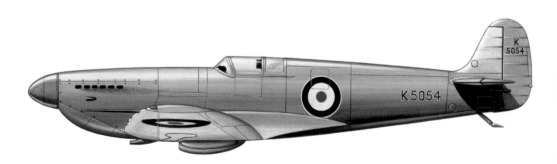

K5054 was the Spitfire prototype, the first of the Spitfire line and the birth of a legend.
Initial production Spitfires resembled the prototype, but wore camouflage paint and included
the eight-gun armament that was such a vital part of the Spitfire's combat prowess.

An evocative study of the Spitfire prototype K5054 in flight. This view illustrates well the distinctive elliptical wing planform that was a hallmark of the Spitfire design.

but there is much, much more about this history-making aircraft during World War Two in the following volume of this work.

Specifications – Supermarine Spitfire Mk.IA

Wingspan	36 ft 10 in
Length	29 ft 11 in
Maximum speed	362 mph at 18,500 ft
Service Ceiling	31,900 ft
Range	approximately 395 miles
Armament	Eight fixed forward-firing 0.303 in machine guns
Engine	One Rolls-Royce Merlin II inline piston engine, of 1,030 hp
Crew	One

Fiat C.R.32

Although in many aircraft-producing countries the biplane fighter was starting to lose its appeal by the early to mid-1930's, in some countries the biplane continued to play an important part in design and procurement plans. In Italy, despite the bombast of Fascist dictator Benito Mussolini, the Italian air force was undergoing a period of bad procurement policy, poor training and lack of funding for many modern programmes. Although it proved effective in the skies over Spain during the Spanish Civil War, the Fiat C.R.32 biplane was outclassed as a front-line type by the time of Italy's involvement in World War Two in June 1940 – even though approximately two-thirds of Italy's front-line fighter force at that time were biplanes. The C.R.32 was a logical development from the C.R.20 of 1926, and the C.R.30, being a more refined and purposeful model that first flew in 1933. Basically a robust and manoeuvrable fighter, the C.R.32

was constructed in four major versions. There were various changes in engine model, armament or equipment between the versions, and some 1,212 of all marks were eventually built. The aircraft's finest hour was in Spain, where the C.R.32 was operated by Italian forces on behalf of the rebel Nationalist forces under General Franco fighting against the Spanish Republican government, and was also flown by the rebel Nationalists themselves. The C.R.32 proved to be successful sometimes against the Russian-built Polikarpov I-15 biplane fighters which were its closest opponent, but it could also gain advantage over the monoplane Polikarpov I-16 if engaging in a close dogfight. Very often the quality of the pilots made the greatest difference in air combat over Spain. Italian pilot Mario Bonzano, and rebel Spaniard Juan Garcia Morato (with 35 victories), were particularly successful in the C.R.32. The type was also

The immediate predecessor of the C.R.32 was the C.R.30 as shown here. All were stocky, purposeful biplanes, the C.R.32 being usefully manoeuvrable (Photo: Philippe Jalabert Collection).

The Fiat C.R.30 as shown here featured a Warren truss-like wing strut arrangement which dated back to the First World War Ansaldo S.V.A.5, and was also used on the Fiat C.R.32 and the later C.R.42 (Photo: Philippe Jalabert Collection).

employed by Italian forces in other conflicts, including air combat early in World War Two for example in East Africa – where it was very quickly outclassed by newer British fighters such as the monoplane Hawker Hurricane. Export models were supplied to several countries, notably Hungary and Austria. A number were also built in Spain.

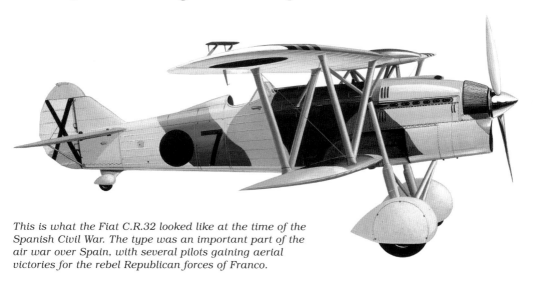

This is what the Fiat C.R.32 looked like at the time of the Spanish Civil War. The type was an important part of the air war over Spain, with several pilots gaining aerial victories for the rebel Republican forces of Franco.

Specifications – Fiat C.R.32 (early production)

Wingspan	31 ft 2 in
Length	24 ft 5.25 in
Maximum speed	233 mph at 9,843 ft
Service Ceiling	28,871.4 ft
Range	466 miles
Armament	Two fixed forward-firing 0.303 in machine guns
Engine	One Fiat A.30 RA inline piston engine, of 600 hp
Crew	One

Heinkel He 115

The Heinkel He 115 was the culmination of a successful series of seaplanes created by Germany's Heinkel company. A direct predecessor was the twin-float biplane Heinkel He 59, which had first flown in the early 1930's, and saw important Luftwaffe service even surviving to operate in World War Two as an air-sea rescue aircraft. Its successor, the He 115, became one of the more important coastal/maritime reconnaissance and attack aircraft of the Second World War. The first He 115, the He 115V1, broke several international seaplane records in March 1938, showing the performance potential of the type. The He 115 became very useful to the Luftwaffe, and was also supplied in small numbers before the war started to Norway and Sweden. Production for the Luftwaffe included various He 115A series versions in 1938, followed by the He 115B series that also served in the early part of the war. The He 115 was able to carry bombs or magnetic mines for maritime work, while some versions could carry a torpedo. It was fitted with a light defensive armament although this was considerably 'beefed-up' with a forward-firing cannon on some of the He 115C models of 1941 after the type's maritime attack potentials had been displayed in action. Production resumed a little later in the war with the He 115E, which was similar to the C series but with various armament variations. A total of some 400 (possibly as high as 500) He 115 of all models was constructed. The He 115 proved especially effective in the early stages of the conflict, particularly in the English Channel, North Sea, and around the Arctic and Baltic coasts. The magnetic mines that were laid by these aircraft were especially destructive, and created considerable problems for the Allies for a time. A small number of the Norwegian export aircraft were able to escape to Britain as a result of the German defeat of Norway in 1940, and at least one was later used on secret operations carrying agents.

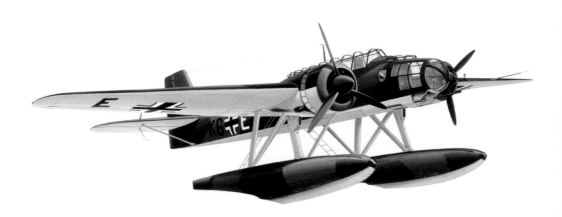

Illustration shows a Luftwaffe-operated aircraft.

The photograph (above), although heavily re-touched, shows the streamlined monoplane lines of the He 115 (in this case an early aircraft), and its large twin floats (Photo: Hans Meier Collection).

Illustration shows side view of a Luftwaffe-operated aircraft.

Specifications – Heinkel He 115B-1

Wingspan	72 ft 2 in
Length	56 ft 9 in
Maximum speed	203 mph at 11,155 ft
Service Ceiling	17,060 ft
Range	2,082 miles
Armament	Two 0.312 in machine guns, various combinations or single loads of magnetic mine or bombs
Engine	Two BMW 132K radial piston engines, of 960-970 hp each
Crew	Three

Savoia-Marchetti S.M.79 and S.M.81

The tri-motor three-engined design layout was much in evidence during the 1920's and 1930's, and was used by such manufacturers as Ford, Junkers and Fokker. In Italy the Savoia-Marchetti organisation, in addition to their twin-hull flying boats (see pages 220-221) and other products, also produced a wide range of tri-motor aircraft for military and civil use. Chief amongst these was the S.M.79, which is one of the select band of aircraft from the first half of the 1930's that were still performing useful tasks at the end of World War Two. The S.M.79 Sparviero (Sparrowhawk) was also one of the new breed of cantilever retractable undercarriage low-wing monoplanes from that time which appeared capable of being both a civil transport and a bomber. The first aircraft flew in late 1934, and was intended to be the basis of an eight-passenger airliner, but its performance was good enough to result in its development as a bomber for Regia Aeronautica (Italian air force) service. The initial bomber model was the S.M.79-I. Like several other Italian and German aircraft types of that period, the S.M.79-I was combat tested in the Spanish Civil War, when it was used by Italian forces

acting on behalf of General Franco's Nationalist rebels. The S.M.79 was then further developed as a torpedo carrier, and the S.M.79-II of 1937-1938 was capable of carrying two torpedoes beneath the fuselage/inner wings. Approximately 1,330 S.M.79 of all models were built in Italy. The type was the main medium bomber of Italy's forces during World War Two, fighting a courageous if ultimately unsuccessful air war in several combat zones. Italy's surrender in 1943 resulted in S.M.79s fighting on both the Allied and Axis sides in the subsequent division of Italian forces, and the type was still in service at the end of hostilities, albeit chiefly in second-line duties. A twin-engine version, which dispensed with the central engine also existed, Romania and Iraq being the main users of this export derivative. Romania in fact proved to be an important operator including licence production. One of Savoia-Marchetti's other three-engined types was the S.M.81 Pipistrello (Bat), which was a bomber and transport with a fixed undercarriage. This type saw action in Spain, Italy's colonial war in Abyssinia, and in World War Two.

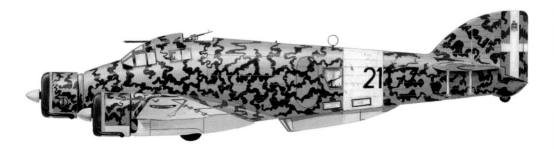

The S.M.79 was the main Italian medium bomber in World War Two.

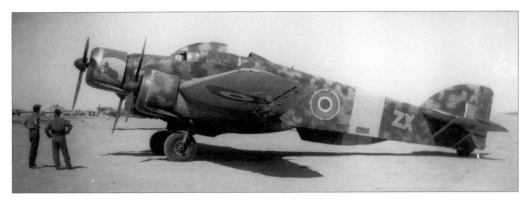

A former Italian-operated S.M.79 captured in North Africa, and wearing British markings (Photo: John Batchelor Collection).

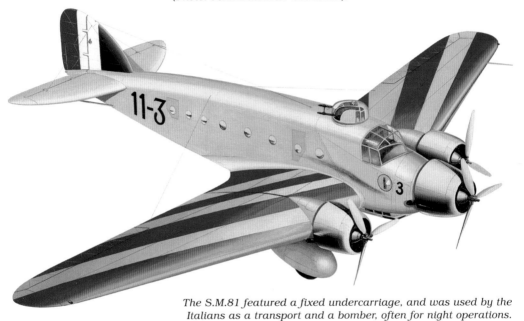

The S.M.81 featured a fixed undercarriage, and was used by the Italians as a transport and a bomber, often for night operations.

Specifications – Savoia-Marchetti S.M.79-I

Wingspan	69 ft 6.75 in
Length	53 ft 1.75 in (sometimes given as 51 ft 10 in)
Maximum speed	270.3 mph at 12,467 ft
Maximum take-off weight	23,148 lb
Range	approximately 1,181 miles
Service Ceiling	22,966 ft
Armament	Three 0.5 in and one 0.303 in machine guns, bomb load of up to 2,756 lb carried internally
Engine	Three Alfa Romeo 126 RC.34 radial piston engines, of 750-780 hp each
Crew	Four or five

Curtiss Hawk/Mohawk Series

Famous for its work on water-borne aircraft and biplane combat/training machines for the U.S. military, the Curtiss company began design work in 1934 on an advanced all-metal monoplane fighter. Known by the Curtiss Model 75 designation, the aircraft was a streamlined monoplane with a retractable undercarriage and enclosed cockpit. The prototype flew in May 1935, and came in second place (behind what became the Seversky P-35 fighter) in a protracted competition to find a new, advanced single-seat fighter for the U.S. Army Air Corps. However, the U.S. government was awakening at last to the fact that its biplane fighter force was sooner or later going to be overtaken by developments in many other countries. The Curtiss fighter was thus ordered into production during July 1937 as the P-36. An initial batch of development Y1P-36 were followed by

the first production model, the P-36A. Deliveries to the U.S.A.A.C. began in the spring of 1938, 180 being ordered plus 30 improved and more heavily-armed P-36C. At that time they were amongst the more modern types in the U.S. inventory. However, by the start of American involvement into World War Two in December 1941 they were outclassed, but some were embroiled in initial combats in the Pacific theatre with the Japanese. The Model 75 also attracted considerable interest from potential overseas buyers, with France, Norway, the Netherlands, and several other countries obtaining the basic Model 75, or related models, either directly or indirectly. A fixed undercarriage derivative was bought (and licence produced) by Argentina, also Thailand and China. The Model 75 had two main engine options, either the Pratt & Whitney Twin Wasp, or the Wright

France received at least 316 Hawk 75 models. This illustration shows an early Hawk 75 A-1 with two wing guns – later versions had four wing-mounted machine guns.

An early production Hawk 75 for the French air force prior to delivery, referred to on its rudder as a Curtiss H 75 C.1 (Photo: Curtiss-Wright).

Cyclone, both radials. The principal overseas customer was France, which flew four different versions of the Hawk 75, one being Cyclone-powered. They were the best fighter available to the French when Germany invaded in May 1940, starting the Battle of France. They proved effective against German aerial opposition if well flown and with good tactics. The surrender of France saw many subsequently used by Vichy French forces, while evacuees plus later aircraft intended for France were diverted to Britain where they were known as Mohawks. Many of these were used as trainers, but some flew against the Japanese over Burma.

A Curtiss P-36A of the U.S.A.A.C.'s 35th Pursuit Squadron, from the colourful period prior to America's entry into World War Two.

Specifications – Curtiss P-36C Hawk

Wingspan	37 ft 4 in
Length	28 ft 6 in
Maximum speed	311 mph at 10,000 ft
Service Ceiling	33,700 ft
Range	approximately 820 miles
Armament	One 0.5 in and three 0.3 in machine guns
Engine	One Pratt & Whitney R-1830-17 Twin Wasp radial piston engine, of 1,200 hp
Crew	One

Hawker Hurricane

Although often overshadowed by the superlative Supermarine Spitfire in accounts of the Second World War, the Hawker Hurricane was a very significant fighter that came before the Spitfire, and was vitally important alongside the Spitfire in Britain's defence during the earlier stages of World War Two. Hawker was a prominent producer of such classic frontline biplane types as the Fury (see pages 252-253). As explained elsewhere in this volume, the high-performance monoplane fighter came to the fore during the mid-1930's, but faced considerable opposition in many (often official) quarters from those who clung to biplane philosophy. Fortunately there were those in Britain who saw the future in the monoplane, resulting in Britain having sufficient modern fighters available to take on the might of Germany's Luftwaffe in World War

Two. In 1933 Hawker's chief designer, Sydney Camm, began private-venture design work on a monoplane fighter. Continuing development work resulted in the modern features of a retractable undercarriage being introduced (of a much wider track than the Spitfire's), and the new Rolls-Royce Merlin engine was introduced into the design. The beautifully streamlined prototype flew on 6 November 1935, several months before the Spitfire. Although modern by contemporary standards, it nonetheless featured major fabric-covered areas on its fuselage and wings, in contrast to the Spitfire and Messerschmitt Bf 109's advanced stressed-skin covering. Hawker was awarded a production contract for 600 aircraft in June 1936 – fortunately Britain's Air Ministry was by then realising the value of monoplane fighters (even though contracts had continued to be placed for some biplane types). The first production

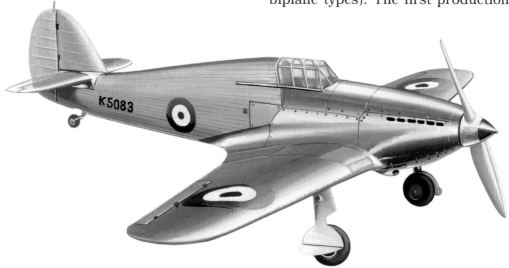

The Hurricane was the R.A.F.'s first monoplane fighter, and was an excellent gun platform with its eight wing-mounted machine guns. This is the Hurricane prototype K5083.

A beautiful painting of the Hurricane prototype in its element.

Hurricane Mk.I flew on 12 October 1937, and deliveries of initial production aircraft were made to the Royal Air Force in late 1937, the first recipient being No.111 Squadron. Considerable interest was shown in the Hurricane from overseas countries, with Yugoslavia and Belgium ordering production aircraft and also setting up for licence production. At first intended to have a four-gun armament, fortunately the Hurricane emerged with the potentially formidable eight-gun wing armament similar to that of early Spitfires. The Hurricane Mk.I bore the brunt of the initial air war during World War Two in several parts of the world, especially during the Battle of Britain. It performed well against some opposition, but was outclassed by others - there is much more about this important aircraft during World War Two in the following volume of this work.

Specifications – Hawker Hurricane Mk.I

Wingspan	40 ft
Length	31 ft 4 in (alternatives sometimes quoted)
Maximum speed	324 mph at 20,000 ft
Service Ceiling	34,200 ft
Range	approximately 525 miles
Armament	Eight fixed forward-firing 0.303 in machine guns
Engine	One Rolls-Royce Merlin II or III inline piston engine, of 1,030 hp
Crew	One

285

Polikarpov I-16

The diminutive Polikarpov I-16 has a number of important claims to fame. Although small and apparently obsolete by the start of Russia's involvement in World War Two, it was one of the principal fighter types in the early part of that conflict, and it fought with distinction in other wars as well. The I-16 was in the vanguard of the movement in the early to mid-1930's towards the adoption of the single-engine, single-seat cantilever monoplane as the future layout of modern fighter design. It was one of the first of this type of fighter to be designed with a retractable undercarriage, and the Russians have often claimed that it was the first-ever modern monoplane fighter with a retractable undercarriage that entered widespread front-line service. The I-16 was devised at around the same time as the I-15 biplane fighter (see Page 248), and it represented a completely different approach to the I-15. The first prototype flew in December

1933. Known initially as the TsKB-12, it was powered by an M-22 radial engine. It was followed in early 1934 by a second aircraft powered by an American Wright Cyclone radial, Soviet-built derivatives of this American radial engine being the power plant used for some subsequent production examples. The I-16 was a small aircraft, which inexperienced pilots found demanding to fly. It comprised a semi-monocoque fuselage mainly of wood construction, with metal structure for the wings which in some versions were partly plywood covered. The initial major production model was the Type 4, powered by the M-22, with the first aircraft being completed in 1934 by a production facility in the Moscow region. Later production took place in Gorky and Novosibirsk, and a selection of gradually improved or modified produc-

tion versions appeared in subsequent years. These included improvements in armament and power output of the engine fitted, culminating in the Types 24 and 29 which were probably the best of the breed. The Type 24 of 1939 was powered by a Shvetsov M-63, derived from the M-62 of some previous production examples, this version becoming the principal production model into 1940. Russian sources state that 9,450 I-16 of all versions were built. There were also two-seat trainers (some of which had a fixed undercarriage), which numbered some 1,895. The I-16 gained a long combat record, flying for the Spanish Republicans in the Spanish Civil War, for the Russians against Japanese forces in 1939, and most notably for the Russian armed forces after the German invasion of the Soviet Union in June 1941. Many were destroyed on the ground in the first days of that conflict, but the type remained in front-line service into 1943, latterly often for ground attack as much as for fighter operations.

Specifications – Polikarpov I-16 (Type 24)

Wingspan	29 ft 6.5 in
Length	20 ft 1.5 in
Maximum speed	303.9 mph at 15,682 ft
Service Ceiling	35,433 ft
Range	248.6 miles plus
Armament	Four fixed forward-firing 0.3 in machine guns, unguided rockets could also be carried under the wings
Engine	One Shvetsov M-63 radial piston engine, of 1,100 hp
Crew	One

Messerschmitt Bf 109B

Destined to become one of history's great fighter aircraft, the Messerschmitt Bf 109 proved to be a significant success over Spain in its first conflict, and later played a key role for Germany in the Second World War. Built in large numbers in many different versions, the origins of this fine aircraft go back to the years immediately after the Nazi take over in Germany. The Bayerische Flugzeugwerke (later Messerschmitt) company began design work on an exceptional all-metal fighter which drew on some aspects of the advanced Bf 108 light touring aircraft. With considerable design input from the talented Willy Messerschmitt himself, the new aircraft emerged as a clean, streamlined cantilever low-wing monoplane with a retractable undercarriage. The tailplane was braced on early models, this bracing later being dispensed

with. The aircraft was designed for the Junkers Jumo inline supercharged engine, but the prototype was powered by a Rolls-Royce Kestrel engine instead. It first flew in September 1935, several months before the Supermarine Spitfire (see pages 274-275) that became one of its main opponents in subsequent years. Known as the Bf 109, it successfully competed against three other designs in a competition for a new standard Luftwaffe fighter, gaining a development contract and going on to become widely-produced. Initial Bf 109B-1 production aircraft were delivered in February 1937. Some of these went to the Luftwaffe's premier fighter wing JG 132 'Richthofen' (named after the First World War ace). There was an immediate opportunity for the Bf 109 to be tried out in combat. In the Spanish Civil War air war, Condor Legion Heinkel He 51

Zo zal een Bf 109B van het Condorlegioen eruit hebben gezien tijdens de Spaanse Burgeroorlog. Het vliegtuig had een metalen propeller, die de eerdere houten schroef van de vroege Bf 109B's verving.

biplanes were hard-pressed against Spanish Republican Polikarpov I-15 biplane fighters. Three development Bf 109s were rapidly sent to Spain, and they were followed in the spring of 1937 by a batch of operational Bf 109B with their German pilots. There is no doubt that the subsequent success of these fighters and those that followed them were a major aid to the eventual victory of the Nationalist rebel forces in the Spanish Civil War. Thoroughly combat proven, the Bf 109 in later models went on to considerable success in the Second World War, as described in the next Volume of this work.

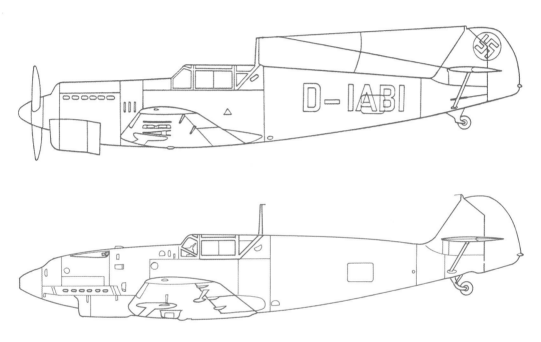

D-IABI was the very first Bf 109, the Bf 109V1, and it was powered – ironically – by the British Rolls-Royce Kestrel engine. The lower side view shows the general configuration of the later Bf 109B, sometimes called the Bf 109B-2.

Specifications – Messerschmitt Bf 109B-1

Wingspan	32 ft 4.5 in
Length	28 ft 0.66 in
Maximum speed	292 mph at 14,764 ft
Service Ceiling	29,528 ft
Range	404 miles
Armament	Two or three fixed forward-firing 0.312 in machine guns
Engine	One Junkers Jumo 210D or Da inline piston engine, of 680 hp
Crew	One

Bristol Blenheim (Early Models)

An important day bomber of the early to mid-World War Two period, the Bristol Blenheim was a huge step-up in capability for the Royal Air Force when it entered service in 1937. Before this, Britain's light to medium bomber capability had principally comprised biplanes such as the Hawker Hart and Hind (see pages 256-257). A streamlined all-metal structure retractable undercarriage monoplane, the Blenheim owed its existence to a private-venture 'one-off' twin-engine transport that was built for a media baron. In March 1934 Lord Rothermere, proprietor of the 'Daily Mail' newspaper, learned of the design at the Bristol company of a sleek, twin-engine monoplane that could form the basis of a light civil transport. On Rothermere's insistence the aircraft was built as the Type 142, and named 'Britain First'. It flew in April 1935 and caused a sensation, having a performance that put some frontline fighters to shame. Britain's Air Ministry and several other countries including Finland at once showed interest in a bomber deriva-

tive of the Type 142. The direct development that duly came out of the Bristol design offices was the Blenheim. In reality the Blenheim was a major re-design of the 'Britain First', with the wing moved upwards to a mid-fuselage position, the installation of a bomb-bay in the lower fuselage, and many other changes to make the type into a fighting machine. The first Blenheim flew on 25 June 1936, and initial deliveries of the production-standard Blenheim Mk.I began in March 1937. The first unit to receive the type was the R.A.F.'s No.114 Squadron. Huge interest was shown in the Blenheim by various countries, and eventually Finland, Yugoslavia, and Turkey received the Blenheim Mk.I, with the first two of these also building Blenheims under licence. In R.A.F. service the Mk.I was used as a day bomber or a fighter (Mk.IF) – for the latter role a gun pack of four 0.303 in machine guns was fitted under the fuselage. British, Finnish and Yugoslav Blenheim I aircraft were fully involved in combat during the early stages of World War Two, but the

The Blenheim Mk.I was much used by the R.A.F. early in World War Two, but it was rather too vulnerable especially to fighter attack in its original form.

The forerunner of the Bristol Blenheim was the private-venture 'Britain First' transport, which had a noteworthy performance and was built for the proprietor of the 'Daily Mail' (Photo: B.A.C. Filton).

type was generally too lightly armed and armoured. Some British fighter Blenheims were used as night fighters with radar installed. Further develop-ment led to the improved and longer-range Blenheim Mk.IV which is described in the next volume.

Approximately 1,415 Blenheim Mk.I were built, by several companies in Britain, and licence production took place in Finland and Yugoslavia.

Specifications – Bristol Blenheim Mk.I

Wingspan	56 ft 4 in
Length	39 ft 9 in
Maximum speed	285 mph at 15,000 ft
Maximum take-off weight	12,250 lb
Range	approximately 1,125 miles
Service Ceiling	27,280 ft
Armament	One fixed forward-firing 0.303 in and one turret-mounted 0.303 in machine gun, up to four 250 lb bombs carried internally
Engine	Two Bristol Mercury VIII radial piston engines, of 840 hp each
Crew	Three

Morane-Saulnier M.S.406

Holding the honour of being France's first really 'modern' fighter, the Morane-Saulnier M.S.406 was in fact a curious mixture of old and new features. It included a retractable undercarriage and enclosed cockpit with a cantilever wing monoplane configuration, but it also featured outdated aspects such as a strut-braced tailplane, tail skid, and a construction that included fabric-covered areas of the main structure. Nevertheless the M.S.406 was numerically the most important fighter available to the French at the start of the German invasion of France on 10 May 1940, but it was found to be lacking real firepower and operational capabilities in action during the rapid and unrelenting air war that followed that fateful time. The M.S.406 actually dated back to 1934, when an official French specification was issued for a modern fighter with (for its time) high performance and useful firepower. Five main contenders emerged, the winning model being the Morane-Saulnier M.S.405. The first M.S.405 flew on 8 August 1935, and was followed by a short series of

pre-production development aircraft ordered in March 1937. Production contracts were placed later in 1937, the production model being renamed M.S.406. Manufacture was shared by several of France's recently-nationalised aircraft factories. In the event production M.S.406C.1 production aircraft were completed by the parent company and by S.N.C.A.O. in Nantes. Construction of the type's Hispano-Suiza engine lagged behind all schedules, however, and the first production aircraft did not appear until late 1938 to early 1939. Ever after then, equipment delays dogged service assimilation. Ten Groupes de Chasse of the Armée de l'Air in France were fully M.S.406-equipped on 10 May 1940. By the time of the French surrender 1,098 M.S.406 had reached the French air force. The M.S.406 also gained some export successes, to Finland, Turkey, and Switzerland. A developed Swiss model was built in Switzerland under licence, and some Finnish aircraft were re-engined with captured Russian engines as the Morko Morane. Finnish-operated air-

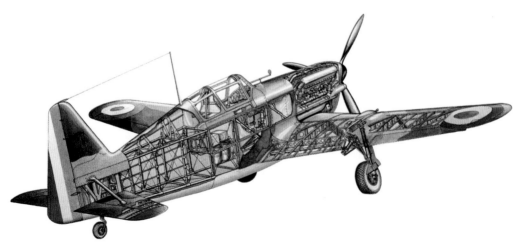

The M.S.406 was of rather traditional construction, with a welded tube fuselage frame, internally wire-braced, and partly fabric-covered. However, the wings and part of the fuselage were covered with 'Plymax' stressed skinning, a bonded plywood and aluminium sheeting.

One of the M.S.405 pre-production/development aircraft in flight.
Production M.S.406 were fitted with an engine-mounted cannon firing through
the propeller hub, although some aircraft do not appear to have been so equipped.

craft flew with some success against Russian forces possibly as late as 1944. A developed M.S.406 model with different wing armament, the M.S.410 appeared in 1939 to 1940.

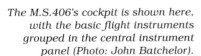

The M.S.406's cockpit is shown here, with the basic flight instruments grouped in the central instrument panel (Photo: John Batchelor).

Specifications – Morane-Saulnier M.S.406C.1

Wingspan	34 ft 9.25 in
Length	26 ft 9 in
Maximum speed	304.5 mph at 14,764 ft
Service Ceiling	32,808 ft
Range	447.4 miles
Armament	One 0.787 in cannon engine-mounted, two fixed forward-firing wing-mounted 0.295 in machine guns
Engine	One Hispano-Suiza 12Y31 inline piston engine, of 860 hp
Crew	One

Boeing Model 247

Although it held the limelight for only a comparatively short time, the Boeing Model 247 can rightly be regarded as the world's first 'modern' airliner. As such it was at the start of the revolution that brought an end to the lumbering biplane airliners so beloved of some manufacturers, and heralded in a new age of fast, efficient air transport. It was a significant in being an important phase in the development of Boeing as a major airliner manufacturer – a status that exists to this day. It was also an important step in the direction towards the later creation of such significant Boeing aircraft as the B-17 Flying Fortress and B-29 Superfortress bombers of World War Two. The first Model 247 flew on 8 February 1933. By that time Boeing had already broken new ground in all-metal aircraft manufacture with the Boeing Monomail mail carrier monoplane, and the all-metal monoplane Y1B-9/Y1B-9A bomber with a retractable undercarriage which was a ground-breaking aircraft for the U.S. Army Air Corps – although it was only ordered in small numbers. The Model 247 airliner was of all-metal construction, a sleek monoplane with retractable undercarriage, de-icing equipment, and good (but not excellent) one-engine-out performance. Early examples had a curious forward-sloping windscreen. It caused a sensation when it first entered service in the airline system that was a part of the Boeing organisation, the first aircraft being delivered in March 1933. On the break-up of this conglomeration, the 247 served principally with United Air Lines which had grown out of the previous Boeing Air Transport. The Model 247 was a huge step forward over the biplane Boeing Model 80/80A airliner that was Boeing's previous production airliner, and it competed well with the Ford Tri-Motors that it rivalled. But it was not long before Douglas had the DC-2 and then the excellent DC-3 (see Pages 214-215) in widespread service, making even the Model 247 look dated. 60 production-standard Model 247s were built, plus 13 of an improved Model 247D to which level many of the original aircraft were refurbished. One example of an armed conversion, the Model 247Y, was supplied to China. The first of United's fleet was 'borrowed' by American Roscoe Turner to compete in the London to Australia air race of 1934 (see pages

United Air Lines was the principal early user of the Boeing Model 247 and 247D.

222-223). With long-range fuel tanks installed in the fuselage, the Boeing came third, but due to a technicality was awarded second place. It had, however, been well beaten by the winning D.H.88 and a DC-2. During World War Two 27 of the Boeings were impressed (requisitioned) for military service as the C-73, some later being returned to airline service. The final examples soldiered on, with small carriers or private individuals, until the 1960's.

The prototype of the Boeing Model 247, X13301. This aircraft first flew in February 1933 (Photo: Boeing Corporation).

Specifications – Boeing Model 247D

Wingspan	74 ft
Length	51 ft 7 in
Maximum speed	202 mph at 8,000 ft
Service Ceiling	25,400 ft
Range	745 miles
Engine	Two Pratt & Whitney S1H1G Wasp radial piston engines, of 550 hp each
Accommodation	Two to three crew, up to 10 passengers

Boeing Model 314

The 1927 solo non-stop crossing of the northern Atlantic by Charles Lindbergh as described on pages 166-167 was one of aviation's great achievements. It was several years later that a number of aircraft manufacturers were designing aircraft that were capable of regular non-stop transatlantic flight, and there were several airlines that were enthusiastic to establish commercial air links across the Atlantic. During the mid-1930's Pan American Airways, the famous American airline that did so much to establish commercial air routes around the world, had approached Boeing to design a flying-boat airliner with genuine transatlantic range. Already the Martin M-130 and Sikorsky S-42 long-haul commercial flying-boats were in existence, but Pan Am wanted something new and with longer range for its planned fast passenger/air mail route

across the northern Atlantic. Boeing's solution was to build what became the largest and greatest production flying-boat of its day. Although the fuselage/hull of this aircraft was basically a new design, the wings in particular were borrowed from Boeing's mighty XB-15 bomber project that had not itself entered production. Known as the Boeing Model 314, the transatlantic flying-boat was bought by Pan Am in July 1936 with an order for six initial aircraft. The name Clipper is often used for this line of fabulous flying-boats, which could carry 74 passengers. The first flight was made in 1938, and regular transatlantic mail services began in May 1939. The first passengers were carried in late June. Unfortunately, this was only weeks before the outbreak of World War Two. What had looked like a giant step into the future was now interrupted by war. Pan Am

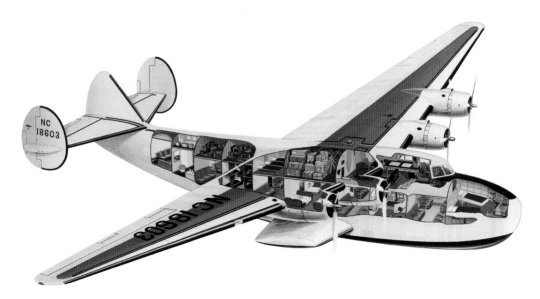

A cutaway of the Boeing Model 314. Although the civil flying career of these aircraft was curtailed by war, they helped to pioneer non-stop transatlantic commercial flying.

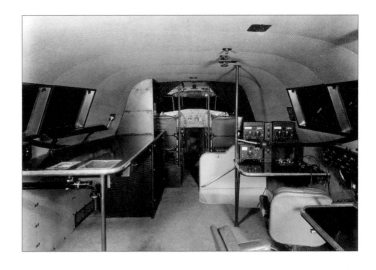

The cockpit/forward cabin of a Boeing Model 314. There was a lot of room aboard these fabulous flying-boats, but sadly they were never given the chance to really prove their worth as commercial airliners in peacetime (Photo: Boeing Corporation).

also ordered six more of the big Boeings, in a slightly refined and more powerful version, the 314A, and these were delivered in 1941/1942. Five of the original Model 314 were brought up to this standard. Three of the later 314A were operated by Britain's airline B.O.A.C. for services on the Foynes (Ireland) to Lagos (Nigeria) wartime communications route. Four of Pan Am's fleet were impressed (requisitioned) for the U.S. Army Air Force as C-98 transports, while the U.S. Navy eventually operated five. Post-war, commercial flying ultimately resumed but the days of the passenger-carrying flying-boats were already starting to end, with long-haul landplanes increasingly coming into service.

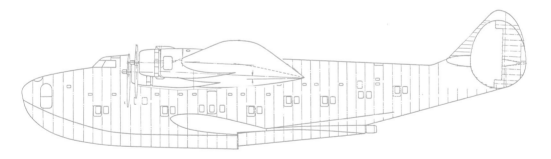

Specifications – Boeing Model 314A

Wingspan	152 ft
Length	106 ft
Maximum speed	193 mph at 10,000 ft
Service Ceiling	13,400 ft
Range	3,500 miles
Engine	Four Wright R-2600 Double Cyclone radial piston engines, of 1,600 hp each
Accommodation	Eight crew, up to 77 passengers

Heinkel He 178

One of the principal developments that led to the creation of powered, manned and controlled flight at the start of the twentieth century was the birth of the internal combustion engine. Yet it was less than four decades later that an equally revolutionary new source of power for aircraft started to evolve. This was jet propulsion, and the development of the turbojet engine. Its influence on aviation in the decades after this was to be as profound as the appearance of the petrol engine had been to pioneers such as the Wright brothers. In two countries in particular, Germany and Britain, far-sighted individuals were working on the concept of jet propulsion in the 1930's. In Britain, Frank Whittle doggedly pursued his research into creating jet propulsion. In Germany, similar official hurdles and particularly indifference existed. At least in Germany, however, research into jet propulsion was able to progress somewhat further, quicker and in the short-term more profoundly. In particular the researchers Hans Joachim Pabst von Ohain and

Max Hahn had been privately working on jet propulsion during the 1930's. In 1936 both were taken on by the Heinkel company, and the development of a viable jet engine and the aircraft to fly it in really began. In the autumn of 1937 the first successful demonstration jet engine was bench running. This was the Heinkel HeS 1. Successful air testing followed in mid-1939 of the HeS 3a in a He 118 test-bed aircraft, and the stage was set for the new jet-powered Heinkel He 178 to fly. An unscheduled hop was made during taxiing trials on 24 August. On 27 August 1939, at Heinkel's factory airfield at Rostock-Marienehe, with test pilot Erich Warsitz at the controls, the He 178V1 powered by a HeS 3b became the first-ever aircraft to fly solely under the power of a turbojet engine. Ironically, this momentous event received little official accolade in Germany, and it was not until October – November 1939 that representatives of the German air ministry really began to take an interest in the project. Eventually a He S6 jet

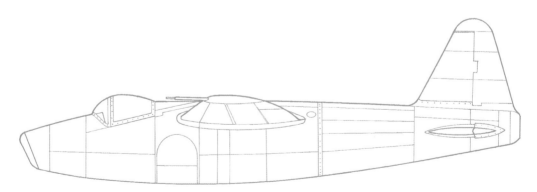

The illustrations on these two pages show the unique Heinkel He 178, and its revolutionary Heinkel turbojet engine. The He 178 was purely an experimental aircraft, not intended for production. It was several years before operational jet-powered aircraft took to the skies.

of some 1,301 lb st was designed for the He 178, which made approximately 12 flights under jet power. The jet age had commenced, but it was several years before operational jet-powered aircraft became operational. In September 1939, the Second World War commenced.

The Ohain engine which only powered the He 178V1.

Specifications – Heinkel He 178V1

Wingspan	23 ft 7.5 in
Length	24 ft 5.25 in
Maximum speed	approximately 392.7 mph at sea level
Maximum take-off weight	4,405 lb
Engine	One Heinkel HeS 3b turbojet engine, of approximately 750 lb st (although c.1,000 lb st intended)
Crew	One

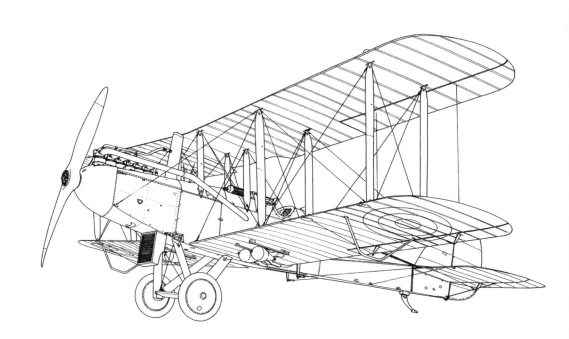

Index

Index

Index